WHAT INDOOR PLANT IS THAT?

WHAT INDOOR PLANT IS THAT?

STIRLING MACOBOY

SUMMIT BOOKS
Published by Paul Hamlyn Pty Limited
Sydney·Auckland·London·New York

To convert
my mother,
who still prefers
her gardens outdoors . . .

Unless specifically credited, all photographs are by the author
Line drawings by Bob Arnold

Summit Books
Published by Paul Hamlyn Pty Limited
176 South Creek Road, Dee Why West, NSW, Australia, 2099
First published 1976
2nd impression 1977
3rd impression 1977
4th impression 1978
© Copyright Stirling Macoboy 1976
Produced in Australia by the Publisher
Typeset in Australia by David Graphic Typesetting
Printed in Hong Kong

National Library of Australia Cataloguing-in-Publication Data

Macoboy, Stirling
  What indoor plant is that?

  Index.
  ISBN 0 7271 0108 0

  1. House plants — Identification. I. Title.

  635.965

THE VANISHING GARDEN

As population explodes in the world's great cities, so gardens vanish in direct proportion. Not so much the daily more crowded parks of worn grass and newly polluted trees, but the private gardens — those cool oases of green tranquillity created by a million families.

It's an old story, and sadly familiar. Population grows, the city spreads and residential land is priced so high that no family can afford the taxes to live there privately.

So down come the houses and the trees that sheltered them for generations, and up go high-rise apartments and condominiums with underground concrete parking lots boring their way into secret places once known only to tree roots, earthworms and bulbs awaiting the coming of spring.

Dry figures buried in the files of national census departments reveal the same picture all over the world.

In Japan, Tokyo spreads like a cancer over country once famous for its exquisite gardens. It has become the most densely populated, widest-spreading industrial metropolis on earth.

In the vast United States, the 1970 census revealed that 31 per cent of that country's 69 million dwelling units were in multiple unit structures (i.e., apartments).

In Australia, in the year ended June 1974, more than 45,000 of the 153,000 dwelling units completed were not houses (i.e., they were apartments). In this most lightly populated of all continents, more than half a million families now live in flats, home units or co-operative apartments with the country-side many miles away.

But if the gardens are vanishing fast, what about the plants that once flourished unnoticed in their shadows?

They are certainly not giving up without a fight.

Plants have come to terms with the enemy and moved right indoors to become part of our family groups in the same way as pet animals. They are keeping a watch on us in our offices; are taking over our hotels and airline terminals; and are even in the process of setting up an industry to cater to their every whim and need!

Notice the way they set to work!

A perfectly normal ten-floor apartment block is completed, bare and empty of anything except a decorator's demonstration unit. Families set up house in sterile splendour, until, late one Sunday, a single pot of Daffodils sneaks in with a tenant fresh from a country weekend.

Pretty soon some Ivy appears cheekily on the next floor; then a Palm; a Rubber plant; a row of Cacti; a whole hanging basket overflowing with flowers.

Before you can say 'Jack and the Beanstalk', every apartment in the district is bursting at the seams with green, growing life.

The next thing you know, those plants will be taking over the world!

EXODUS

In recent times, I have been obliged to move from a large house in a large garden, with land developers hot on my tail.

Geographically speaking, it was not very far. But stimulated by unseasonably wet weather, I decided to take as much of the garden with me as possible, rather than leave my old friends to their fate.

It was a traumatic experience after twenty years in the one place, and I had to keep reminding both myself and my plants that even the Israelite Exodus from Egypt finally turned out all right.

So we all set off down the road, myself in a large car bursting with my favourite plants, the others following behind in a fleet of trucks, like tumbrils full of gaudy aristocrats on their way to Madame Guillotine.

It was a foolhardy idea really. The new garden was even smaller than I'd feared, and almost all the family had to take up residence in pots — literally hundreds of them. But by and large they've adapted very well to the container life, either indoors or in courtyard conditions.

This book is the result of many things we learned in adjusting ourselves to a new form of gardening activity — both the plants and myself. The photos show, I think, that we have been successful.

Overseas readers will have to forgive my inclusion of a few plants I grow indoors in Australia and which may not readily be available to them in their own countries. If they are real plant people, however, they'll know that where there's a will there's a way of getting hold of them.

They may also be puzzled at some of my omissions, such as Australia's own *ACACIA* (or Wattle) and *GREVILLEA* (or Silky Oak), both of which are certainly grown indoors in many parts of the world.

I just happen to prefer my *BOUGAINVILLEAS* and night-flowering Cacti, and the pastel *AZALEAS* and Orchids that light up my home almost the entire year round.

Sydney's climate is generous and varied — rarely cold enough to need much winter heating, a bit more humid than other places on hot summer days. With the help of a few awnings I can leave the house wide open whenever I am there. This enables me, perhaps, to grow a far wider range of plants indoors than would be possible in other places. But a large proportion of them are bound to enjoy life in your home, wherever you live.

Some of the more spectacular pictures in this book were taken on visits to California, Hawaii and Tahiti, where imaginative indoor gardeners have been doing wonderful things with potted plants for years.

The great majority of plants however, were photographed in or about my own house, which accounts for a certain repetition of backgrounds.

Exploring the world of indoor plants has been a rewarding experience for me, and I sincerely hope my pleasure can be shared with plant lovers everywhere.

Stirling Macoboy

THE GREEN INVASION

The popular 'Swiss Cheese Plant', MONSTERA, can be grown in well-supported hanging containers.

My own pleasurable experience to the contrary, there is nothing especially novel about bringing plants indoors. History records that there have been house-plants almost as long as there have been houses.

There is strong evidence, for instance, that the famed Hanging Gardens of Babylon were actually a series of covered terraces built one on top of another just like a modern apartment block. But they were built to shelter not people but a massive collection of plants, watered by their own pumping system to compensate for the searing desert heat of Mesopotamia.

Ancient Chinese emperors filled their palaces with exquisitely cultivated trees in pots — a fashion that spread to the Japanese islands and ultimately developed into the art of bonsai.

Egypt's only female pharaoh, Hat-Shepsut, made a political visit to the neighbouring land of Punt. Whether she got the treaty she was after, history does not record — but the carved stone murals of her triumphant return illustrate exotic potted plants she brought back as gifts from the king of that currently unidentified land! It is even possible to recognise what species some of them were.

The Greeks and the Romans certainly practised indoor gardening, and in Louis XIV's splendid palace of Versailles, the now empty gallery of mirrors was lined on festive occasions with flowering Lemon trees in tubs of solid silver!

In the great houses of the landed gentry from one end of Europe to the other, and for hundreds of years, there were orangeries: heated, glass-walled pavilions where exotic trees were brought indoors to survive and brighten up the cruel European winters.

The point is that while indoor plants have always been with us, they were, until comparatively recent times, the pleasure and privilege only of the very rich and very powerful.

The foyer of the author's home features an indoor garden with an ever-changing display of colourful plants.

The *Orangerie* at the Palace of Bagatelle in Paris dates from the 18th century.

This elegant Juniper has been trained in the ancient Chinese tradition. (De Young Museum, San Francisco).

A row of PHILODENDRONS being grown under ideal conditions of heat, diffused light and humidity. (Green Fingers Nursery, Warriewood, NSW).

Plants must have light to grow indoors; they must have heat to survive the winter; they must have water at all times — and until the industrial revolution began to bring glass and electricity and plumbing within the reach of all, one had to be pretty well-heeled to waste any of these expensive commodities on the survival of a mere plant.

But now our homes are well lit and warmed, and water is available at the turn of a tap. We can all aspire to perform horticultural wonders in every room of the house.

Plant hunters have combed the world to find new and exotic subjects to suit our indoor environment. Nurseries have propagated them by the million. Chemists have developed pills and hormones and fertilisers and fungicides to keep plants happy in their adopted homes and all seems right with the indoor botanical world.

Within a mere quarter of a century the fashion for growing things indoors has snowballed into a universally popular leisure pastime and a major industry.

We use the phrase 'indoor plants' loosely to cover a whole army of species that are grown in containers — whether they spend their time wholly or only partly inside the home itself, or on the balconies, terraces, courtyards and patios that are so much part of the modern pattern of living.

For it is not only apartment dwellers who have learned to enjoy indoor gardening.

Suburban commuters have chosen to brighten the offices where they spend so much of their lives with favourite plants, on either a permanent or an exchange basis.

Owners of quite large houses often elect to garden indoors because they don't have the leisure time to cope with a big garden any more. They enjoy the decorative value of their botanical friends in the evenings, and willingly accept the many responsibilities inherent in sharing the same house with growing plants.

For invalids and the housebound, indoor plants are sometimes their only link with the world of changing seasons outdoors.

Add the great hordes of Orchid fanciers, bonsai growers, African Violet fans, Fern fanatics, Bromeliad buffs and followers of other plant hobbies and you have a mighty host indeed — all dedicated to the joys of container gardening of some sort throughout the year.

Success, one regrets to say, does not always crown their efforts in the way they would wish.

Eagerly awaited flowers fail to appear. The lush firm foliage that caught the eye all too frequently dwindles into pale, spindly shoots that trail away to nothing. Rich colours fade, and the plant promised to grow at a great rate gradually dies away leaf by leaf.

Where did they all go wrong?

Be sure of one thing. It was rarely the fault of the plant — but of the environment provided for it.

In nature, plants are the most adaptable things of all creation. When the soil dries out, they send down roots to where it is damp. Rob them of light and they grow upward until their leaves reach the sun. Exhaust the nutriment in the soil and they'll quickly send out feeding roots to where the soil is rich and the growing green.

But that's all in the outdoors, where plants can do their own thing and find a way to survive. Shut

This large planter in a modern office foyer contains *STRELITZIA, PHILODENDRON* bipinnatifidum and Ferns.

The elegant 'Boston Fern', *NEPHROLEPIS*, is among the most widely grown of indoor plants.

them up in a pot where the roots cannot grow out or down, and where they cannot reach the moisture, light and nutriment they need — then they're as helpless as animals in a cage.

And without human help, they have about as much chance of survival.

From the moment you carry that first plant inside your home, you are going to need the taste of an artist, the patience of a parent and the judgement of a skilled doctor.

In return, your life will become enriched by what the plant can teach you. A sense of responsibility, a feeling for living things, the fulfillment of watching your own creation grow, develop and burst into maturity beneath your very hands.

All of these talents take time to acquire, of course, and the rewards may take even longer to be received. But where's the hurry? Indoor gardening should above all things be relaxing, and nobody with a well-lit window and a watering can will fail to get results and a great deal of satisfaction.

There are no real limitations, beyond your personal taste, your income and the space available. Any plant that can be grown successfully in a pot can be brought inside for a time at least.

Whether it will enjoy life there and flourish is a different question. The air inside the average home tends to be drier than in the garden or shadehouse. Daylight is far less intense indoors, and there is less air movement as well.

The biggest difference of all between indoors and out is generally in temperature, particularly when the house has some form of winter heating or summer air-conditioning.

All of these variations from nature are hazards to indoor cultivation, and the ideal indoor plant is one that can survive for long periods in spite of them.

This book brings you colour photographs of more than five hundred plants that are tried and proven indoors, and tells you about many hundreds more.

In tropical climates, the shaded courtyard becomes a cool summer oasis. (Kahala Condominium, Honolulu).

Some of them will be familiar to you, some not, but in the majority of cases they fall into one of two main divisions — the flowering pot plants and the true houseplants.

The former are chosen for the beauty of their flowers (and sometimes fruit) at certain times of the year, but must be looked on as temporary house-guests at best. They are usually raised outdoors or in greenhouses, brought indoors as they begin to bloom, and hurriedly returned outside after the flowers fade.

Most of them need plenty of light and sun, with regular water and feeding. In the case of flowering shrubs, a long spell outdoors is necessary so that the plants can build up reserves of energy to flower again another year.

Annual flowers are discarded after one season indoors. Most flowering bulbs need to be ripened naturally — and then spend a year in the open garden before they recover strength for another season in pots. For city dwellers who don't have gardens, that normally means discarding them as well.

The most popular flowering pot plants include bulbs and tuberous plants of many kinds, *AZALEAS, FUCHSIAS, GARDENIAS,* Geraniums, Orchids and Poinsettias.

True houseplants, on the other hand, do not need so much light and can be grown away from windows.

They are mostly tropical in origin, used to the lower light levels of the jungle floor, and not averse to the warmer temperatures found indoors during the winter. When properly sited and well cared for, they can be left indoors permanently to increase in size and beauty from year to year.

Many of them develop a dramatic sculptured appearance as they age, and can indeed be thought of as living sculpture for indoor decoration.

The most popular of these houseplants (which are illustrated later in the book) include such favourites as *AGLAONEMA, DIZYGOTHECA, FATSIA, MONSTERA, PHILODENDRON* and *SANSEVIERIA* — Evergreen every one of them, with leaves in a myriad of shapes and shades of green.

Some houseplants on the other hand have foliage as gaily coloured as any flower, particularly varieties of *CALADIUM, CODIAEUM, CORDYLINE, MARANTA* and many of the Bromeliads. These may be used as striking colour accents in a modern all-white decor, but will need as much light as you can give them, for they are lacking in natural chlorophyll.

The same craving for light applies to the white and cream variegated varieties of many plants, all of which bring a refreshing dash of coolness to more heavily coloured interiors.

Indoor plants are very much part of our decoration, but are best displayed in groups where the contrasts of leaf shape and colour can make an ever-changing display.

There are many ways in which this can be done, as you will see from the illustrations in the next chapter.

THE INDOOR JUNGLE

This window grouping of individual pots includes *FICUS benjamina, SPATHIPHYLLUM, HEDERA, DIZYGOTHECA* and *CHRYSANTHEMUMS.*

Indoor plants help link our living areas with the changing seasons beyond our walls. There is pleasure in watching them grow, and when we have become used to their habits, they can teach us many other things as well. Plants act as nature's barometer for conditions to which we are insensitive ourselves. They can beat any forecasting service with their predictions of unseasonable climatic change.

How often have I thought to myself: 'Those buds are developing fast — it's going to be an early spring'. And generally the plant's predictions turn out to be pretty much correct and enable me to update my indoor planting and take advantage of the coming change.

In nature, plants believe in communal living, and take pleasure in each other's company. Indoors, the same thing applies — they look better, do better, displayed in groups, where the contrasts of leaf shape and colour can make an ever-changing display. Rising humidity from small plants helps keep the big ones fresh — the big plants in turn help shade the small; spreading ones help mulch and cool the roots of more vertical growing types. It is even believed that some deep-rooting plants bring minerals to the surface for the benefit of nearby, shallow-rooting companions.

Grouping plants indoors is not quite so easy as it is outdoors but there are ways in which it can be done.

GROUPING IN POTS
Grouping single plants in individual pots is the simplest way, but it has several inconveniences. Small single pots dry out quickly and need more frequent replacement of soil due to constant washing away of vital minerals. And, because all pots need drainage holes to rid themselves of excess stale water, this means a choice between marked furniture or floors, and the use of pot-saucers, which are unsightly in large groups.

One solution is to group the individual pots in a larger outer container such as a preserving pan or tray-lined picnic basket. Another is to use one of the many types of plant stands or *étagères* that are currently on the market. These are available in light cane construction, cast aluminium or plastic-coated heavy wire; many of them are quite decorative and have room for up to two dozen individual plants. Alternatively, special waterproof trays can be made up to fit in large window sills or on traymobiles, and the individual pots arranged in them on a bed of moisture-retaining gravel or tanbark.

By grouping the pots, flowering plants can be mixed with evergreens — at least within the limitations of their individual light requirements — and the arrangement continually changed about for interest. Single plants can be taken outside for a rest, for pruning, training or re-potting.

13

If there's a home handyman in the family, plant grouping can be taken a stage further with the construction of attractive end-tables or coffee tables with waterproof pot-holders made of copper or galvanised iron and sunk below the surface level. Individually potted plants can then be grouped in these on a bed of charcoal or pebbles and switched about all year. The surface of the pots in their inbuilt holder can be covered with peat or fine gravel so that the whole arrangement looks like a permanent planting.

In my own home I have a similar idea on a much larger scale in the entry foyer. Here a stone-walled planter was constructed over a deep gravel bed that takes away excess water through an agricultural drain. At first the entire planter was filled with potting compost, and a variety of plants was grown satisfactorily. Unfortunately I reckoned without the natural habits of my otherwise house-trained cats. They found the idea of an indoor garden irresistible in rainy weather, with mildly unhygienic results. Treatment with various products alleged to be cat-repellent made not the slightest difference, so out went the plants, soil and all, to be replaced by a large quantity of heavy fir-bark chips of the type used for growing Orchids. In these I sink large plants in individual containers, raking the chips over the pot rims. I probably owe the disappointed cats a vote of thanks, for the new arrangement works much better — the opportunity to change the plants about results in a fresher, better appearance all year.

PLANT GROUPINGS

Groups of complementary plants can also be grown together in larger containers as living permanent arrangements. Any large nursery or indoor plant shop these days will stock a selection of special containers, planted with quite charming arrangements of popular indoor plants — miniature Palms, Crotons, Ivy, Bromeliads, Ferns and Mosses, all in together, sometimes with the addition of small evergreen flowering plants.

These group plantings make wonderful gifts, so why not try planting some of them yourself? You will need either an outer container partly filled with a good layer of drainage material, and some sort of inner container to hold the soil and let excess water through — or you could opt for a single fully-drained container with matching tray to catch excess moisture as it flows away.

Follow the normal instructions for potting (in a later chapter) and arrange the planting to your own taste. This will use principally smaller, younger plants than you would normally buy; and you'll find them a lot cheaper, often only a few cents each. Just make sure you include at least one taller plant (a Palm or Fern) to add height. Trailing and cascading plants to spill over the edge, and something in the nature of a ground cover, will put the arrangement together.

You might use all plants with variegated leaves, or others with foliage of any colour but green. You'll find plenty of ideas in the Dictionary section of this book.

Some of these plantings have almost the appearance of landscape in miniature, and the idea can be taken a step further by deliberately arranging plantings (for instance) solely of Cacti and succulents in

This mixed planting at London's Chelsea Flower Show includes
BEGONIA, HYDRANGEA, PELARGONIUM and *TRADESCANTIA.*

14

Several individual pots in one outer container reduce the number of pot saucers. Here CYCLAMEN in a copper preserving pan strike a cheerful fireside note.

An indoor garden in the author's home changes with the seasons. Here, in midsummer, are Lilies, Gloxinia, Fishbone Fern and Cape Primrose.

Typical of mixed indoor plantings available at many nurseries and shops is this grouping of COLLINIA, BEGONIA, AGLAONEMA and DIEFFENBACHIA.

Rich massed planting in the lobby of Honolulu's Kahala Hilton Hotel includes RHAPHIDOPHORA, PHILODENDRON, ASPARAGUS and many species of DENDROBIUM Orchids.

the form of a miniature desert garden, or of dwarfed trees, grasses, rock and mosses in the Japanese style, perhaps with the addition of a miniature oriental figurine, bridge or pagoda.

PLANTERS AND JARDINIÈRES

Special decorative containers for raising groups of plants indoors have been made in one form or another for hundreds of years, but like all antiques, they have become very expensive in recent times.

Instead, we have a number of new designs in lightweight fibreglass or pressed metal or wood and woven cane. These are relatively portable, easy to manage, and can be most attractive when properly planted.

The *jardinière* is a pot or planter usually of a more horizontal design, to allow a spread of roots and volume of soil sufficient for larger plants (even small trees). Planters retain moisture longer than individual pots, and as a rule drain better. Some of them have double bottoms to catch draining water. Some come on legs or even wheels so they can be shifted about. Large planters can be sited permanently on a terrace or balcony, and their most spectacular indoor use is to mount them permanently on the inside of an east- or west-facing window and fill them with a display of plants that thrive on maximum natural light. In colder climates, though, this may require double glazing to minimise heat loss due to low outside winter temperatures.

PLANT WINDOWS AND TERRARIUMS

The siting of plant groups in well-lit windows can be carried a step further by the creation of a special plant window, or *blumenfenster* as they are known in Europe. This can be done in several ways. First, there is the simple form where glass shelves are arranged across a fixed window. For preference, this should be double glazed to prevent summer scorch of delicate leaves, and winter heat loss; but a cheaper alternative is to have the window coated on the outside with one of the many heat-reflecting plastic coatings that are now available. The shelves can be mounted on brackets or rods, and should be removeable for easy cleaning. On these glass shelves, you can arrange a mass display of small plants on many levels, some spilling down from shelf to shelf. The window arrangement brings the plants maximum winter light, and lends a cooling effect to any room in summer.

More elaborate and expensive is to fit up a deep window recess as a miniature glasshouse by having glass doors fitted on the *inside* of the bay in addition to normal glazing. This effect can be adapted to many modern homes and flats, which are without great window depth, by building the glassed extension *outside* the window onto a terrace. The floor of the recess should be lined with a waterproof tray or tiling, and used to display a collection of tropical plants that need constant summer humidity to survive. These may be separately potted or (more decoratively) planted around an old tree branch or

Grouping in a sunny window of the author's kitchen includes *PHILODENDRONS oxycardium* and *warscewiczii*, *PEPEROMIA* varieties and a Pygmy Date Palm.

Bromeliads of many types thrive on a dead tree stump in this heavily planted and humidified conservatory.

rock. Provided a blind is fitted outside to protect the more delicate plants from direct summer sun, superb displays of Orchids, Bromeliads and other tropical exotica can be raised in this way.

GARDEN ROOMS AND WINTER GARDENS

Larger European houses of the nineteenth century often included a winter garden or conservatory — a separate room, largely of glass, heated and humidified to ensure an indoor display of flowers all through the cold weather. It was usually fitted with a tiled floor and often had cane or wire furniture so that tea could be taken amid the pleasant surroundings of growing plants.

Today, similar arrangements on a smaller scale can often be organised in sunrooms or glassed-in

Plant grouping in the form of a miniature landscape. A dwarf Conifer with *CAMPANULA, DIANTHUS, SCHIZOCENTRON* and *SABINA* (Irish Moss).

16

Old stone sinks and troughs can be used for terrace or courtyard plantings of smaller specimens. Here, a collection of *DIANTHUS, AUBRIETA* and Thyme.

A well-drained built-in planter is a permanent feature of this modern home. Grouped in it are *CALATHEA, BEGONIA, HEDERA, ZEBRINA, MONSTERA* and *NEPHROLEPIS.*

Hybrid *CYMBIDIUM* Orchids flourish in the humid atmosphere of the author's bathroom for four months of the year.

balconies that can be closed off from the rest of the house in cold weather. This is best done with clear glass doors so plants may be viewed from the rest of the house — and so that really striking displays of spring-flowering shrubs and bulbs can be obtained months ahead of time.

Such a 'garden room' is the perfect place for vines and other climbing plants, which can be trained up small panels of trellis or wire mesh mounted on the wall, or even next to the windows.

The principal problem to be faced is drainage. If the room has a wooden floor, tiles can be laid over a waterproofing compound. Sometimes the best solution is to provide wide shelves on several sides of the room. These must be supported on stout legs and topped with a series of heavy trays made from galvanised steel and filled with moistened gravel on which the pots are stood.

It is naturally a great help if water can be piped in for occasional sprinkling in warm weather — so much easier than the endless carrying of cans!

A simpler form of winter garden can be arranged in a well-lit bathroom. Here the level of humidity is often the highest of any room in the house, and a wide variety of tropical and semi-tropical plants will revel in the steamy atmosphere. They can be arranged at windows to give privacy, or in large plantings at the end of the bath. The ingenious and enthusiastic indoor gardener will find a thousand places for plants in a single bathroom.

Kitchens however, are not so successful, particularly if there are gas fumes. The best growing area is a well-lit window above the sink, or on top of cupboards where trailing plants can spill down. Hanging baskets can also be used, for most kitchens have moisture-resistant floors.

In my own house I have a rather cramped garden room adapted from an old laundry, unused for many years. Here the floor has been recemented to drain properly, the roof tiles replaced with translucent fibreglass, and two sides of the room fitted with solidly supported shelves. With the good light and constant humidity, the entire available space is a mass of greenery at all times of the year. I find the room very useful to freshen up any houseplant that looks a little jaded after long spells inside. Light-loving plants go on the shelves, shade lovers on the floor. Hanging baskets of Orchids and tropical Cacti are suspended by hooks from the original heavy roof beams. When the weather is too hot, and the humidity reaches saturation point, I just open the windows during the daytime, and close them again at night.

GOING POTTY

Terracotta pots are still the most useful of all, and are now available in many new shapes and designs, both glazed and unglazed. (Green Fingers Nursery, Sydney).

Plants in general have a wide range of needs to be filled if they are to be kept as happy indoors as in ideal garden conditions.

The art of indoor gardening, then, becomes largely a matter of learning what these needs are, and how to compensate for the lack of them.

Let's start from the bottom with a few words about pots, and work our way up.

There are almost as many kinds of containers for indoor plants as there are plants themselves, but I believe the most practical are still the unglazed terracotta (burnt clay) pots that are made in many countries in sizes from 2 in (5 cm) to 24 in (60 cm) in diameter, with matching undersaucers for the larger types.

These terracotta pots generally have one or more good-sized drainage holes, and are completely porous. This means excess moisture will evaporate through the sides of the pot, and conversely, moisture can enter. This evaporative effect helps prevent roots scorching in hot weather, and also permits the entry of air (important to plant growth) through the pot walls. The usual type is taller than it is wide, and rather unattractive, both in shape and colour.

Large nurseries will stock terracotta pots in a wide variety of shapes. The wider, shallower types known as Azalea or bulb pots are useful for shallow-rooted plants, and less likely to tip over.

The curved, bowl-shaped types are perhaps more decorative and are available in diameters up to 4 ft (120 cm). There are also Strawberry jars with a number of openings in the side for growing small trailing plants, and collections of herbs and succulents. These are available both in upright and hanging types, and in several sizes.

The Cadillac of terracotta is the large Italian pot designed especially for Lemons and other Citrus fruits, and unchanged for centuries. These are decorated with masks and garlands in deep relief, and the larger types have classic figures copied from ancient Roman urns. They are expensive, but a pair of them makes a marvellous feature on a balcony or courtyard. The Italians also make horizontal terracotta troughs decorated in the same way. These rather resemble small sarcophagi.

Lightweight fibreglass planters can be quite expensive but hold many plants, as in this courtyard display of dwarf *ZINNIAS.*

Japanese terracotta pots are available in more subdued tones of brown and mauve, both glazed and unglazed, in keeping with the Japanese belief that the pot should not detract from the plant's own beauty.

In a more expensive range (and suitable for period interiors) are reproduction antique urns in lead, copper, cement, reconstituted stone and fibreglass. These are very heavy, particularly when filled.

A more sensible idea (if the plants are to be moved around much) is to buy one of the lightweight moulded plastic urns as an outer pot holder. Use a normal terracotta for the actual planting inside, packing the space between with sphagnum moss or tanbark.

Larger pots in many shapes and sizes are available in both asbestos cement and cement. The former are comparatively lightweight, but rather expensive.

New cement pots of all types should be used with caution, since cement naturally contains lime, which is anathema to acid-loving plants. These include most of the indoor types.

It is best to leave cement pots to age naturally for a year or, if this cannot be done, make sure they are filled and drained with fresh water several times, and use more than usual acid content in the compost with which you ultimately fill them.

Modern nurseries stock a wide range of flatter planters in anodized aluminium and various types of fibreglass and plastic. These are most suited to modern interiors, but are not all porous. Great care must be exercised in watering the plants placed in them.

On terraces, balconies and other outdoor positions, wooden planters are often effective. Their designs vary greatly, and because of the individual labour involved, they are often costly. Home handymen will find a wide range of patterns in their design manuals and in monthly magazines.

The thin plastic pots so often seen these days are as a general rule neither decorative nor functional, and are best abandoned after the plant has been brought home from the nursery.

The best source of decorative plant containers is often one of the many shops specialising in goods from the Far East. Manufacturers in China, Taiwan, Japan, Thailand and Vietnam produce a wide range of tasteful pots in every colour of the rainbow, and

This metal-lined wooden planter holds several miniature Palms (SYAGRUS weddeliana) and adds a strong architectural note to a light stairwell.

Indoor plants can be switched and changed in a group of matching, inexpensive pot holders, here arranged on an aluminium plant stand.

have been doing so for hundreds of years.

To me, the most attractive of these are probably the earthenware pots with a vivid jade glaze, from China. They are wonderfully suited to flowering plants, as are the similar, better-finished pots from Japan, finished in either a pure white, pale turquoise or deep blue glaze.

Some of the best bargains are undoubtedly the large 'Ali Baba' jars from Thailand, glazed in various shades of brown and green and modelled with dragons and other eastern motifs. These are large enough for the tallest indoor tree. But be cautious! They are not made as water jars (as often claimed) but to store dried foodstuffs, and are not completely waterproof. I've found there is a certain amount of seepage from the sides. This is to the good as far as the plants are concerned, but may mark your floors badly, so only invest in them if you can find some particularly large pot-saucers to place underneath. These saucers should always be fully glazed inside and out to prevent passage of water.

Casa Pupo and other Spanish, Portuguese and Italian companies manufacture white-glazed containers in a myriad shapes and textures. Most interesting are those finished with a basket or rope weave, while others imitate bamboo or seashells.

POT HOLDERS

As a general rule it is wiser to stick to old-fashioned terracotta pots, complete with drainage holes, and invest in a series of attractive pot-holders or *cachepots* to hold them when the plants are brought indoors.

But do buy your pot holders in sets of a single colour or in related styles. All white or all yellow, all wood or all cane, or all gold-anodised metal — whatever suits your own interior best.

The range is limited only by your pocketbook, and includes such luxury items as reproduction wooden Versailles planters, modern copies of blue-and-white Chinese porcelain, and many beautiful containers in copper and brass from Holland or the Middle East. Some of these resemble Victorian coal scuttles and 18th-century preserving pans.

From Asia there are pine soya barrels, and more elaborate tubs in brass-bound teak. Both Far East and Mediterranean areas export a wide range of baskets, which are most effective. They are quite porous, however, and care must be taken to locate some form of saucer to fit *inside* them. Very often, cheap baking pans will do.

The discerning indoor plant fan will soon develop a hawk-eye for suitable outer containers, including old bread crocks, teapots, earthenware mugs and 19th-century washbowl-and-jug sets, which can be beautifully adapted.

Some bowls intended for flower arrangement can be converted by simply piercing holes in the bottom with a masonry drill.

Just remember that whether they are kept in simple pots or grouped in large containers, all indoor plants need perfect drainage. It is no use even *trying* to grow them directly in containers without drainage holes, no matter how attractive they are.

EARTH, AIR, FIRE AND WATER

A simple recirculating water cascade provides all the humidity that indoor plants can use, either indoors or on a terrace.

To the ancients, all living things were composed from four elements: Earth, Air, Fire and Water. Modern scientists have learned to break things down more accurately, and expanded the table of elements into three figures.

But for indoor gardening, we might do well to recall the ancients' simple belief in four elements, substituting only temperature for real fire. Let's take them in the old order.

EARTH

It must be stressed that ordinary garden soil just will not do for pot culture. It is not porous enough, and does not drain properly. It tends to cake hard so that all the water you give the plant finds its way down the side of the pot instead of to the roots.

We must use instead composts (or mixtures) of materials balanced to the liking of the individual plant. Plant preferences vary widely, but fortunately the main ingredients of these composts do not — only their proportions, and the minor additions to them, do.

If your needs are small, it is obviously easier to buy a ready-mixed potting compost from your local nursery — but these leave a great deal to be desired and are relatively expensive. Enthusiastic indoor gardeners prefer to make their own formulas.

This may pose certain problems if you live in a small apartment, but you can always work in your kitchen, where there are scales and containers handy.

Quite a number of potting mixtures have been devised by various horticultural institutions, including some American universities, but the best and most versatile are probably the series of John Innes composts. These were developed in England to suit all types of plants growing in enclosed conditions.

The basic formula for all John Innes composts is:

7 parts of medium garden loam steamed for 20 minutes to destroy pests, seeds and disease spores.

3 parts granulated peat moss or leaf mould.

2 parts coarse river sand (not salt-water sand).

The ingredients are measured by loose bulk, not by weight, and must be mixed thoroughly.

There is also a basic fertiliser mix, which is added in different proportions to suit different conditions. It consists of:

2 parts hoof and horn meal
2 parts superphosphate
1 part potassium sulphate

These three items are measured by weight and thoroughly mixed also.

For **delicate hothouse plants,** or **small plants in small pots,** mix four ounces (114 grams) of the fertiliser mix into each *bushel* of the basic compost (a bushel is approximately 1½ cubic feet or .036 cubic meters).

For **less delicate plants** and those in pots of 5 in (13 cm) or larger diameter, use *double* the amount of

21

Cacti and succulents prefer a gritty, well-drained plant mix. This is *EUPHORBIA pseudocactus.*

Many plants can be grown in pure water with no soil at all. Here is a sprouting Hyacinth bulb in a special glass container.

PHILODENDRON X 'Imbe' likes an acid, well-drained compost, and regular leaf spraying with warm water.

the fertiliser mix to each bushel of basic compost.

For **really large plants,** in pots more than 8 in (20 cm) in diameter, or those that are to be kept permanently indoors, use *three times* the fertiliser mix to each bushel of basic compost.

The John Innes composts retain moisture, drain well and provide all the nutrient a plant will use until it outgrows the pot.

Caution: These composts are designed for lime-hating plants (calcifuges), which include most of the tropical types of house plant.

For plants that prefer lime (and you'll learn which ones do in the individual listings later in the book), you'll need to add ¾ ounce (21 grams) of dolomite to each 4 ounces (114 grams) of the prepared fertiliser mix.

Some special plants will require slight variations.

Plump-rooted plants, like bulbs and tubers, require a more porous mix; omit some loam; add sand or vermiculite.

Cacti and succulents like fast drainage; double the sand, reduce the loam.

Gross feeders like *COLEUS, PETUNIAS* and many annuals do better with a ration of aged animal manure in the mix.

Please don't let the compost variations rob you of any sleep. All that is necessary is to mix up a few bushels of the basic John Innes compost and keep it under cover until needed.

Then, a few pounds of the fertiliser mix can be kept separately and will last you for weeks. Extra ingredients you'll need occasionally can be kept in small containers, just as you'd keep cooking ingredients.

These might include coarse sand, sphagnum moss, leaf mould, declayed tanbark, charcoal, vermiculite, Polyurethane granules, pebbles and animal manure.

In custom-blending your composts for individual plants, just keep the following facts in mind:

Sand has no food value, is used to promote fast drainage and stimulate root growth.

Peatmoss and decayed tanbark are very acid and moisture-retaining.

Leaf mould is equally acid and richer in nutritive elements.

Animal manure is richest in growth elements, but scarcely acid at all. It may even be alkaline.

Vermiculite has no nutritive value, but absorbs many times its own weight in water to keep a compost moist.

Charcoal is pure carbon. All plants love it, and it prevents the soil souring due to over-watering and clogged drainage. Many Orchid growers raise prize blooms in pots of pure charcoal.

AIR

The second of the ancient elements is often overlooked in indoor gardening, but the fact is, plants appreciate fresh air as much as you do, and react as badly to cold draughts or an over-dry atmosphere. Most of them are sensitive to household gas and will not do well in the same room as a gas fire or cooker.

When practical (even in the winter months on a fine day the air outdoors is at the same temperature or warmer than an unheated room) it is helpful to open all the windows and let both room and plants freshen up.

Don't place them in strong draughts, however, whether hot or cold. These tend to dehydrate the foliage. The same degree of humidity you would find comfortable indoors is good for your plants.

Plants are great air fresheners indoors, because one of their more useful functions is to produce and distribute oxygen by breathing in stale carbon

This ornate mirror reflects a number of indoor plantings in an airy Californian interior.

This heavy planting grouped around an old statue revels in the humidity from a recirculating indoor fountain.

dioxide. The carbon they use as nutriment; the oxygen they expel back into the air.

Plants perform this valuable gas exchange through millions of tiny leaf-pores called *stomata* — and it is as necessary to their well being as the absorption of water through the roots.

To carry it out, their leaves must be clean. The best way to ensure this is to place the plants out-doors on a terrace occasionally, in a rain shower.

If this is not practical, a short spell under the bathroom shower set at room temperature, will remove any coating of clogging dust. Exceptions are furry-leafed plants, which prefer a light brushing.

FIRE

In the indoor gardening sense, we read this to mean temperature.

Plants, particularly the tropical types usually grown indoors, are greatly affected by changes in room temperature. In nature, the heat goes up as the days grow longer; the temperature falls as they grow short. But since houses are designed for people and not plants, the opposite is usually true. We turn on the heat during the short days, and try to lower the temperature in summer by pulling down blinds and turning on fans and air-conditioning.

Yet most plants must have a season of lower temperature to rest and consolidate their energies, with warmth during the long days to make maximum growth and develop flowers. What to do?

Many growers will try to give their valuable plants a warm-weather spell outdoors to really burst out all over; but with a little commonsense we can adapt indoor conditions to suit the plants as well as ourselves. A sunny windowsill, for instance, will have a higher summer temperature during the day than the rest of the room. The same windowsill may be colder than the room in winter and need a light curtaining between plants and glass to prevent cold damage.

Bay Trees *(LAURUS)* in wooden Versailles planters are out for a summer airing at Empress Josephine's Chateau of Malmaison near Paris. They will be carried indoors for decoration, and in winter.

Room temperatures for plants can be varied by moving them away from the source of heat, or nearer to it, depending on individual plant preferences.

Caution: Make sure any movements into the sun are gradual. A plant which has not known direct sun will burn more badly than you on your first swimming day of summer. The big difference is that a plant can't shed any skin, so the affected leaves scorch and die.

Remember too that heat rises, so valuable plants shouldn't be positioned close to central-heating ducts in the cold weather. Move them well away. Under-window heaters can be utilised, however, by building an insulated shelf above them and topping it with a tray of damp gravel on which the plants can be positioned. Rising humidity from the gravel (which must be kept wet) will help prevent leaf scorch and keep the foliage fresh. Unheated rooms (such as glassed-in sunrooms) can be warmed economically on chill winter nights by using a cheap kerosene heater. Variations of these are made especially for plant heating, and incorporate a tray that can be filled with water for humidifying.

Individual minimum temperature requirements for each plant are shown in the Dictionary. You will find most of them are happy with a winter night minimum of 60° F (15° C), which is not hard to achieve in average home conditions, particularly where curtained windows minimise heat loss through large areas of glass.

Light humidity automatically provides a cooling effect in dry summer heat, particularly where there is air movement. Placing the plants together above trays of moistened gravel or peat is beneficial, as is regular syringeing of the foliage with clear water.

WATER

Control of water, humidity and drainage is the key to success in indoor gardening. Indoor plants need more moisture than plants in natural garden conditions, yet paradoxically, more of them are lost through drowning than any other cause.

Plant roots need air as well as water, and cannot breathe if the soil does not drain well and is constantly soggy. Never judge watering needs by the condition of the surface soil. If it appears dry, poke your finger well in. If it is damp an inch or so down, no water is needed. Water when the plant shows signs of distress, not just when it is convenient for you. The need for water will vary according to the plant's size and leaf area; the size and type of pot; the temperature and humidity of the room it lives in.

Plants absorb water through their roots, filter it up through the stem and breathe out water vapour through the leaves. The more leaf area, the more water a plant can dispose of, especially in dry or windy conditions.

Porous terracotta, wood or cement pots allow moisture to evaporate through their sides, especially when they are in the sun. Glazed ceramic, plastic and metal containers are not porous. Water cannot evaporate through the sides and they become so hot in the sun that the roots will literally boil.

All plants require more water in summer, when they are making growth, than in winter, when they are resting — and it is a wise rule to water rarely and deeply rather than lightly and often. Best of all is to soak the plant in a sink or a larger container so that it absorbs water through the entire root mass. Leave the pot and its contents under water until the bubbles have ceased to rise, then put it aside to drain before returning the plant to its regular position.

Exceptions to this rule are soft-stemmed plants such as Gesneriads (see Dictionary entry). It is not wise to cover the stems of these with water. Stand their pot in a shallower container and let the water filter up naturally until the surface is barely damp.

Tropical plants in particular absorb water through their leaves as well as their roots, and suffer from the over-dry atmosphere indoors. They cannot compensate by the absorption of natural dew and rain as they do ourdoors. During the summer months, stand them in a large tray of water or moist gravel so that evaporation can bring the necessary humidity to the leaves, and spray all the foliage at least twice a week with an atomiser. This can be done at close range withour damage to furnishings.

Indoor plants prefer water slightly warm or at room temperature, particularly in winter. Most tap water is suitable, though some indoor gardeners prefer to let it stand a while to let excess minerals settle to the bottom. The Japanese, the most skilled indoor gardeners of all, prefer to use rain water, and set aside a large barrel to collect it as run-off from the roof — but this is rarely practical for apartment dwellers.

POTTING, REPOTTING, POTTING ON

Flowering bulbs can be crowded into a pot for indoor use, but will last only one season.

A suggestion of repetition in the chapter heading is completely intentional. Potting of one sort or another is a continuous process if your indoor plants are to grow and remain in generally good condition. There are a few plants that like to be crowded and resent disturbance, but these exceptions to the rule are noted in the entries of the Dictionary section. Here we are concerned with the majority.

THE POT
Whichever one you select should be completely clean, and if used before, should be thoroughly scrubbed and sterilised in boiling water. This is essential to destroy disease spores and insect eggs, which have a great instinct for survival.

POTTING ON:
The pot must never be too big for the plant. Small plants are always started in the smallest possible pot, and gradually repotted in fresh compost and larger pots as they grow. This process is called potting on or potting up, and there are many reasons for it — not the least being that the roots of small plants cannot reach out into the compost of a large pot to convert the moisture and food, with the result that the compost may sour and retain too much water, leading to root rot and other diseases.

An additional good reason for not using over-large pots is that plants tend to flower more heavily when the roots are crowded. It's a sort of panic reaction against potential starvation, in which the plant rushes to flower and reproduce as quickly as possible.

POTTING
I always start by covering the drainage holes with a simple cupboard ventilator or sink strainer, costing only a few pence or cents at any hardware store. This helps prevent the entry of unwelcome insect visitors.

Next, I add a couple of pieces of broken terracotta to prevent precious compost from being washed away, and a layer of coarse gravel mixed with charcoal. This draining layer may be as much as one fifth the depth of the pot.

Fill with compost as far as necessary to support the root mass of the new plant. This will be deep enough in the pot so that the nursery soil mark on the stem falls slightly below the rim.

Spread the roots out horizontally, then fill the container to the soil mark level. Do not press the compost in, for you want to retain its open porous nature.

Instead, lift the pot and tap its bottom sharply on a flat surface several times. This will encourage the compost to settle, firmly supporting the roots.

If a small stake or cane is necessary to support the plant, it should be placed in position *before* topping up, and the plant attached to it with a flexible plant tie, not a wire.

REPOTTING
As a general rule, indoor plants should be repotted only when they have used up the nutrients in the compost. This can sometimes be signalled by the plant's roots appearing through the drainage holes in search of more food.

Seedling Umbrella Trees *(BRASSAIA)* are raised in 2 in (5 cm) pots until large enough to transplant.

Gradually repotted to a 16 in (41 cm) pot, the *BRASSAIA* will reach 6 ft (2 m) in a container.

Remember that the bulk of a plant's roots will correspond with the bulk of its leaves, and a year of particularly heavy growth will generally mean a larger pot.

Repotting is generally done in early spring, though some growers prefer to wait till summer is nearly over so that the plant will look fresh for winter. It should be carried out on a large table, out of sunlight and away from drying wind. Having prepared the new compost, place the necessary drainage material in the bottom of the new pot, which should be no more than 2 in (5 cm) larger all around than the old and, again, should have been sterilised.

Water the patient several hours before the operation, and leave to drain. Then, tip the old pot upside down, placing a hand flat on the surface and around the stem or trunk. Tap the pot sharply on all sides with a stick, or on the edge of a table. It should now be possible merely to turn the plant rightside up and have the old pot fall away. If it still sticks, run an old knife around the inside of the pot.

Plant and root ball should slide out easily in one mass, and it will not be necessary to disturb the roots further unless there are signs that the pot has not been draining well. This will generally be signalled by dead roots on the outside of the root ball, and these should immediately be cut away.

How do you know if a root is dead? Well, generally, a live, growing root will have a plump green or white tip, and will be of a light colour, with whitish feeding hairs. Dead roots are generally dark, almost black. Their feeding hairs fall off and the outer shell sloughs away. Cut right back to fresh, live root tissue with a very sharp, clean knife.

On other occasions, you may find the roots have been travelling round and round the inside surface of the pot. This generally means that the compost has dried out and water has been penetrating only down the pot's inner surface. Untangle the roots with a light stick or dessert fork and cut them away

to a more reasonable length, shaking away the dried mass of compost you'll find in the centre.

After completing any of these three alternatives, place the old root mass on top of fresh compost in the larger pot and pack the new compost all around the sides and a little on top, still leaving space for water below the pot rim.

Settle the new compost in firmly by tapping the pot as outlined above — do not press hard in case you damage delicate roots. Instead, after either potting or repotting, soak the plant by placing it almost up to the rim in a large container of water, then set aside to drain. The soaking may cause the compost to settle, and additional compost can be added on top.

If it is necessary or desirable to keep the plant the same size, or to return it to the same pot, you must take a razor-sharp knife and cut away some of the root mass at the bottom and on all sides, to make room for new compost. You might also tease the roots out and cut away any stragglers. But be sure to leave no cut root ends behind — these might decay and start an infection.

Ideally, root pruning should be balanced by removing some of the foliage as well, otherwise the plant will lose more moisture by leaf-evaporation than it can absorb through its shortened root system. If cutting back the foliage would spoil the shape, then water the plant and cover it (pot and all) with a large clear plastic bag. Leave this in place for a week or more to conserve humidity while the plant is starting to replace the lost roots.

Through all of these potting processes, it is vitally important that the roots should never be allowed to dry out. If you've started work on too many plants at once and have to break for lunch, cover all of the roots with dampened hessian or newspaper until work can resume. Do not wait until you have several freshly potted plants ready to soak. Water them one at a time before starting the next.

LET THERE BE LIGHT

Well-lit interior of the author's house makes possible an ever-changing display of indoor *AZALEAS, CAMELLIAS* and other flowering shrubs. (Photo by 'Home Beautiful' magazine).

Many factors interact to induce healthy growth in a plant. We have now dealt with the potting mixture and the pots themselves, the necessary water, air and temperature, and the humidity that comes about as a combination of them.

Finally, we must deal with light. No plant can grow properly without it, for light is the catalyst that enables the plant to convert food to its own use. It does this by means of a process called photosynthesis, in which light reacts on the green chlorophyll in the leaves and enables them to extract the necessary sugar and oxygen from absorbed carbon dioxide and water.

Without sugar and water, no plant can grow satisfactorily — you will find in the Dictionary section several freak plants that are without chlorophyll and have to be grafted on to other host plants to survive at all.

As a general rule, flowering plants need more light than foliage plants if they are to bloom properly. This is because they need to convert vast quantities of food to use solely for the production of the flowers and, later, fruit. And in addition to the flowers, the plant still has to keep its leaves in a healthy condition. So — more light, more flowers.

The foliage plants we call 'houseplants' are quite a different story. The deeper the jungles they come from, the less light they need indoors to survive.

Their dark leaves are particularly rich in chlorophyll, which makes them sensitive to a minimal amount of light. They won't grow much, and they'll never produce flowers, but they will stay healthy so long as they are not watered too heavily. If this seems in contradiction to normal practice, just remember that without strong light, the plants are unable to convert the water to food, and will in consequence drown. Leaf drop is the first sign of distress in such circumstances, and one of the best revival techniques is to move the plant to a lighter position so it can use up the excess moisture — but not directly into the sun, for the leaves, unused to strong light, would burn badly, and the plant be worse off than before.

Sudden light changes of any sort affect all types of indoor plants — a new position, a change of curtaining or even wall colour in the room where it lives.

New plants brought straight from the plant shop or nursery should be given as much light as possible initially and only gradually moved to their final positions. This may be well away from windows in the case of dark-leafed plants.

Great attention has been given to lighting for plants in the unbelievable 17-floor-high lobby of San Francisco's Hyatt Regency Hotel. The row of 30 ft (10 m) high Indian Laurel Trees (*FICUS retusa*) flourish in the natural daylight of high-set windows, boosted by low hanging spots over each tree. (Photo by Akinari Takeuchi).

Overhead Gro-lux lighting keeps this hanging *NEPHROLEPIS* Fern happy and healthy in an otherwise dark interior. (Crossley's Flowers, Beverly Hills).

Pale or variegated leaves pose an additional set of problems, for their white leaf areas contain little or no chlorophyll and are unable to carry on the food conversion process. So the more variegations a plant has, the more light it needs merely to survive, let alone continue healthy growth.

In choosing a permanent position for an indoor plant, remember that:

Windows facing away from the equator give even light without sun at all times of the year.

Windows facing toward the equator give direct sunlight in the colder months, but less sunlight in summer when the sun is overhead — sometimes none at all when you take into account overhanging eaves or awnings.

East and west-facing windows will give the most direct sunlight on a year round basis, though only for half the day. They may need morning or afternoon diffusion of a light curtain during the summer.

Since lack of light is sometimes the major barrier to plant growth in sunless rooms, it is worthwhile giving some thought to increasing its intensity. You can help do this by painting all window woodwork in a light colour, preferably white, and having the walls directly opposite the window in a light, reflective tone. Use venetian blinds rather than roller blinds if privacy is a problem, but preferably none at all; and make sure that any curtains can be drawn completely away from the windows. You may even be able to help by thinning any outdoor vegetation that comes between your window and the sun.

Many plants need a minimum number of daylight hours to flower or produce leaf colourings, or to hold onto their leaves at all. In winter months, particularly in areas well away from the equator where days are very short, this may be quite a serious matter, however well heated and humidified the plant may be.

So you may find your plants will benefit at this time from a few extra hours of light — not ordinary room incandescent light, but fluorescent tubes, which are cooler and radiate the wavelengths most closely approximating natural sunlight. There are special types of fluorescent tubes manufactured solely for the benefit of plants — Sylvania is one manufacturer, Grolux is a trade name.

There are special planters incorporating light tubes on the market, but they are pretty unsightly for living room use. You will probably find it more acceptable to mount the light fixtures in a bookcase or window frame, with the plants directly underneath.

For larger dish plantings, a special fixture can be made up and suspended right over the planter with hanging chains or wires. These can be moved nearer to or further away from the plant according to the season and growth.

However you use them, the special tubes designed for plant growth always come with details of correct placement distances for many types of plants. They fluoresce in a combination of red and blue light that is even better for plants than daylight. They also enhance the colours of flowers and leaves (particularly

Tropical houseplants stay healthy in dim light well away from windows. Here is a mixed planting of *AGLAONEMA* and *DIEFFENBACHIA.*

Variegated and coloured-leaf plants like these Crotons, are weak in chlorophyll, and need the strongest available light.

Flowering plants, including bulbs, need all the natural light they can get, and do best by a sunny window.

Flowering shrubs, Palms and many other plants prefer the full light of a large window.

pink or red ones), in much the way that special lighting in a butcher's window makes the meat look so appetising.

OTHER POINTS WORTH REMEMBERING

In winter, foliage houseplants need all the light you can give them and are best moved closer to a window — in summer, the opposite applies.

Plants that live naturally in or under trees (such as epiphytic Ferns, Bromeliads and Orchids) need less light than those that are found in the open (such as most Cacti, succulents and many Palms). These may be exposed to direct sun.

Most flowering plants need an average of fourteen hours of light per day in the flowering season, but there are others that flower around winter in which the bloom is actually triggered by the shrinking hours of light. These include *CYCLAMEN,* Crab Cactus, many *BEGONIAS* and succulents, and in particular Poinsettias, which will not develop their colourful bracts at all if they receive much illumination out of daylight hours, and are best not brought into the living room until they are in full colour.

Nurserymen raise them in special 'darkhouses' where the light can be deliberately cut out at a certain point to force flowering at any time of the year, but elsewhere their flowering cycle can be upset by nearby night lighting in streets or from houses, resulting in a very poor display of colour.

So for all your indoor plants the rule is 'Let There be Light' — but not necessarily as much of it as you might think!

GARDENING IN THE AIR

This decorative Tunisian birdcage has been planted by the author with
CHLOROPHYTUM, trailing *COLEUS, PHILODENDRON* and Ivy. See text for details.

Baskets and other hanging containers have been used to grow plants since the beginning of civilisation as we know it. They are still a decorative solution where space is short, and the only satisfactory way of displaying many epiphytic plants, whose flowers are borne on the underside of trailing stems, or are produced in some way that makes them clearly visible only at eye level or above.

I use hanging containers for many types of Orchids and Ferns, for creeping *COLEUS* and *CAMPANULAS*, for *BEGONIAS, BROWALLIA* and epiphytic Cacti such as *EPIPHYLLUM, RHIPSALIDOPSIS, WINTERIA* and *ZYGOCACTUS*.

Until recently the only containers available were either made of wire, which rusted, or from wooden slats, which rotted. Both types dripped water and potting soil all over the place and could be used only out of doors — unless you were prepared to do a great deal of cleaning up.

But now, the green invasion of our houses has generated a host of new container ideas, and modern technology has solved most of the problems.

WHERE TO USE HANGING CONTAINERS
Outdoors: under house eaves or pergolas; beneath covered walkways; suspended from brackets of the type used for hanging signs; from balcony roofs to give privacy or frame a view.

Indoors: in window reveals or doorways; in the bathroom, kitchen or sunroom; in the living room, dining room or anywhere a strong hook can be screwed into solid support.

30

Colourful 'Basket Begonias' (*B. tuberhybrida Pendula*) make stunning hanging plants for a garden room or glassed-in sunroom.

A good solution to dripping hanging pots is to hang a waterproof under-saucer, merely standing the container on top.

In good light or bad, dependent on the choice of plant. Just remember to hang them high enough to clear the tallest person in a traffic area. Nobody wants to dodge heavy baskets as they move around.

Remember, too, that the ceiling hooks, brackets, chains or whatever you use to support your hanging gardens must be really strong and properly attached either to solid wood or concrete. A container full of wet soil weighs a great deal, and would certainly not get sufficient support from a plaster ceiling or window trim. Proper fixing is the only way to avoid accidents.

One of the great advantages of hanging gardens is that they are portable and can be moved indoors or out according to the season.

But 'portable' is a word with many shades of meaning — the important one being can *you* handle it without help? A cubic yard or cubic metre of soil and pot can weigh as much as one ton (1000 kg)! — even a full 10 in (25 cm) pot can weigh 30 or 40 pounds (15 kg).

Let us assume you won't be doing too much moving of the hanging planters once they're in place! Still, you must be able to get at them for watering, fertilising, pruning, etc. Outdoors, this could be solved by the use of a stepladder, but if you live in an apartment, that leads to additional storage problems.

It is far easier and more satisfactory to install some type of pulley system so the basket can be lowered to a reasonable working height. I'm not suggesting this should be done with every basket, but it is a practical way of getting at one or two special containers, or for changing containers around in a special position.

The rope or wire supporting a basket is merely run through a single pulley wheel attached to a ceiling hook, and needs a wall bracket nearby to which it can be attached.

HANGING YOUR GARDEN

At most nurseries or plant shops there are now a number of attractive gadgets to support your hanging garden. These include macramé slings, brass chandelier chains, and 'Hangups' (which are ingenious little clear perspex platforms supported by transparent and adjustable plastic lines); heavy plaited nylon cords in white or various colours can be used for larger containers; lightweight plastic chains are decorative for plastic planters in modern shapes; plaited leather cords are effective outdoors with stained wood planters.

Any well-furnished hanging garden is stunning on its own, particularly when almost hidden by cascading greenery and flowers, but the effect is multiplied many times by hanging plants in groups — say three matching containers hung at different heights and staggered a little to each side of one another.

THE CONTAINERS

In addition to wire or wood baskets, which are now available in improved forms (the wire plastic-coated to prevent rust, the wood treated with preservative compounds), a number of new hanging containers have also come onto the market. The most important are hemispherical baskets of natural fibre compressed over a wire frame. The fibre is impregnated with plastic and looks very like a bathroom loofah sponge in its texture. They hold soil perfectly, and are so porous that many plants actually shoot out through the fabric, making it possible to have a hanging garden with plants on all sides, not just on top. In Australia these are called 'Mulchmats'.

There are clear plastic containers, usually globular or hemispherical, and quite drip-proof. These are attractive in modern interiors.

There are eye-catching designs in porous terracotta — dull brown and black as well as lighter

Most colourful of hanging plants are the glorious 'Column Flowers' or *COLUMNEAS,* available in many shades of red, orange and yellow.

colours. Some of these are conical or pear shaped, others spherical. A few have side holes like old fashioned 'Strawberry' pots, others are dish-shaped and completely open at the top (these are usually supported on slings).

There are plastic or anodised metal planters in many shapes, usually attached to their own drip tray. I do not find these in the least attractive, but they seem to sell by the thousands in unlikely colours like orange or purple, which harmonise with no known plant.

Finally, I have seen many ceramic designs, often interestingly textured and coloured and pierced with holes for hanging chains.

Containers already pierced with drainage holes will need some sort of plant saucer suspended underneath. This can often be overcome by hanging the drip saucer itself, and merely standing the pot on top of it.

Alternatively, the pierced pot can be given an inner lining or inner saucer to prevent water spillage.

Pots without drainage holes will need a deep layer of coke, charcoal or rubble where excess moisture can lodge and evaporate rather than rot the roots.

Porous containers of terracotta, clay, cork or wood will dry out quickly, but do allow excess water to evaporate.

Water cannot evaporate through plastic, aluminium or glazed ceramic. These must be watered lightly and emptied regularly to prevent the plants damping off.

The choice is up to you.

For every design and shape of hanging basket or pot, there is an equivalent half-basket or pot, designed to be hung flush against a wall, mounted on brackets. These are often most effective in sunny positions, filled with succulents or flowering annuals — but please use them in groups, not just singly.

Travelling around, I am constantly amazed at the originality used by many plant fanciers in their choice of hanging containers. Among these are: hollowed-out lengths of treefern trunk (Hawaii); the outer husks of coconuts filled with epiphytic Cacti (Tahiti); kitchen colanders, lettuce baskets and the tiers of three wire-mesh hanging baskets used to hold fruit and vegetables in the kitchen.

Finally of course, in the luxury class, are ornamental birdcages. But birdcages need some adaptation if they are to be really satisfactory, for they can rarely hold sufficient depth of soil to satisfy plants. I have illustrated one of my own, a fantastic Tunisian affair planted with *COLEUS, CHLOROPHYTUM* and *PHILODENDRON.*

This was adapted by cutting a square hole in the base and inserting a square, lipped pot, glazed the same white as the cage.

Other cages have a gravel tray, which clips over the outside of the wire frame. This can be deepened sufficiently either to take a good depth of soil or to act as a supporting base for a collection of pots placed inside.

Cages designed for small birds usually have too many wires to let growing plants through, and I adapt mine by clipping away every second wire.

As a general rule the charming Japanese cages, which look like many tiered pagodas, are not satisfactory, for the light cane of which they are constructed rots too quickly. Wire or wrought-iron cages are the best for plant work.

Mixed planting of hybrid *DENDROBIUM* Orchids arranged in an umbrella-shaped hanging container of beaten copper. (Kahala Hilton Hotel).

32

PLANTING A BASKET

Hanging baskets, whether of wire, cane or wood, must be lined with some other material if the potting mix is to remain intact.

If a coarse mixture of treefern chunks, sphagnum and rubble is to be used (as for many Orchids) I prefer merely a light lining of plastic insect mesh. This keeps everything together and ensures the free movement of air so important to epiphytic plants.

Wire baskets to hold more conventional potting mixes must be completely lined. In the case of square ones, this can be done easily with cork tiles. More conventionally shaped hemispherical baskets are best lined with a double layer of fine bark (available by the roll at many nurseries), or with a thick mat of natural sphagnum moss. These are kept in place by the weight of the potting mix. You can even use sheets of natural moss, turned growing side out. This last is far and away the most attractive, turning brown in dry weather, and greening up again in humid shade.

For indoor use, it is a work-saving plan to partly line the basket (the lower half) with either foil or horticultural Polythene. This is placed *inside* the moss before the basket is filled, and helps retain soil moisture as well as prevent drips.

COMPOST FOR HANGING GARDENS

Any commercial houseplant mix will be fine for hanging baskets or containers, but if you are mixing your own it's not a bad idea to keep the potential weight of the mix in mind. Composts can be made lighter by using a large proportion of vermiculite, perlite or Polyurethane pebbles. All of these ingredients are extremely lightweight but moisture-retaining.

The main thing is that the mix for a hanging basket be porous so that water and fertiliser can easily penetrate to all parts. Each basketful of mix should also contain a loose handful of milled cow manure and bone meal mixed thoroughly through to give the plants continuing nutrition.

After they are thoroughly established, your hanging gardens will still require a twice-monthly feeding with diluted natural fertiliser such as fish emulsion or liquefied cow manure, because soil nutrients are continually washed away with water draining from the container.

WATERING HANGING GARDENS

It is only natural that hanging baskets and porous hanging pots will dry out far more quickly than other types. Air movement and the natural process of evaporation quickly take moisture from all sides of the container — though just how quickly depends on the location and the weather. Containers will need watering at least once a day in hot weather, preferably in the evening. This is best done with a long-spouted watering can or small hose, the water being slowly dribbled around the plant so that it sinks well in. Nevertheless, at least twice a month

Epiphytic Cacti such as *RHIPSALIDOPSIS* are seen at their best in hanging containers.

the entire plant, basket and all, should be thoroughly soaked in a large tub, or even the kitchen sink or bath. This could be combined with the twice-monthly feeding.

After soaking, the basket should be set aside to drain thoroughly before rehanging.

In dry or windy weather, a close-up spray from an atomiser will help keep the plants fresh-looking.

Pests, fortunately, are not a great problem in containers although you may still need to spray against caterpillars and flying insects such as thrip.

PLANTING HANGING GARDENS

Most hanging pots seen in nursery and plant shop displays contain a single trailing plant, but the most attractive result is obtained by mixing your plantings in a single container. The vertical interest of a *DRACAENA* or *CORDYLINE*, or one of the taller growing *PTERIS* Ferns, brings many a hanging display to life.

In Victorian days there was quite a vogue for mixed hanging plantings of Ferns, small Palms, Ivy, *FUCHSIAS* and small trailing annuals.

The last can be planted through the sides of a wire basket as it is being filled, layer by layer. They will quickly learn to grow upside down once the roots become established and give a far more profuse effect than merely planting the top of the container. Wild Strawberries, *CAMPANULAS* and *SAXIFRAGAS* lend themselves particularly well to this treatment.

Ivies, *HOYAS*, *TRADESCANTIAS* and *ZEBRINAS* are useful trailing plants, while Geraniums, *LOBELIA*, *PETUNIAS* and *VERBENA* are among the many flowering plants that add colour in basket work.

Almost anything can be used, and you'll find hundreds of possibilities in the illustrated Dictionary, which occupies the greater part of this book.

GARDENING IN GLASS

Delicate Maidenhair Ferns (*ADIANTUM* spp.) thrive in the moist, humid
enclosure of an old-fashioned witch- bowl, planted as a terrarium.

For indoor gardeners who love green growing things but really don't have the time to look after them properly, bottle gardens or terrariums may be the ideal solution. They can be bought ready planted at most indoor plant shops — but creating them for yourself is half the pleasure.

Insulated from the world outside, many types of plants flourish and stay fresh for months, even years, in the sparkling glass container of their very own universe. They need no water, no fresh air, but constantly use and replenish their own humid atmosphere.

Terrariums (as they are popularly but incorrectly called) were first made in the 1830s by a London botanist, Dr N. Ward, and the idea quickly caught on both for its educational and decorative value.

Thousands of strangely shaped glass containers known as 'Wardian Cases' were manufactured. As evidence of a scientific turn of mind they were interesting, but as items of interior decoration, monstrosities. It is not surprising that the originals now exist only in illustrations.

Today, in the revival of Dr Ward's idea, containers of many kinds are being used, and a vast range of specialised bottles are manufactured and sold purely for the enjoyment of this charming hobby.

Our airy, modern houses and apartments are a far cry from gloomy Victorian drawing rooms where plants were shrivelled by the gas lighting and open coal fires. But bottle gardens still have advantages when the matter of aftercare is taken into account.

They enable us to grow many interesting plants out of season, just as in an expensive heated conservatory. They are particularly useful for flat or apartment dwellers who can display fascinating collections of rare plants in a wide choice of decorative settings.

Once the right balance of moisture has been achieved, the 'garden' can be left for months without further attention. There is no problem if the owner must go away on vacation and leave it unattended.

CHOOSING THE PLANTS
It is impossible to produce dry atmospheric conditions in a glass garden, so that eliminates most Cacti and other xerophytic plants. Choose from the many types that love or tolerate humidity, particularly tropical ones. Another obvious choice is a

grouping of small Mosses and Ferns, of which many interesting types can be bought from nurseries and indoor plant shops.

In general, choose plants that don't grow to any great size or, if they do, are slow growing.

Even seedling trees can be grown. A stunted seedling might give a bonsai effect for a time, and you could create a landscape at its base, using moss for grass and some interesting stones.

Some of the tiniest, least-considered native plants may be of value in this 'new' kind of garden.

But be careful about flowering plants. Dead blooms may spoil the effect of a bottle garden and, more importantly, may harbour a spreading fungus disease. So don't put these plants in a narrow-necked bottle; grow them in a glass dome (more about these later) or in a wide container with a removeable glass cover.

And try not to introduce pests or diseases into the bottle world when planting it. You might prefer to spray the plants first.

FINDING THE CONTAINER

Many kinds of container are suitable — ingenuity is the keynote in glass gardening — but be sure it is pleasantly proportioned. Attempts to grow pretty

Fairy Rose "Climbing Baby Masquerade" and *CAMPANULA* growing under a glass dome in the author's home. (Photo by courtesy 'Australian Women's Weekly').

A handsome terrarium by 'Green Fingers' nursery. The planting includes variegated Ivy, African Violets, *AGLAONEMA* and Ferns.

plants in ugly vessels would surely be too thorough a revival of Dr Ward's hobby.

Everyday suggestions would include old candy jars, presentation liqueur bottles, perfume decanters, vinegar or wine flagons, glass carafes.

A hunt for old glass in antique shops would reveal some more exotic (and expensive) possibilities: acid carboys, chemist's jars and even goldfish bowls.

It is not essential to keep the container closed. Some growers prefer to leave them unstoppered; the loss of moisture is fairly slow with a small opening, because much of it still condenses on the sides of the bottle and trickles down again into the soil. It would still not be necessary to water the garden very often.

But a goldfish bowl, or any really wide-mouthed jar, is more likely to need a glass lid. Get a handyman friend to cut a piece of sheet glass to the right diameter or inquire at a glass dealer — it doesn't cost much to have it done.

THE SOIL

Soil should be treated to avoid introducing pests or weed seeds. You should use a commercial plant compost, available from nurseries and many hardware stores, that has been steam sterilised. It will require a little additional sand for drainage and some granulated charcoal to prevent the soil from becoming sour.

THE TOOLS

Tools for planting bottle gardens can be extemporised. These, I suggest, would be useful.

A barbecue fork with extending handle (for weeding).

A length of strong wire bent into an almost right-angled loop at one end (to hold plants).

Antique glass acid carboys are most sought after for planting as terrariums. This one houses a varied collection of tropical plants including *DRACAENA*, Ivy, *CTENANTHE*, and *TRADESCANTIA*.

A length of bamboo to push plants in and tamp down soil.
A funnel for pouring compost.
A rolled cardboard tube, slightly narrower than the neck of the bottle.
A long-necked fine spray or syringe for watering the planting.

METHOD OF PLANTING

First wash and polish the bottle, making sure it is clean and perfectly dry inside. Crusted deposits of old contents can be removed by shaking some lead shot or small pebbles inside the bottle with warm water and detergent.

Insert garden moss, a piece at a time, and line the bottom of the bottle with it, growing-side out.

Now, through the tube inserted into the neck of the bottle and lowered as far as possible, cover the moss first with a layer of sand and then with pebbles mixed with small pieces of charcoal. Spread these out with the bamboo.

Through the tube, again, pour a layer of granulated peat moss. This will later hold moisture well, but it is easier to introduce when quite dry.

Finally, pour in several inches of the soil mixture, still using the funnel and tube. The tube is important because it prevents fine particles of soil from flying around and adhering to the inside of the bottle, where they are difficult to remove.

With the length of bamboo, tamp the soil firmly in position, but leave the natural hill contour from the pouring. Finally use the same tool to poke a hollow for the first plant.

Tip the plant out of its container and loosen most of the soil from the roots. Sit it on the looped end of the planting wire and lower gently through the neck

a. Partly line container with moss pieces, growing side out. Through a cardboard tube, add pebbles and charcoal for drainage, then planting mix. (above)

b. After making a hollow, add plants one at a time, supported on a wire loop. Slip it through the neck of the bottle, guiding the leaves by hand. (opposite)

c. Tamp soil over the roots with a blunt stick. Complete planting with ground covers, add surface pebbles for decoration. Water gently with a very fine spray. (above)

African Violets *(SAINTPAULIAS)* love the humid conditions inside a brandy snifter fitted with the lid from an old candy jar.

Quite the opposite to most terrariums, this one is completely dry — a bed of dried moss and lichen supports an arrangement of artificially preserved flowers and butterflies, keeping out the humidity that would otherwise rot them. (Eschbachs Flowers, Laguna Beach, Calif.).

of the bottle. Use your other hand as a funnel to fold the plant leaves together so they will pass through the small opening.

With the plant in position in the hollow, move soil over the roots with the bamboo and slip the loop out. Tamp soil into place and repeat this procedure until all plants are in position.

With the funnel and tube introduce a soil cover of fine sand or pebbles and spray water through the neck of the bottle with the syringe.

Be tentative with the watering; too little is easier to correct than too much. Give plenty of time for the moisture to settle into the soil. When only a light film of vapour remains on the glass, the amount of water is probably right for a healthy garden.

Put the planted bottle in a shady place for a day or two until the plants have established themselves, and finally bring it into the position you have chosen for its display. Near a sunless window is probably best, for direct sun might very well boil the plants in their glass container.

If the planting looks too continuously wet, leave the container open for a few days. Ideally the glass should be slightly misted over on a warm day, and quite clear in the early morning.

Weeding can later be done with the fork, loop or an extended clothes peg. If a plant is growing too fast, choking the others and looking out of proportion in the tiny garden, it can be removed in the same way, though you might have to saw it up first, using a serrated vegetable knife bound to a bamboo stake.

GLASS DOMES

In Victorian times, large glass domes were used to protect a number of household items from dust.

This Victorian glass specimen dome keeps the atmosphere moist and fresh around an arrangement of Croton, *COLEUS, SELAGINELLA, SYNGONIUM* and *DAVALLIA* grown on a driftwood branch.

These included clocks, stuffed birds, dried flowers, shells and various arrangements of natural and artificial objects.

They came in all shapes and sizes and you can sometimes find them by haunting antique and junk shops. The domes are usually made of better quality glass and are very suitable for covering plant groups.

However, throw away the wooden bases which come with them. A little more searching will usually reveal a more suitable base to contain soil. Salad bowls, float bowls and soup tureens are a few possibilities, and the wide, flat containers made for bonsai plants are ideal, provided they have an undersaucer so that excess moisture won't ruin the furniture on which they are placed.

It is certainly easier to plant a dome than a bottle — you can even landscape it attractively. Variations can be made by including an interesting piece of rock, driftwood or piece of treefern trunk for climbing plants to ramble over.

No special tools are needed, and fast-growing plants can easily be trimmed or thinned.

But this type of garden cannot be left without attention for as long as the completely closed types. A certain amount of water is bound to escape. It will be necessary to spray the soil and plants every week or two, particularly when flowers are developing.

Most Victorian domes are taller than they are wide, but lower, wider types can sometimes be found. They are easier to group plants in.

As in any mixed planting, place the taller plants first, toward the centre and back. Lower-growing types with interesting leaves can be introduced in front of them, and finally some ground cover plants to hide the soil and break the line of any bare stems.

The finished planting is sprayed, as with the sealed containers, and finally the dome is lifted into place. Hold it with a soft cloth to avoid fingerprints.

Beware the sharp edges on these domes. For safety, bind them with plastic tape.

FURTHER IDEAS

Skill in planting glass gardens is quickly acquired, but the pleasure is there from the very first attempt. Why not spread it around by preparing one for an invalid or elderly friend? A small container of growing things can be an endless source of interest and delight.

Glass gardens are splendid for decorative relief from dull office surroundings and easily survive the lack of water over a weekend.

They also make fascinating school projects. Help the children plant one entirely with grasses or native plants, or using only plants from a particular country. The possibilities are endless.

PLANTS FOR GLASS GARDENS

All plants for glass gardens must have a love of humidity and a tolerance of shade. Here is a partial list, but others will be found in the Dictionary.

Ferns: Any small varieties of *ADIANTUM, ASPLENIUM* bulbiferum, *ATHYRIUM, DAVALLIA, NEPHROLEPIS, PHYLLITIS, PTERIS* and *SELAGINELLA.*

Foliage plants (small specimens of any of the following): *AGLAONEMA,* Bromeliads (especially *CRYPTANTHUS* and *TILLANDSIA), CALATHEA, CODIAEUM, COLLINIA, DRACAENA, FITTONIA, HELXINE, MARANTA, PEPEROMIA, PILEA, PLEOMELE, SANSEVIERIA* hahnii, *SAXIFRAGA* sarmentosa, *SYNGONIUM, TRADESCANTIA, TOLMEIA, ZEBRINA.*

Flowering plants (only under removable cover): *ANTHURIUM, BEGONIA, COLEUS, CROSSANDRA, CHLOROPHYTUM, EPISCIA, IMPATIENS* (dwarf varieties), *SAINTPAULIA.*

Alpine or rock plants (under removable cover): *CAMPANULA, DIANTHUS, FUCHSIA* procumbens, *SCHIZOCENTRON, VIOLETS.*

Miniature roses: Miniature or 'Fairy' Roses do well under glass domes for a limited time, blooming longer than usual, with freedom from pests. All dead flowers must be removed immediately, and the plant dusted with Zineb to prevent mildew and other fungus diseases. Varieties include:

'Baby Masquerade' — yellow fading to cerise.
'Bits o'Gold' — yellow
'Desert Charm' — deep red
'Elf' — dark red
'Fairy' — appleblossom pink
'Lavender Lace' — mauve-pink
'Over the Rainbow' — multicoloured
'Peon' — crimson, white centre
'Perla d'Alcanada' — light crimson
'Pixie' — white, flushed pink
'Simple Simon' — candy pink
'Starglo' — cream
'Yellow Jewel' — almost single lemon

Almost 200 named varieties are available if you cannot find any of the above. Also several small climbing Fairy Roses which may reach a height of three feet (90 cm).

UPSTAIRS — DOWNSTAIRS:
BALCONIES, COURTYARDS AND PATIOS

The tiny shaded courtyard of this Melbourne terrace house becomes a spring showplace with potted Camellias and Daffodils. The grapes on the trellis are frankly fake.

BALCONY GARDENING

Many apartments these days come with one or more balconies, often small, always narrow — and irresistible to the gardening instinct in all of us.

Shall we turn our balcony into an oasis of green where we can enjoy summer breakfasts or have friends out for drinks? Well, we can try, but there are likely to be a few problems before we can produce a mini-jungle.

The first difficulty is exposure — exposure to drying wind, to baking sun, to biting cold, to soaking rain and to salt air (if we're near the sea). Before we can grow anything, we must try to correct this.

Does the balcony have a roof, or another balcony overhanging it? If it does, good, for that will give shelter from the worst of the midday sun in summer, and break the force of heavy rainstorms. There will also be something to hang baskets from, and they are an essential part of balcony gardening. If there's no roof over your balcony, you'll have to arrange

protection (with the permission of your landlord or fellow tenants, of course). This might take the form of a lightweight pergola built of wood or aluminium piping. This could support an awning in summer, or in time a densely leafed climbing plant.

Whether or not there's a roof, a canvas awning or 'Tuscan Blind' can be a great advantage. These work from a roller mounted as high as possible above your doors, and cantilever out on a pair of metal arms that slide up rails screwed to the building. They can be locked in place, and you pull them up and down on a rope. Tuscan blinds can be fixed in almost any position from horizontal to almost vertical, and if made of cotton canvas have quite a cooling effect in summer. They come in a wide range of colours, plain or striped, and are normally backed in green.

They also give good protection against rain and frosts, but can be rolled away in cooler weather to bring in as much sun as possible. We won't even mention snow because in a climate *that* cold, your balcony garden can only be a very temporary summer affair.

Next we must consider protection from wind. If your balcony has the more common type of railing made of vertical wrought-iron rods, it should be closed in, at least partially. This can be done with panels of wire mesh, wire-reinforced glass or translucent plastic. These will protect young plants from drying wind, but will still let through a deal of light.

Alternatively, you could plant a quick-growing vine such as Honeysuckle, and train it to fill the gaps.

Are the ends of your balcony open to wind? Then consider fixing some vertical screens to shelter your plants from that direction, and perhaps give climbing support. The screens might be made of wire mesh or wooden trellis, or again a panel of reinforced glass supported by vertical uprights. I have a screen of expanding PVC trellis at the end of my balcony to hide some apartments next door, and it is quickly covered in warm weather by the rampantly growing leaves of *CALONYCTION*, the 'Moonflower', and several pots of Bamboo (*PHYLLOSTACHYS*).

Balcony screens can be used to grow annual climbers such as Sweet Peas, Morning Glories or even a crop of green beans for the kitchen. Passion-flowers, Grapes, climbing Roses and Jasmine are other more permanent possibilities — and so too are large scrambling tropical plants such as *MONSTERA*, *SOLANDRA* ('Hawaiian Lily') or *BOU-GAINVILLEA* if your climate is warm enough.

Now, are you anxious to retain the view, or create privacy? That will dictate the size and position of the plants you use. If you're retaining the view, you'll plant *below* the rail level, or confine the plants to both ends. Plum Pine, Privet, Bamboo, Palms and Box all make suitable privacy screens, and the idea can be taken a little further by growing light, lacy climbers up vertical wires. Plants like Jasmine, *ANTIGONON* and several species of *QUAMOCLIT* grow into an

The narrow but sheltered balconies of these modern apartments face the morning sun and have each been developed into a mini-jungle.

In a more tropical climate, the end of this seaside balcony has been arranged with a ship's mast and rigging to support a climbing *MONSTERA*.

In Paris, the 5 ft (1.6 m) terrace of Mme. Louise Coleman's apartment bursts into a lavish summer display of *PETUNIAS, VERBENA* and Catmint. The *treillage* end panels support Jasmine and Banksia Roses.

Ideal for mass displays in summer courtyards, dwarf species of the Aztec Marigold come in many shades of yellow and orange.

airy screen that lets you see out, but keeps your neighbours at a distance.

Use several large planters rather than many smaller pots. They will hold more soil and won't dry out so quickly. Plant a flowering shrub or small tree in each, surrounded by quick-growing annuals or bulbs. Make up a set of long boxes that can be mounted with brackets — preferably on both sides of the railing, which will help them balance. Try Nasturtiums in these, or PETUNIAS, VERBENAS, LOBELIAS and other trailing annuals. Brilliantly flowered Geraniums are also ideal for boxes, particularly dwarf-growing or ivy-leafed types.

If part of your balcony faces a wall rather than a window, fix up a trellis and grow more flowering climbers, or mount a series of brackets to hold wall planters or half baskets, and fill them with BEGONIAS, epiphytic Cacti like ZYGOCACTUS, or Asparagus Ferns, (but not true Ferns, because balcony life is too tough for them). And don't forget to try some hanging containers if you have a roof overhead — you'll find all you need to know about them in an earlier chapter.

Just remember the cardinal rules for balcony growing: use large containers for moisture retention, provide as much shelter as you can, and move everything possible off the floor and onto the walls and railings. Keep an eye on the watering and drainage. Nothing is more annoying to your downstairs

neighbours than a constant drip-drip-drip onto their balcony.

COURTYARD GARDENING
Most of what we've said about balcony gardening applies equally well to small courtyards and patios, though as a general rule they are well protected from drying winds by their boundary walls. However, it is still a good idea to plant around the walls, leaving as much space as possible for entertaining and movement. It is also wise to provide partial overhead protection with a pergola or awning, for sunny courtyards become very hot indeed on summer days, with heat bouncing back from walls and paving.

Courtyards as we know them have their origins in the Mediterranean and Middle East areas, and we can't do much better than to go back and find how our forefathers used them as winter suntraps and oases of summer coolness. For both seasons, the sight and sound of moving water is agreeable to the senses, whether in the form of a wall fountain or a small fountain pool. Surround the water with tropical plants that revel in humidity, and plant baskets of Papyrus, Iris or Waterlilies in the pool.

Grow a deciduous tree in a large tub or sunken planter to give you shade against the worst of summer but let winter sun through. A Sydney friend has a delightful courtyard garden planted with Weeping Willows in large containers. He surrounds these with Ivy and Polyanthus Primroses in winter, 'White Cascade' *PETUNIAS* in summer.

Grow *CLEMATIS* on the shaded side of the courtyard, with support so they can climb up into the sun (the sort of conditions they love). If the courtyard has a permanently shaded side you can grow *CAMELLIAS*, *AZALEAS* and cool-climate bulbs, Primroses and Violets, Ferns and Ivy. If there's a side that receives sun all year, think in terms of *GARDENIAS*, potted *CITRUS* trees and lush foliage plants like Bananas, *CORDYLINE* and *YUCCA* for a really tropical effect.

All of these are best planted in large containers, or grouped in a permanent planter raised above court-

The elegant leaves of many *HOSTA* species delight in a permanently shaded courtyard garden. The flowers are a summer bonus.

In courtyard and balcony gardens, colourful *CLEMATIS* thrive with their roots in shade, their flowers in sun.

Courtyard gardens come alive with the sound and humidity of modern recirculating fountains and cascades.

yard level right along one wall. If it's a wall backing onto the inside of your house, or that of a neighbour, the height will be dictated by the level of the damp course. The soil must always be below this, or the planter permanently lined with waterproofing material such as lead or fibreglass.

SHADED COURTYARDS

If your courtyard is on the shady side of the building, or shaded for most of the year by other nearby apartments (as is often the case), you'll plan rather differently. Don't plant trees, for you'll need as much light as you can get all year — and I do hope your favourite colour is green, because that's the one you'll be seeing most of. Very few plants flower well without sun. Use as much white as you can: white lacy furniture, white gravel instead of paving, white containers for your shrubs, white trellises to make a stunning background for climbing Ivy or espaliered *CAMELLIAS*. Bamboos enjoy shaded conditions — look for species with variegated leaves or golden stems (*SASA* and *PHYLLOSTACHYS*).

HOSTA, FUCHSIA, TRILLIUM, PRIMULA, IMPATIENS and Ferns are other plants that like shade in cool temperate climates; among the bulbs, Lilies of The Valley, Snowdrops, Bluebells and many *LILIUMS* revel in it.

In more tropical areas, the problem is quite different. Many tropical plants are used to the heavily shaded conditions of jungle life and will do well in shade, at least in summer months. Try *ANTHURIUMS, AGLAONEMA, RHOEO, SPA-THIPHYLLUM, MONSTERA, TRADESCANTIA* and others you'll find in the Dictionary section.

Just remember not to water them too heavily, for as was said in an earlier chapter, plants without light cannot use too much water.

GARDENING IN MINIATURE — BONSAI

This small Fir has been planted to resemble a windswept tree, its roots
trained over the rock into the container below.

The Japanese word *bonsai* means simply 'planted in a container' or, more loosely, 'pot plant'; but in recent years it has become the key to a new pleasure for plant enthusiasts all over the Western world. They have discovered what the Chinese and Japanese have known for centuries — that there is a way to train large trees and shrubs so they remain in perfect health, but never exceed the precise height you want them to be.

Bonsai is a slow and painstaking hobby, as is the creation of all true art. And make no mistake, bonsai trees owe as much to human artistry as they do to nature.

At the outset, it is just as well to get several facts in their right perspective:

Bonsai must be grown in small containers to control the dwarfing process. Planted in over-large pots or in the open ground they quickly assume natural size.

Bonsai are not house-plants, though they can be brought inside occasionally. They must have natural sun, rain and air.

Bonsai are amazingly hardy when properly planted. Many famous Japanese specimens have survived for hundreds of years.

From personal experience I have found that any keen plant hobbyist, with a deal of common sense and an eye for the beautiful, can raise and train bonsai trees.

There are several techniques to be mastered, notably root pruning and wiring, but apart from these there is only minor variation from standard potting procedure and aftercare.

WHERE DO YOU GROW BONSAI

Outdoors, in containers. These can be raised on a table or wall to put them at good viewing and working height, or kept on a paved area. They should be open to rain and a certain amount of sunlight, but need protection from strong wind, full summer sun and really heavy deluges — shelter under a lightly covered pergola or canopy of sarlon mesh is close to ideal.

However, a great advantage of bonsai is that they are relatively portable and can be moved to a position that suits them at different times of the year. Cold-climate plants might well be moved to a more shaded place in summer. Tropical plants could be taken into a sunroom for the winter.

WHAT TYPE OF TREES CAN YOU GROW AS BONSAI

Almost anything — but it's best if the leaves are naturally fairly small. A Chinese Elm, which has ½ in (1 cm) leaves even on a mature specimen, would be ideal.

It is true that flowers and fruits on bonsai tend to be much the same size as on their giant counterparts, but they can be thinned judiciously, and are not on the tree all the time. A small-berried Firethorn could be trained most effectively to resemble a mature, gnarled, apple tree.

WHAT SIZE CAN BONSAI BE?

There is no fixed rule. There are bonsai as big as your thumb-joint, grown in containers no bigger than a tooth — and there are others as tall as a man and grown in very large containers.

Miniature and small sizes require a lot of care in hot weather. Medium and large sizes are more practical and give a real opportunity to create an acceptable work of art.

HOW DO YOU START?

The best beginning might be a study of trees and how they grow in natural conditions, the textures of trunks, the angles and forms of branches, the shapes they assume when buffeted by years of wind, or when forced to grow in unfavourable, rocky conditions.

Then, when you have formed a good mental picture of just how trees look and grow, try to get to see a few bonsai created by other people. There are commercial bonsai nurseries in many states and cities, and specimens in many botanic gardens.

As soon as you have seen a few live bonsai, you'll want to train your own — so buy a reliable book on the subject that shows plenty of examples.

The best written on the subject in English are probably *Bonsai*, by Nori Kobayashi (published by the Japan Tourist Association); *The Japanese Art of Miniature Trees and Landscapes*, by Yoshimura and Halford; and *Bonsai*, published by the Californian 'Sunset' Magazine. The Yoshimura book is expensive, but amazingly comprehensive.

SELECTING A PLANT

You will find that, according to variety, bonsai in Japan are raised from seed, layers, cuttings and graftings. All of these techniques are within the skill of the enthusiastic gardener, but are very slow.

A quick short-cut is to look around plant nurseries (particularly in the back rows of neglected ones) for small trees and shrubs that have been cramped into containers that are too small for them. Many of these older plants have already begun to assume an interesting shape . . . a thickened trunk or a gnarled branch or two.

They will make ideal material, for they are already used to growing in constricted conditions and will actually welcome the transplanting operation.

Look especially for plants that have begun to develop a horizontal shape, or those with double or triple trunks. These are particularly valued, for they can be trained to resemble a small clump of trees in a forest.

AZALEAS are among the easiest to train, for they grow well in cramped conditions and shallow containers, but it is hard to find one with a developed trunk because they are much given to suckering and low branching.

Maples are probably the next easiest, and quite cheap when small, as are Pine seedlings. Or you

Perfect for the display of a bonsai collection, these open tables give back and overhead shelter from direct sun and heavy rain. They could be copied in any courtyard. (Huntington Gardens, San Marino, Calif.).

Hybrid Azalea "Paul Schame" makes a colourful bonsai specimen, and flowers twice a year at least.

These four-year-old Hawthorn seedlings have been group-planted as a forest glade, complete with bronze deer.

might like to try Kumquats that have been grown from cuttings, Box, Junipers or *CAMELLIA sasanqua*.

Try to avoid choosing a plant that has an unsightly graft. If it is bad in appearance to start with, it is unlikely that time will bring about any improvement.

CHOOSING A CONTAINER

A great variety of special bonsai pots can now be found at most nurseries and many department stores. They are generally in dull colours, such as red, liver, brown and grey, because the Japanese quite rightly believe that nothing should detract from the plant itself. White and yellow are sometimes used for plants that colour in the autumn, and blues for plants that have pink or white flowers in the spring.

The containers can be shallow or deep; square, round or hexagonal. They will be unglazed inside and have one or more large drainage holes.

These are best covered with a small grille or piece of insect screen to prevent pests entering and to stop the precious soil draining out.

As a general rule, a tree of formal shape will be placed two thirds of the distance along an oval or rectangular pot, or in the centre of a round container. Weeping or windswept plants are seen to best advantage in tall containers.

Plants trained to grow on a rock with exposed roots are displayed in very wide shallow containers without drainage holes. These are often filled with water or sand to give the impression of a tree growing on a small rocky island.

PREPARATIONS FOR PLANTING

You must decide at the outset just what you want to do with the plant you have obtained — a general idea of the shape or style, and whether you want to reduce its size or encourage it to grow further. Remember, an over-large pot will encourage growth that you may not want.

The Japanese consider the ideal container should be from one fifth to one seventh of the total bulk of foliage of the plant it is to house. When you remember that the spread of a plant's roots balance the spread of its branches almost exactly, you get an idea of how much root must be pruned away.

If the root amputation is to be very great, you would be wise to minimise the shock by getting rid of any really useless top hamper of twigs and leaves. Extreme care must be exercised, because it is very difficult to replace a branch once it has been cut away — though it can in fact be done — by grafting.

When pre-pruning has been done, you can start to plant in earnest. This will be done only in late winter or early spring for deciduous trees (when they're dormant) or in late summer for evergreens.

Choose a sheltered place to work, out of sun and wind. Soak the plant thoroughly in its nursery container. Tap it out, or if in a tin cut it out with tin snips.

This will reveal most of the root structure. Now, begin to peck away the soil with a pointed stick or small fork, gradually reducing the bulk. If the plant is really rootbound, it may be necessary to use a garden hose or kitchen tap to wash all the soil away so you can make out the growth of the roots.

With a very sharp knife cut away any old roots as you go. This will include some of the main roots, even the tap root, for the idea is to encourage the growth of new fibrous roots near the surface, where they can easily absorb food and water. Work to a shape that corresponds with the chosen container, and remember that the soil line will be well above the lip of the new container.

When the root pruning is complete, leaving as many young, white surface roots as possible, cover

A beautifully trained bonsai in the cascade style, this is *PINUS pentaphylla*, the Japanese 'Five-needle Pine'.

A mass-planting of dwarf Conifers and mosses has turned this carefully chosen rock into a miniature hilltop, bonsai-style.

the root mass with a damp bag to prevent it from drying out.

Now begin to fill the pot. First, some sharp pebbles for drainage, then a layer of finer gravel mixed with crushed charcoal to keep the soil sweet. This layer might be from one quarter to one half an inch deep (½ to 1 cm).

With a medium-fine sieve (a kitchen type is fine) sieve some coarse granular under-soil (you'll get good quality from any nearby building excavation). This is where bonsai treatment is different — *the soil to throw away* is the fine powdery material that goes through the sieve, for this would only be washed out the drainage holes with hard watering.

Mix some of the coarse sieved soil with a little sharp sand (this encourages root development), and place it in the pot. Mix the balance with some fine leaf mould and a small portion of standard packaged bonsai mix.

Use more sand for Conifers, more leaf mould for deciduous trees, more nutriment and even fertiliser for flowering and fruiting trees.

THE PLANTING

The tree can now be placed in position on top of the under-soil and in the container, with the exposed trunk to the front, and any interesting large roots exposed in the manner of a mature tree.

The plant will probably need a little bracing at first, so thread a piece of fine bamboo or cane through the roots and jam it against either side of the container. Alternatively, a strand of copper wire can be passed over the roots and out the drainage holes to meet underneath. Spread the root mass out and proceed to fill the pot, layer by layer, poking each lot of soil mix gently among the roots with a sharp stick.

When you've nearly reached the top (about a quarter of an inch — 0.5 cm — below the rim of the

container at the edges to hold water, and sloping up to the trunk in the centre), give the plant a good soaking with the finest of sprays.

Top up the surface with a thin layer of good quality sterile garden soil, and finally sprinkle it with finely powdered dry moss. This will soon sprout and cover the entire surface of the soil with a delicate green layer that will prevent erosion and conserve precious moisture. The Japanese say 'Healthy moss, healthy tree', and its greenness will give you an indication of when the plant needs water.

The newly planted tree can now be placed in a cool shaded position for several weeks to allow roots to grow and begin supporting the plant. Daily spraying (several times a day if possible) will help this establishment — but do not let the container become too sodden, or rot could develop in the cut root ends.

TRAINING TO SHAPE

When the plant is established and growing, training can begin in earnest. Be careful with deciduous trees — their branches are very brittle in the dormant period. You would be wise to wait until the sap is running.

Evergreens are usually trained in late spring after the new growth is complete.

Branches are trained to the desired position and shaped by several methods: (a) wiring, (b) hanging weights, (c) bracing, (d) tying down to the container. Wiring is the most usual.

You will need copper wire in various thicknesses. Galvanised wire is no good, for it sets up irritation where it touches the tree.

Begin with the trunk. You will not wish unsightly wire marks to mar its appearance, so first wrap the trunk in raffia or paper to protect the young bark.

Take a heavy grade of copper wire, cut to about two and a half times the height of the trunk. Dig one end in deeply beside the trunk. Begin to coil it (not too tightly) around the trunk, beginning at the bottom, with equal spacing.

When you've reached the top you will find that the wire can be bent gently between thumb and forefinger at intervals. As it is bent, it takes the trunk with it.

Then proceed with the largest branches in the same manner, using a progressively lighter gauge of wire, and finishing with the smallest twigs. Bend and train completely to the desired shape, making sure the wire of any branch continues for several coils down its supporting trunk or larger branch. All wires on all branches will go in the same direction, clockwise or anti-clockwise.

It is customary to reveal as much trunk as possible at the front for almost the full height of the tree. The Japanese greatly admire the weather-beaten appearance of tree trunks, which are visible all year, even when the leaves come and go.

Branches should be trained so that they are clear of one another looking from above, so each gets its own share of sun and rain.

It is worth noting that most older trees have the branches sloping slightly downwards under the weight of the leaves, and this is an ageing effect you might like to try and achieve.

The wires may be left in place from two months to a year, depending on the speed of growth of the

Bonsai *BOUGAINVILLEAS* give a cheerful welcome to a Honolulu home.

tree. If wires are biting into expanding branches, loosen or remove the coils immediately.

MAINTENANCE
When the bonsai is thoroughly established and the wiring removed, there is still work to be done year after year. New leaf growths must be pinched back to the first pair of leaves to encourage branching — remember, you can only achieve the effect of a mature tree if there are many fine branches.

Deciduous bonsai will need to be repotted every two or three years, and Conifers every five. At this time the outer inch or two of roots will be removed to give new ones a chance to develop.

WATERING AND FEEDING
Young bonsai should be sprayed daily with the finest mist of water — this includes the leaves as well as the soil. In hot weather the spraying should take place twice a day or whenever the plant shows signs of distress.

When you water bonsai, the coarse open soil allows the water to penetrate rapidly and force out stale air around the roots. The water drains swiftly away and fresh air is sucked in.

This cycle, prolonged indefinitely, keeps the plant alive while encouraging it to stay the same size (in fact, it's rather like an extremely low calorie diet for humans).

An occasional feeding (say once a month) with a light, water-soluble plant food at half normal strength is beneficial. The principal exceptions to this are fruiting and flowering trees, which will need several light applications of manure while the blossoms are developing.

Try this delightful hobby for yourself. But be prepared to give your plants a minute or two of time every day. One day without water in the summer months and you may lose your precious bonsai forever.

Tropical trees can be trained as bonsai too. This superb Banyan (*FICUS religiosa*) is in a private collection at Pearl City, Hawaii.

PREVENTION AND CURE
OF PESTS AND DISEASES

Indoor gardeners are rarely troubled by snails and slugs, those two voracious marauders of the outdoor garden, but their precious plants are sitting targets for insects and a variety of fungus infections. This is because the plants are exposed neither to natural rain nor normal air movement, both of which discourage pests outdoors.

The majority of these indoor problems arrive with the plants. They cannot appear spontaneously. So, as always, an ounce of prevention is worth a pound of cure later. Keep both plants and pots clean at all times, and give them the occasional treat either of an evening outdoors in the rain, or a bracing session under the bathroom shower. Remove all dead or damaged flowers and leaves regularly and destroy them.

If a plant is obviously sick or diseased, do not let it infect the others. Instead, place it outdoors in quarantine until it has either been nursed back to health or sent to that great conservatory in the sky.

Wash down the leaves occasionally with lukewarm soapy water. This is as effective as any insecticide on many pests, and is non-poisonous to anything else.

That brings us to the question of pesticides in general. To be effective, most of them have been formulated so strong that they become a danger to forms of life other than the targets for which they were specifically designed. Only you can decide whether to take the risk of using them.

If you have pets (birds, fish, dogs and cats) the risk of accidental poisoning is considerable. If you have small children, your store of 'plant medicines' must be kept under lock and key at all times — and, for your own safety, in their original labelled containers.

If you do decide the well-being of your plants is dependent on chemicals, then make sure you carry out the treatment out of doors, on a windless day, in a sheltered position. This is so that dangerous sprays will not be carried indiscriminately to other nearby plants that may be part of the diet of birds or beneficial insects of many kinds.

For those who find it necessary to 'make with the cure', the principal indoor plant pests and the remedies against them are:

Ants: These will be attracted by Aphids (which they milk). Ants may be destroyed by various proprietary ant-killers (Ded-Ant is one). If they have nested in the pot, they may destroy roots and upset the drainage. Soak them out by watering in a solution of 1½ teaspoons of chlordane to one gallon (5 litres) of water.

ANTS
(enlarged)

Aphids: Sometimes known as greenfly, blackfly or plant lice, aphids are attracted to the young growth of many plants and cluster about tip shoots. They are sap-suckers and cause discolouring and distortion of leaves. Ants carry them about and they secrete a sticky honeydew on which black mould forms. Preferably, blast them off outdoors with a jet of water from a hose. Soapy water and White Oil may help, but as a last resort, spray them with a pressurised house-plant spray containing Rogor or Malathion.

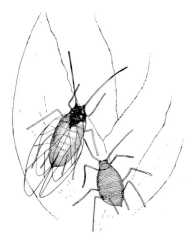

APHIDS
(enlarged)

Botrytis, or grey mould, is a furry greyish fungus that forms on indoor plants when the humidity is too high, usually in cool weather. The spores are carried in the air. Improve ventilation, lower the humidity and destroy all infected leaves and stems, finally spraying with Benlate, Zineb or similar fungicides.

Caterpillars hatch from eggs laid by moths and butterflies, which may enter through open windows. The eggs may also be present in the soil or under leaves. The first sign of their presence, when small, is often a scattering of excrement on large leaves or other surfaces, or sometimes leaves rolled or stuck together. Pick them off by hand and destroy them if you can. Otherwise spray with Derris dust.

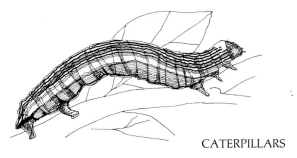

CATERPILLARS

Earthworms: Beneficial in the garden, worms are a pest in pots where their tunnelling upsets the drainage so that water pours right through, rather than reaching the roots. A watering with diluted Permanganate of Potash (Condy's Crystals) will bring them to the surface.

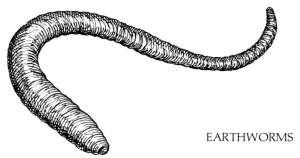

EARTHWORMS

Mealybugs: These are furry, white sucking insects that cluster about leaf veins or stems and lay eggs like a mass of pinkish spun sugar. They feed on plant juices and distort new growth. Swab them with diluted methylated spirit and pick them off. Sometimes, however, they suck from the roots of softer plants such as *PRIMULA* or *CYCLAMEN.* Here the plant is best destroyed.

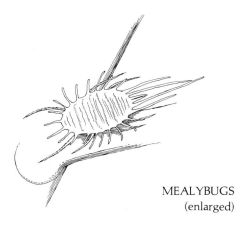

MEALYBUGS
(enlarged)

Mildew is the commonest plant fungus when humidity is too high. It appears as a cloudy greyish coating on new leaves and buds, which then distort badly. Improve the ventilation, pick off affected leaves and spray with Benlate, Zineb or other fungicide.

Red spider mites: These almost invisible pests proliferate when humidity is low, causing leaf discolouration and fall, and the abrupt death (sometimes) of whole branches, particularly on Conifers. The infected plant should be taken outside and thoroughly saturated with preventative sprays, under as well as over leaves. A solution of Malathion and White Oil in water is most suitable.

Rust covers a number of different fungi that cause rust-coloured patches and spots on leaves, particularly on *ANTIRRHINUM, AZALEAS, DIANTHUS* and *PELARGONIUMS.* Destroy affected foliage and spray the plant with Zineb or other fungicide powder.

Scales: Black and brown scales and white wax scales form as hard lumps on stems and the underside of leaves. These lumps are the home of a variety of sap-sucking scale insects, which should be brushed away with an old toothbrush. The plant should then be sprayed with White Oil or soapy water to prevent recurrence.

Slaters (sometimes called sowbugs or wood lice) are small grey shield-shaped critters that may grow from eggs present in either pot or compost. They damage roots of young plants and can be eradicated by laying BHC powders or a piece of potato sprayed with poison.

SLATERS
(enlarged)

Thrips: These small black sucking insects cause distortion of flowers and leaves and are particularly prevalent after prolonged spells of dry weather. Eliminate them by outdoor spraying with dilute Malathion and White Oil in soapy water.

When in doubt as to just what is plaguing your plant, don't hesitate to ask your nearest nurseryman or indoor plant shop — they are the plant doctors. It will make their diagnosis a lot easier if you take some of the affected foliage along in an envelope.

THE WELL-FED PLANT

Ferns such as *NEPHROLEPIS* prefer natural fertilisers like fish emulsion or diluted animal manure.

In fertilising your indoor plants, it is important to draw the line between nourishment and over-feeding. It is certainly not necessary or advisable to fertilise with every watering. The plant does not need feeding when it is resting or dormant (mostly in cold weather), but only when it is growing, or building up strength for a spurt of flowering, or after pruning when it must make strong new growth.

Properly prepared composts contain all the nourishment a plant needs for healthy, normal growth; but there is a danger in indoor gardening that the nutritive elements in the compost will be washed away through the drainage holes.

Your local nursery or plant shop will be able to help you with many types of fertiliser to replace the lost elements and promote healthy growth, but be sure to specify your needs so they can help you select the best formula for the purpose. Many suitable fertilisers for foliage plants, for instance, are not right for flowering plants because they force growth at the expense of bloom. Ferns do not like artificial chemical fertilisers at all, preferring mild solutions of animal and fish manure. *CITRUS* plants require a different fertiliser mix from *AZALEAS*, and different again from Roses.

Most fertilisers for houseplants are supplied in soluble form — either liquid, powder or tablets — to be dissolved in a large quantity of water. Follow the package directions as carefully as you would a kitchen recipe.

There are also slow-release fertilisers, in granular or tablet form, that release their nutriment over months at a time as the plant is watered.

Whichever form you use, remember to add the fertiliser in dilution, and only on damp soil — dry concentrations of chemical will harm more plants than they help.

The rule should be: water, fertilise, water again.

If a chemical crust does form on the soil surface and prevent the entry of air, break it up with a small kitchen fork and turn the surface soil over before re-watering.

Although natural fertilisers such as horse, cow and poultry manure are beneficial to almost all growing plants, they are not greatly used indoors in solid form. There is the problem of odour and their attraction to flies and other insects but most importantly the problem of their 'bulking' up the potting mix in small containers.

In any case, no plant can absorb solid nutriment, so it is necessary to prepare the solid manure by soaking it in water until it breaks down into liquid form. This is a messy business at best, and neither hygienic nor practical around the house. The only 'natural' fertiliser on the market in liquid form is Fish Emulsion, which can be diluted in your watering can and is not too smelly.

WHAT INDOOR PLANT IS THAT?
PICTURE DICTIONARY FROM A-Z

Four popular house plants in an attractive grouping. They are:
(indoors) *COLLINIA* elegans, the 'Parlour Palm' and *CYCLAMEN*; (outdoors)
FICUS Lyrata, the 'Fiddle-leaf Fig', and *HOYA* carnosa, the 'Honey Flower'.

This illustrated dictionary is arranged alphabetically by the botanical names of included plants. These scientific names may he hard to remember, for they are based on Latin and Greek; but they are also fixed and internationally recognised, which popular names are not.

If you already know the botanical name of a plant, just turn through the alphabetical section until you find it, in words or pictures.

If you don't know the botanical name, or what the plant looks like, turn to the index at the back, where you'll find both the botanical and the more common popular names listed alphabetically, with page reference numbers.

Each dictionary entry is headed with the name of a plant's botanical *genus*, which corresponds to your family name, e.g. PHILODENDRON. These *generic* names are printed in capitals everywhere in the book; a large Roman type face is used for the headings, smaller Italic capitals are used within the entries for clarity.

Seven special entries are exceptions to the above rule. They are headed with the names of the seven most popular *groups* of indoor plants; the *AROIDS*, the *BROMELIADS*, the *CACTI*, the *FERNS*, the *GESNERIADS*, the *ORCHIDS* and the *PALMS*. Included in each group entry is a cross-reference to all group members found elsewhere in the book, together with notes on the special likes and dislikes that are common to most of them; this saves repeating data in individual entries.

Beneath each heading (e.g. PHILODENDRON) you will find two other words. The first, printed in small letters within brackets, is a simple phonetic guide to the pronunciation of the plant's generic name. Many people wrote to me after the publication of earlier books, saying that while they appreciated knowing at last the name of their favourite plant — they would be even happier if they knew how to pronounce it!

Well, this phonetic guide should help. Using it, the spelling will inevitably differ from the actual spelling of the generic name above. This is because the whole aim of a phonetic guide is to give <u>constant</u> pronunciation values to the symbols used.

Vowels, and some consonants, can be pronounced in many different ways in English (look at the vowel 'a' in f<u>a</u>t, f<u>a</u>te, f<u>a</u>ther and f<u>a</u>re; or the consonant 'c' in <u>c</u>at and a<u>c</u>e. A phonetic guide makes it necessary to select one special letter or group of letters to represent each specific sound, and that sound only. Because there are more sounds in English than there are letters in the English language, we also use one extra symbol (ə) to represent the many indeterminate vowel sounds heard in words like <u>a</u>lone, syst<u>e</u>m, terr<u>i</u>ble, gall<u>o</u>p and circ<u>u</u>s.

Beyond that, we have separated each syllable from the next by a space, and used an apostrophe (') immediately after the stressed syllable. Each separate letter or letter combination is <u>always</u> pronounced according to the following table.

a	f<u>a</u>t	**d**	<u>d</u>o, co<u>d</u>
ae	p<u>ay</u>, f<u>a</u>te	**f**	<u>f</u>eef, rou<u>gh</u>, <u>ph</u>one
ah	m<u>a</u>rk, f<u>a</u>ther	**g**	<u>g</u>as, ba<u>g</u>
ai	<u>i</u>ce, h<u>igh</u>, b<u>uy</u>	**h**	<u>h</u>elp, a<u>h</u>oy
ə	<u>a</u>lone, syst<u>e</u>m	**j**	<u>j</u>aws, <u>g</u>em, ra<u>ge</u>
	terr<u>i</u>ble, gall<u>o</u>p,	**k**	<u>c</u>at, sa<u>ck</u>
	circ<u>u</u>s	**l**	<u>l</u>imb, mi<u>ll</u>
e	d<u>ea</u>f, d<u>e</u>n	**m**	<u>m</u>ore, ru<u>mm</u>y
ee	t<u>ea</u>ch, l<u>ee</u>	**n**	to<u>n</u>, to<u>n</u>ight
eə	<u>ai</u>r, d<u>a</u>red	**p**	<u>p</u>al, la<u>p</u>
i	f<u>i</u>t, t<u>i</u>ff	**r**	<u>r</u>ot, t<u>r</u>ot
o	s<u>o</u>t, t<u>o</u>ss	**s**	<u>s</u>ale, la<u>c</u>e
oh	<u>oa</u>th, b<u>o</u>th, cr<u>ow</u>	**sh**	<u>sh</u>ade, mo<u>ti</u>on
oo	pr<u>o</u>ve, p<u>oo</u>l	**t**	<u>t</u>one, no<u>t</u>e
or	<u>ough</u>t, m<u>o</u>re, r<u>oar</u>	**th**	<u>th</u>in, bo<u>th</u>
ou	c<u>ow</u>, cr<u>ou</u>ch, sl<u>ough</u>	**v**	<u>v</u>at, ca<u>v</u>e
u	s<u>u</u>ck, s<u>o</u>n	**w**	<u>w</u>in, t<u>w</u>in
ur	<u>err</u>, c<u>ir</u>cus	**y**	<u>y</u>ellow
b	<u>b</u>at, ta<u>b</u>	**z**	<u>z</u>ip, to<u>es</u>, ro<u>s</u>e
ch	<u>ch</u>ip, pa<u>tch</u>	**zh**	mea<u>s</u>ure, inva<u>si</u>on

The sound of each phonetic letter or letter-group always remains constant. As examples, here are the first five dictionary entries with their generic names and the phonetic pronunciations:

ABUTILON	ə byoo′ til on
ACALYPHA	a kə lai′ fə
ACER	ae′ sə
ACHIMENES	a kə mee′neez
ADENIUM	a dee′ nee əm

The second word following the generic name is in smaller capitals and is the name of the botanical *family* to which the plant belongs (in the case of PHILODENDRON, it is ARACEAE, the Aroids). In botany, the family is a larger group consisting of many related genera with similar characteristics — as an example, the family ARACEAE also includes *ANTHURIUM, CALADIUM, SPATHIPHYLLUM* and many others with flowers like Arum Lilies.

Within each dictionary entry you'll find reference to some of the most popular *species* of the genus which are grown (*specific* or *species* names correspond to our given or personal name). Specific names are printed in small Italic type. Where a species is described, the generic name is abbreviated to its initial capital with a full stop to save space.

Sometimes, the generic and specific names will be followed by yet a third name. This is the *varietal* or *cultivar* name, which further identifies the plant when two varieties have the same generic and specific names. *Varietal* names are used when it is necessary to distinguish some small natural point of difference — a consistent flower colour or leaf-marking, or a particular habit of growth. Varietal names are printed in small type with an initial capital and sometimes within quotes. *Cultivar* names fall in the same position (in place of varietal names) when it is necessary to refer to some characteristic or sport of the plant that has proved capable of cultivation only by means of cuttings; (raised from seed it might revert to the original). Cultivar names are often in a modern language instead of Latin or Greek.

Another word you'll run across is 'hybrid' or 'hybrida'. This is used when each of a plant's parents is of a different species. Hybrids are often raised by seedsmen to produce superior new species, just as breeders of horses and cattle try to improve their stock. A hybrid is often indicated by a large X between the generic and specific names.

Individual dictionary entries give all sorts of additional information such as size, flowering time, country of origin, method of propagation, type of potting mix required, minimum necessary winter temperature, ideal position or light intensity, popular names and many other things.

A number printed in **heavy** type at the end of any entry is the page number on which a colour illustration will be found if it is not immediately adjacent.

Under every illustration is a brief caption giving the plant's correct botanical names, and also the most common of its popular names.

ABUTILON
(ə byoo' til on)　　　　MALVACEAE

ABUTILON X *'Golden Fleece'*
Chinese Lantern

ABUTILON *megapotamicum Variegatum*
Big River Abutilon

Mostly native to tropical South America, *ABUTILONS* grow easily from cuttings struck at any time of the year, and flower throughout the warmer months. They enjoy a rich soil, plenty of summer water and feeding, and free circulation of air at all times. They do best on a sunny terrace, and will not withstand winter temperatures much below 50°F (10°C). Pinching out will lead to a bushier habit and more flowers. *ABUTILONS* can be trained as standards, as compact bushes in large pots, or to weep from hanging baskets. Varieties with variegated leaves are most effective when not in flower.

A. darwinii Two-inch (5 cm) flowers, tomato red veined crimson.

A. X hybridum 'Chinese Lantern'. A cross between *A. darwinii* and *A. striatum*. Flowers in many colours include:
　　'Apricot' — orange.
　　'Boule de Neige' — white.
　　'Delicatum' — rose.
　　'Golden Fleece' — yellow.
　　'Vesuvius' — red.
A. megapotamicum 'Big River Abutilon'. Toothed oval leaves. Lantern-shaped yellow flowers with red calyx and stamens.
A. striatum 'Flowering Maple'. Green maple-shaped leaves. Veined orange flowers.

ACALYPHA
(a kə lae' fə)　　　　EUPHORBIACEAE

ACALYPHA *hispida*
Red-hot Cat's Tail

ACALYPHA *wilkesiana*
Beefsteak Plant

Warmth, high humidity and plenty of liquid fertiliser are the keys to success with these striking plants, native to Southeast Asia and the Pacific Islands. The 'Red-Hot Cat's Tail', *ACALYPHA hispida*, from New Guinea, is the most difficult to cultivate, requiring almost tropical conditions of winter heat (at least 60°F or 16°C). All in all the coloured-leaf varieties are more within the scope of the average indoor gardener. They will survive winter temperatures down to 45°F (7°C), though with some loss of leaves, and strike easily from cuttings in warm weather. Plant several of them in a large pot for maximum display; cut back to about 10 in (25 cm) and fertilize in late winter to stimulate growth. They'll look good all year round in a sheltered courtyard or sunroom. Good varieties include:

A. godseffiana Cream-edged toothed green leaves.
A. g. Heterophylla Divided leaves, same colour.
A. hispida 'Red-Hot Cat's Tail'. Green leaves. Long red tassel flowers.
A. wilkesiana 'Beefsteak Plant'. Leaves variegated green, pink, cream and red.
A. w. Macafeana 'Fire Dragon Plant'. Red, crimson and bronze leaves.
A. w. Macrophylla 'Copperleaf'. Bronze and copper leaves.

ACER
(ai' sə)   ACERACEAE

ACER palmatum Dissectum
Japanese Mountain Maple

Available in a myriad varieties of leaf shape and colour, the decorative and deciduous 'Japanese Mountain Maples', *ACER palmatum* spp. are ideal pot subjects. Taller varieties make beautiful house trees; smaller fancy-leafed types assume natural bonsai shapes and remain a reasonable size. I have used them successfully in my home from first leaf to

autumn colour, keeping their leaves fresh with regular spraying and an occasional treat under the bathroom shower. Give them good light, but not direct sun. Plant in a well-drained, porous, acid soil mix, and do not over-water. Feed periodically with diluted fish emulsion or an acid-based plant food suitable for *Azaleas* and *Camellias*. Good varieties include:

A. palmatum Dissectum Much-divided green leaves.
A. p. D. 'Atropurpureum' Divided purple-bronze leaves.
A. p. 'Roseo-ornatum' Delicate pink and pale green leaves.
A. p. Scolopendrifolium Divided thread-like leaves.
A. p. 'Seigen' Yellow-green leaves; new growth pink. Stems turn scarlet in winter.

All of these Maples are frost hardy, and do well with summer shelter in mild climates.

ACHIMENES
(a kə mee' neez)   GESNERIACEAE

ACHIMENES longiflora
Hot Water Plant

Related to African Violets and Gloxinias, the many species of *ACHIMENES* are found wild in Central America. Their name means 'cold-suffering' and a cold snap in the growing season may make them go dormant unless they can be given warm water — hence one of their popular names, 'Hot Water Plant'. Put the small scaly tubers in a sandy-acid soil mixture with plenty of leaf-mould, and maintain a constant level of moisture until flowers appear. They like sun in the spring, but more sheltered conditions in summer. The many varieties (which include white, pink, blue, purple, orange and red-spotted yellow flowers) are hybrids from original species, and have varying habits — upright, bushy or trailing. The handsome foliage is shiny, toothed and hairy; the flowers, generally open in shape, resemble Petunias. In late summer the stems will die back and the pots should be stored under cover in a shaded warm place.

ACHIMENES are particularly spectacular in hanging baskets.

ADENIUM
(e dee ny əm) APOCYNACEAE

ADENIUM obesum
Desert Rose

A rare and beautiful plant from Northeast Africa, the 'Desert Rose', *ADENIUM*, is related to *Plumeria*, and is often seen growing in similar conditions. It develops a gross, succulent trunk and is completely bare in winter. In spring, the dark green blunt-ended leaves appear; in summer, the gorgeous clusters of carmine trumpet flowers; white and gold centred. *ADENIUM* is often seen potted in courtyard gardens of tropical climates. Perfect drainage and an acid sandy soil are necessary. But be warned—it is not a common plant, and you may have to grow it from seed, or from a plump cutting of old growth thoroughly dried out before striking in sand. Recently, German plantsmen have found a way to graft it onto Oleander.

ADIANTUM
(a dee an' təm) POLYPODIACEAE

A popular fern genus for indoor use, the delicate 'Maidenhairs' or *ADIANTUM* include more than 200 species from almost every part of the world. They favour moist semi-shaded places, and that gives the clue to their indoor requirements. Give them an acid, peaty compost with some sand for drainage and a little powdered charcoal. Propagate by divisions and start them into life in early spring in

ADIANTUM aethiopicum
Maidenhair Fern

ADIANTUM hispidulum
Maidenhair Fern

a shaded place (even in the bathroom). As the wiry fronds unfurl, *ADIANTUMS* can be moved indoors among other groups of plants. Always keep them out of direct sun, and raise the humidity by placing their pot in a tray of damp gravel. Feed during the warm months with diluted natural fertiliser like fish emulsion — never with chemicals. The fronds will brown and dry off at the approach of winter. Snip them away and store the pot in a warm sheltered place, never allowing it to dry out completely. Varieties grown depend on which country you live in, but species *A. aethiopicum, A. capillis-veneris, A. hispidulum, A. tenerum* and *A. venustum* are most common, all looking rather alike. *A. micropinnulum* has finer, more delicate leaflets; *A. trapeziforme* has larger and more angular leaflets. (See also plate page 34).

AECHMEA
(ak' mee ə)   BROMELIACEAE

AECHMEA chantinii Mooreana
Amazon Zebra Plant

AECHMEA distichantha Schlombergerii
Vase Plant

Bewildering in their variety, *AECHMEAS* are fancy-dress members of the Pineapple family (or Bromeliads) from tropical America. They aré air-feeders, collecting nourishment from water and decaying matter in the upturned cup of their leaves. They can be grown wired onto pieces of driftwood (the roots covered in sphagnum moss), or supported among clusters of large pebbles in open containers. *AECHMEAS* also thrive in open mixtures of leaf mould and fibre with small additions of charcoal and sand. They are winter-hardy provided they receive shelter from frost. Fertilise only once a year. A diluted solution of calcium carbonate in the leaf vase

AECHMEA X 'Foster's Favourite'
Lacquered Wine Cup

will produce flowers in about six weeks in warm weather. Good species and varieties include:

A. caudata 'Variegata' 'Living Vase Plant'. Cream-striped leaves. Yellow, orange and midnight-blue flowers. *A. chantinii* Striped grey leaves. Yellow flowers, salmon-orange bracts. *A. fasciata* 'Urn Plant'. Grey-green leaves, cross-banded in silver. Tufted pale blue flowers in pink bracts.
A. X 'Foster's Favourite' Dark red leaves. Red and blue flowers with chains of coral berries.
A. fulgens Discolor Leaves purplish underneath. Purple flowers with scarlet stems and sepals.

AEONIUM
(ae oh' nyəm)   CRASSULACEAE

AEONIUM tabulaeforme
Aeonium

Succulents from North Africa and various Atlantic islands, *AEONIUMS* are excellent for terraces, courtyards and dry sunny positions. A poor quality porous soil mixture, with plenty of sand and limestone chips, grows them to perfection. Grown from offsets, the plants form a formal rosette of leaves (often on a long stalk) and produce tall spikes of starry flowers in branched clusters, after which they die off. Minimum outdoor winter temperature is 50°F (10°C) — give plenty of water in hot summers. Some species are:

A. arboreum Stem to 3 ft (90 cm), topped with green rosette, yellow flowers.
A. decorum Copper leaves. White flowers. 30 in (75 cm).
A. nobile Olive-green leaves. Coral flowers. 24 in (60 cm).
A. tabulaeforme Green leaves in a dense flat rosette. Yellow flowers in a many-branched cluster.

AESCHYNANTHUS
(ash ee nan' thəs)   GESNERIACEAE

AESCHYNANTHUS lobbianus
Lipstick Vine

Mid-summer flowering relatives of the African Violet, *AESCHYNANTHUS* are succulent-leafed trailers from Southern Asia. They are generally grown in baskets of moist, acid compost and hung in a warm humid position in semi-shade. They need plenty of water in the warm weather growing season. The flowers look like an orange-scarlet lipstick poking out of a dark red-green holder. Propagate in spring or late summer from hardened stem-tip cuttings. Some species are:

A. lobbianus 'Lipstick Vine'. Glossy light green leaves. Yellow-lined red flowers.
A. marmoratus 'Zebra Basket Vine'. Handsome

dark leaves veined with yellow, backed with purple. The brown-spotted flowers are green.
A. speciosus Light green leaves. Orange flowers shading to yellow at base.

AGAVE
(ə gah' vae)   AMARYLLIDACEAE

AGAVE americana Marginata
Century Plant

Hardy enough for the most exposed courtyard or balcony, *AGAVES* are slow growing and ought to be abandoned for pot culture when they reach 24 in (61 cm) across. By this time they'll have produced many offshoots which can be potted up so that you can start over again. Give them poor sandy soil with just a little leaf mould, and water sparingly. All *AGAVES* grow formally-shaped rosettes of spine-tipped leaves which can be quite dangerous to children and pets. They will not bloom in a pot. But outdoors, where the plant may reach 6 ft (2 m) in diameter, enormous flower spikes will shoot up as tall as 25 ft (8 m). Good species are:

A. americana Marginata 'Century Plant'. Yellow-edged grey-green leaves.
A. attenuata Smaller grey-green rosettes on a short trunk.
A. filifera 'Thread-leaf Agave'. Bright green leaves with silvery threads in place of spines. Flower spike to 12 ft (4 m).
A. victoria reginae 'Victoria Agave'. A superb dwarf species, rarely reaching 12 in (30 cm) across.

AGLAONEMA
(a glə oh nee' mə)   ARACEAE

Members of the Arum family, *AGLAONEMAS* make ideal house plants and thrive indoors in warm, poorly lighted places, where their beautifully

AGLAONEMA *pseudo-bracteata*
Chinese Evergreen

AGLAONEMA *roebelinii*
Painted Drop-tongue

marked leaves are most striking. 55°F (13°C) is the minimum winter temperature required for them to stay in good condition, but they'll recover from occasional colder spells. Plant them in a peaty compost. Do not over-water in cold weather, but build up the supply gradually as the temperatures climb. Check root moisture before re-watering.

AGLAONEMAS produce flowers like small green or white Arum lilies and propagate easily from stem cuttings (with at least two joints) placed firmly in a damp mixture of sand and peat. Good species are:

A. commutatum Silver-marked green leaves.
A. modestum 'Chinese Evergreen'. Plain bright green leaves. Will grow in plain water.
A. pictum Dark, silver-spotted leaves. A dwarf for terrariums.
A. X 'Pseudo-bracteata' Cream-splashed green foliage.

A. roebelinii 'Silver Queen' 'Painted Drop-tongue'. Dark leaves heavily variegated with silver.
A. treubii 'Ribbon Aglaonema'. A compact plant with ribbon-shaped blue-green leaves marked silver. Many AGLAONEMAS bear red berries after flowering. (See also plate page 29).

ALLAMANDA
(al ə man' də)   APOCYNACEAE

ALLAMANDA *neriifolia*
Golden Trumpet Bush

Showy-flowered shrubs from South America, ALLAMANDAS mostly climb and sprawl untidily. However one species. *A. neriifolia* the 'Golden Trumpet Bush', can make a spectacular pot specimen for a sunny courtyard or balcony in temperate climates. Propagated from cuttings in warm weather, it grows into a many-branched compact bush in a large pot of good loam with leaf mould and decayed manure. Water only occasionally in winter, top-dress and cut back in spring, then increase the water as the weather gets hotter. Basically evergreen, ALLAMANDAS will drop many leaves in cooler areas and produce showy clusters of orange-striped yellow trumpet flowers in summer. Keep up water and humidity during hot weather; give shade from the midday sun.

ALOCASIA
(al oh kae' shə)   ARACEAE

Arum relatives from Southeast Asia, ALOCASIAS are grown purely for their spectacular leaves, and are rarely successful outside conservatories except in mild climates. They grow from tubers planted in spring in a rich peaty compost, and do best sheltered

ALOCASIA X *amazonica*
Giant Caladium

ALOCASIA *indica Metallica*
Elephant's Ears

from direct sun. Feed regularly with diluted fertiliser, and check the drainage for they can easily damp off. Species include:

A. amazonica Metallic blue-green leaves, dramatically veined in white. To 24 in (60 cm).
A. cuprea 'Giant Caladium'. Develops dark metallic leaves, bronze on top, purplish underneath.
A. indica Metallica 'Elephant's Ears'. The hardiest of the family. Often seen outdoors in temperate climates where it develops masses of metallic leaves on purplish stems and spreads from runners.
A. macrorhiza 'Spoon Lily' or 'Cunjevoi'. Develops giant arrow-shaped leaves which may be 6 ft (2 m) long. The yellow boat-shaped flowers are highly perfumed.

ALOË
(a loh' ae)   LILIACEAE

ALOË spp.
Aloe

When not in flower, *ALOËS* are sometimes mistaken for the American *Agaves* (which see), but they belong to a different family and are all native to Africa. Both genera have toothed leaf margins, but unlike *Agaves*, *ALOËS* bloom almost every year and do not die back after flowering. They make good balcony or courtyard plants in large pots of well-drained sandy soil with infrequent watering. *ALOES* rarely flower inside, but in full sun produce tall candelabra spikes of tubular flowers in scarlet, pink, orange and yellow. They tolerate drought and salt sea air. There are hundreds of species and varieties, including:

A. arborescens 'Candelabra Aloë'. May reach 10 ft (3 m). Orange flowers.
A. ferox The leaves have a reddish-brown tinge and are covered with spines. Scarlet flowers in 3 ft (90 cm) spikes.
A. nobilis 'Gold-spined Aloë'. Grows to 24 in (60 cm). Green leaves edged with yellow.
A. variegata 'Partridge-breasted Aloë'. The green triangular leaves are backed with white flecks. A manageable size.

ANANAS
(an' a nəs)   BROMELIACEAE

The edible Pineapple is *ANANAS comosus*, but a rare and more delicate cousin *ANANAS bracteata*, the 'Striped Wild Pineapple', is one of the most popular Bromeliads among collectors. The 5 ft (150 cm) spiny leaves are banded in green and cream, often flushed with pink. The flowers are violet, with bright red bracts and stems, later developing into a brilliantly coloured miniature Pineapple.

ANANAS bracteatus Striatus
Striped Wild Pineapple

ANANAS is a native of Brazil, and less tolerant of winter cold than its edible cousin. It prefers a sandy compost with leaf mould and charcoal, and moderate watering at all times. Small specimens can be grown in pots, larger ones may require a tub. This highly decorative plant can be propagated from suckers or from the leaf rosette on the fruit. *A. comosus* also makes a decorative indoor plant, particularly bearing its formal leaf rosette and large fruit above a classic urn. Avoid winter temperatures of less than 50°F (10°C).

ANTHURIUM
(an thoo' ree əm)   ARACEAE

ANTHURIUM andreanum Rubrum
Palette Flower

ANTHURIUM scherzerianum
Flamingo Flower

ANTHURIUM species *A.giganteum,
A.scherzerianum, A.warocqueanum*

ANTHURIUMS are often grown and shown with Orchids, although they are not related in any way. They form a splendid genus of more than 500 species within the Arum family, and like a rich moisture-retaining compost, perfect drainage and high humidity all through the warm weather. They like a winter minimum of not less than 60°F (15°C); Fortunately, this can be maintained near the window of a sunny livingroom. Propagation is possible by division of older plants. This, and the necessary re-potting, is best done in early spring. The many species include:

A. andreanum 'Palette Flower'. This has heart-shaped leaves. Flowers red, white, coral, pink or green according to variety. All flowers have a highly lacquered appearance.
A. crystallinum Grown for the striking velvety leaves, which appear to be coated with some

sparkling material. The flowers are uninteresting.

A. X ferrierense 'Little Boy Flower'. Pink spathe and spadix.

A. scherzerianum 'Flamingo Flower'. This is much smaller than the others. The leaves are spear-shaped. The flowers are usually red with a coiled spadix.

A. waroqueanum Is grown for its elongated 30 in (75 cm) leaves, veined with chartreuse. Has small yellow flower spathes.

As with all members of the Arum family, the spadix or column of *ANTHURIUM* consists of a myriad tiny flowers; the highly coloured shield or spathe is merely a specially developed protective leaf. *ANTHURIUM* flowers last for months.

APHELANDRA
(a fə lan' drə)   ACANTHACEAE

APHELANDRA squarrosa 'Louisae'
Zebra Plant

Popularly known as 'Zebra Plants', *APHELANDRAS* take readily to indoor cultivation. They are inclined to grow leggy after flowering, but are quite easy to start afresh from cuttings. Native to South America, they have the usual tropical needs — a rich porous soil, plenty of water in the warmer months, little in winter. They suffer when the temperature drops below 50°F (10°C) but can usually get through winter in a warm corner (perhaps in a bathroom). Grown in relatively small pots, they make a memorable summer display. Few of them reach more than 20 in (50 cm) high indoors. Good species are:

A. aurantiaca Orange-red flowers.
A. aurantiaca var. Roezlii Scarlet flowers.
A. squarrosa 'Louisae' Deep yellow flowers. Red stems.

APOROCACTUS
(ə po roh kak' təs)   CACTACEAE

APOROCACTUS flagelliformis
Rat's Tail Cactus (Photo: Hamlyn Library)

Once one of the most popular of Cacti for home use, the 'Rat's Tail', *APOROCACTUS flagelliformis*, now seems to be a little out of favour. It is very easy to grow from cuttings dried off a few days before planting. It is an epiphyte, native to Mexican jungles, so it needs a rich compost with plenty of leaf mould, sharp sand and some charcoal. *APOROCACTUS* is best grown in small hanging pots because of its weeping habit, but is sometimes grafted onto sturdier tall cactus to make a weeping standard. The slim trailing stems are covered with brown spines and are not much more than a centimetre thick. They are frequently branched. The 1½ in (4 cm) cerise flowers appear in late spring. *APOROCACTUS* prefers only part sun, and makes an intriguing indoor plant.

ARAUCARIA
(a roh keə' ree yə)   ARAUCARIACEAE

Potted 'Norfolk Island Pines' have many indoor uses, not the least being as the annual Christmas Tree. How strange that this giant among conifers (up to 200 ft or 60 m tall on its native island) will remain happily potbound year after year, seldom attempting to pass 4 ft (120 cm) in height. It enjoys a compost of loam, sharp sand and a little peat, appreciating an occasional deep soaking in a bucket of water. Give your *ARAUCARIA heterophylla* bright light and plenty of fresh air: an occasional syringeing will keep red spider at bay. It is not particular about temperature and seems to enjoy the same range as human beings.

ARAUCARIA heterophylla
Norfolk Island Pine

ARDISIA
(ah dis' ee yə)   MYRSINACEAE

ARDISIA crenata
Coral Berry

One of winter's most colourful indoor plants (and popular in the Northern hemisphere for the Christmas season), the 'Coral Berry', *ARDISIA*, is a shade lover. It prefers a woodsy compost rich in leaf mould, and is grown particularly for the vivid red (or, in some species, white) fruits. The habit is dwarf, the shape vertical with a leafy crown of glossy *Camellia*-like leaves. The small white flowers appear on short stems right around the upright trunk in spring and are long lasting. At this time the plant is best left outdoors so that the bees can do their work of pollination. It may be returned indoors when the

berries have begun to form. *ARDISIA* likes to be kept moist at all times and is not pruned. Grown species are:

A. crenata   'Coral Berry'. 30 m (75 cm).
A. japonica   'Snow Berry'. 18 in (45 cm).

A pink-berried hybrid is also sometimes seen.

THE AROIDS
(eə' roidz)   ARACEAE

Typical *AROIDS* — young plants of *PHILODENDRON panduraeforme*

This is a particularly large botanical family, almost entirely of tropical or warm climate origin, and is particularly suited to indoor cultivation. Members are generally characterised by roughly heart-shaped leaves, and by the appearance of flowers very much like those of the popular Arum or Calla lily—this is, a long spear-shaped mass of tiny florets (called a spadix) set in a large and often colourful bract called a spathe. Most *AROIDS* prefer a temperature of 60-70°F (15-20°C), and need frequent warm-weather watering. They like a porous compost including some charcoal, and very good drainage. Diffused light suits them, with protection from sun in summer. The *AROID* family includes many popular indoor plants illustrated in this book. They are:

Aglaonema (Chinese Evergreen), *Alocasia* (Elephant's Ears), *Anthurium* (Flamingo Flower), *Caladium* (The Rainbow Plant), *Dieffenbachia* (Dumb Cane), *Monstera* (Swiss Cheese Plant), *Philodendron*, *Rhaphidophora* (Hunter's Robe), *Scindapsus*, *Spathiphyllum* (Peace Lily), *Syngonium* (Arrowhead) and *Xanthosoma*.

ASPARAGUS
(əs pa' rə gəs)   LILIACEAE

ASPARAGUS densiflorus 'Sprengeri'
Emerald Feather

Toughest of indoor subjects for a soft, profuse effect, the many species of Asparagus Fern are not Ferns at all, but members of the Lily family. Easy to grow in pots or baskets, they remain fresh indoors the whole year round and grow in any light. *ASPARAGUS* species grow from large masses of succulent tuberous roots which send up soft stems. These rapidly burst into a fine mass of leaves—feathery, tinsel-like or sickle-shaped according to species. The tiny white or pink spring flowers are followed by scarlet, black or green berries. There are more than 150 species, including:

A. asparagoides 'Smilax'. 3 ft (1 m). Sharp pointed leaves.

ASPARAGUS d. 'Sprengeri' in fruit
Emerald Feather

ASPARAGUS retrofractus
Twisted Asparagus Fern

A. densiflorus 'Sprengeri' 'Emerald Feather'. Most commonly seen species. Grows to 5 ft (150 cm). Fronds like tinsel.
A. meyeri 'Foxtail Asparagus'. Dwarf habit, plumes of needle leaves like green foxtails.
A. plumosus 'Asparagus Fern'. The most delicate fronds imaginable, popular in florists' work. Often develops a climbing habit.
A. retrofractus 'Twisted Asparagus Fern'. Similar to *A. 'Sprengeri'*.

All species need plenty of water in warm weather, and an occasional deep soaking. Though fairly winter-hardy indoors, they may lose leaves, particularly if damp, and can be cut back to ground level. New shoots appear in spring.

ASPIDISTRA
(as pa dis' trə)   LILIACEAE

ASPIDISTRA elatior
Cast Iron Plant

If you haven't been able to develop green fingers, never despair. There is always *ASPIDISTRA*, the most tolerant of all house plants, known with good reason, as the 'Cast Iron Plant'. Pot a group of them up in early spring, using plenty of crocks or pebbles for good drainage. Any houseplant mix is suitable, but preferably one with a trace of charcoal. Light watering is needed only when the soil is on the dry side.

ASPIDISTRAS really do improve with acquaintance. The 24 in (60 cm) leaves have a brilliant gloss which you can maintain with occasional spraying, and periodically small lightly-perfumed chocolate flowers are produced, right at soil level. Strong light will fade the rich green colour of the foliage, except in winter, when the plants appreciate a spell closer to the window. Two varieties are grown:

A. elatior 'Cast Iron Plant'. Shiny green leaves.
A. elatior 'Variegata' Leaves striped white or yellow.

ASPLENIUM
(as plee' nyəm)   POLYPODIACEAE

Natives of Australia and nearby tropical areas, *ASPLENIUMS*, the ubiquitous 'Spleenworts', are grown all over the world in garden, glasshouse and home. They are usually potted in a peaty mix including sand and leaf mould and, like most ferns, prefer as moist an atmosphere as possible, together with a minimum winter temperature of around 50-55°F (10-13°C). Keep them moist (but not wet) at all

ASPLENIUM bulbiferum
Mother Fern

ASPLENIUM nidus-avis
Bird's Nest Fern

times, and syringe the fronds in summer. Never, never try to grow them in full sunlight. Two species are popularly grown:

A. bulbiferum 'Mother Fern' or 'Hen and Chickens'. This has a curiosity value, for new plantlets develop directly on the surface of the feathery fronds. These may drop and take root or can be detached and potted up.
A. nidus-avis 'Bird's Nest Fern'. This popular plant grows as a simple inverted cone of shiny apple-green leaves. It prefers slightly warmer conditions and does well indoors, preferably at floor level, where the architectural effect of the fronds may be seen.

ASTROPHYTUM
(as' troh fai təm)   CACTACEAE

ASTROPHYTUM myriostigma
Bishop's Hat

These curious Mexican Cacti are easy to grow and, what's even better, are easy to handle — for they are completely spineless. Like most terrestrial Cacti, AS-TROPHYTUMS are grown in a gritty, open compost and must have perfect drainage. Water regularly, but leave them overall on the dryish side. They are ideal for a sunny window, terrace or open courtyard and make an effective contrast to other Cactus types in a mixed planter. Viewed from above, the plants are like a perfect eight-pointed star. Each ASTROPHYTUM plant produces a single golden-yellow flower in spring, right on top. More common species include:

A. asterias   'Star Cactus'. Flatter shape.
A. capricorne   Small spines. Grows to 10 in (25 cm).
A. myriostigma   'Bishop's Hat'.

AZALEA
(ə zae' lee ə)   ERICACEAE

Not true indoor plants, AZALEAS grow splendidly in containers. These gorgeous shrubs have surface-rooting habits, and need no particular depth of soil. I grow them in a mixture that is almost entirely peat and sharp sand, with a trace of charcoal — or when I can get it, old decayed tanbark and sand.

They can be potted up at any time, even when in full flower. So if you have a large collection, you can make do with only one or two 'special' display pots. Switch the plants around into the good containers only when it's their turn to come inside. This should be just as the first flowers open, and you can keep them in a softly lighted position for a month or more. The main flowering varies from early spring to early summer, according to variety, with many

AZALEA X kurume 'Kirin'
Kurume Azalea

AZALEA macrantha
Satsuki Azalea

types giving a lighter bonus flowering in the autumn.

AZALEAS like plenty of moisture all year, and lashings of water when in bloom. Avoid overhead sprinkling if possible — dribble the water around the roots or soak the container in the kitchen sink. Spraying overhead might spot the flowers or, even worse, lead to the development of the dreaded 'flower blight' for which there is no real cure except stripping the entire bush.

Do not top-dress AZALEAS, or mulch them heavily, for the tiny surface roots will suffocate and die off. Feed regularly with liquid fertiliser, preferably a special AZALEA mix, but not just before flowering in case the plants bolt to leaf.

AZALEA varieties are numbered in many hundreds — and almost every colour short of a true blue. The types I find most useful for pot work are:

65

AZALEA X 'Flora'
Hybrid Azalea

AZALEA X 'Countess of Asquith'
Belgian Hybrid Azalea

A. indica (Belgian Hybrids). Mostly double or semi-double flowers with bicolor effect. Rugged, compact shape.
A. kurume Small-flowering, tiny-leafed varieties. These will take more sun and are likely to give a second flowering in autumn.
A. macrantha The true Japanese 'Satsuki Azalea' is best of all for pot use, having small leaves and large flowers borne in late spring and early summer.

AZALEAS can be propagated easily from cuttings of half-ripened wood with a heel. All of them can be wired, clipped and trained into almost any shape. They rarely need re-potting. (See also plates pages 6, 27, 45).

BACULARIA
(ba kyoo lea' ree ə)   PALMAE

BACULARIA monostachya
Walking Stick Palm

Little known outside Australia, the handsome 'Walking Stick Palm', *BACULARIA*, is ideal for not-too-roomy modern interiors. In a 9 in (23 cm) pot the trunk stays just the thickness of a walking stick, growing straight and tall. The 12 in (30 cm) fronds are divided into about sixteen segments with a large fishtail effect at the end, almost as if the leaf had been torn across. They are held at an almost vertical angle. *BACULARIA* (sometimes known as Linospadix) likes a warm, humid position out of direct sun. It thrives in well-drained moisture-retaining compost with sand and peat and, like all Palms, needs plenty of water in the warm weather.

BARLERIA
(bah lee' ree ə)   ACANTHACEAE

Dwarf evergreen shrubs, *BARLERIAS* can be grown indoors, or on terraces in warmer climates, but need winter protection under glass where the temperature drops below 55°F (13°C). They are propagated either from seed or by half-ripened cuttings grown in a sharp, moist, rooting medium at any time apart from winter. *BARLERIAS* prefer a rich, peaty soil mix, and demand plenty of fresh air and water all summer long. The leaves are inclined to scorch in direct sun, so light shade should be provided. Available species include:

B. cristata 'Philippine Violet'. Violet-blue flowers.
B. cristata Alba White flowers. From India.
B. lupulina Rosy-gold flowers. From Mauritius.
B. strigosa Blue flowers.

BARLERIA cristata
Philippine Violet

BEAUCARNEA
(boh kah' nee ə)   LILIACEAE

BEAUCARNEA recurvata
Pony Tail

Often sold as Nolina, which name belongs to a totally different plant, the 'Pony Tail'. *BEAU-CARNEA* is native to Mexico. A member of the Lily family, it grows from seed or cuttings in pots of well-drained sandy loam. The trunk develops a bulbous shape at ground level, reminiscent of an oversized onion, and the tall stem breaks into a spray of leaves at the end — rather like a young girl's ponytail hairdo. In the wild, *BEAUCARNEA* grows to a considerable height, but in pots rarely exceeds 3 ft (1 m). *BEAUCARNEA* is suitable for courtyard or

balcony culture, and enjoys a dry winter climate. It does not like prolonged temperatures below 50°F (10°C).

BEGONIA
(bə goh' nee ə)   BEGONIACEAE

BEGONIA caroliniaefolia
Hand Begonia

BEGONIA X 'Cleopatra'
Cleopatra Begonia

Probably the most widely grown hobby plants in the world, *BEGONIAS* are almost beyond the scope of an entire book, so bewildering is their seemingly infinite variety. Countries of origin include Central and South America, Africa, Asia, the East and West Indies, and New Guinea.
What have they in common? A succulent nature, love of humidity, and waxy leaves of very curious

BEGONIA fuchsioides
Fuchsia Begonia

BEGONIA masoniana
Iron Cross Begonia

BEGONIA haageana
Haageana Begonia

BEGONIA rex-cultorum
Rex Begonia 'Fairy'

shapes. None of them is frost hardy, but many can be grown in a sunny window during the colder months.

The flowers are borne in clusters and are generally pink or white, small and insignificant. Exceptions both in size and colour are principally among the tuberous types where hybridising has produced a rainbow of colours and variegations, in sizes as big as a saucer. All *BEGONIAS* enjoy a moist, well-drained peaty compost and plenty of water in the warmer weather. They are usually propagated from leaf or stem cuttings taken in spring. The small 'Bedding' or 'Wax Begonias' may be grown from seed sown under glass.

For convenience, *BEGONIAS* are usually separated into three classes: fibrous-rooted, tuberous-rooted and rhizomatous.

Fibrous Begonias

Most common of these are hybrids of *B. semperflorens*, the 'Wax' or 'Bedding Begonia'. These are small plants from 6-18 in (15-45 cm) according to variety. They have rather rounded leaves, varying in colour from apple green to a deep bronze-red. The flowers may be single, double or anywhere in between, in shades from white to deep red. They flower almost the entire year, but most heavily in summer. Other fibrous-rooted *BEGONIAS* include:

B. coccinea 'Angel Wing Begonia'. May grow to 4 ft (120 cm). Makes a spectacular pot plant with shiny wing-shaped leaves.
B. fuchsioides Small Fuchsia-shaped leaves on long weeping stems. Pink or red flowers.
B. haageana A tall hairy-leafed plant with clusters of salmon flowers in early spring.

BEGONIA *semperflorens*
Wax Begonia

BEGONIA *tuberhybrida*
Tuberous Begonia

B. maculata 'Trout Begonia'. Many-lobed leaves marked in silver.
B. X 'Orange Rubra' To 3 ft (1 m). Clear green leaves marked in silver. Orange flowers.

Tuberous Begonias
These are strictly summer-flowering types, grown from spring-planted tubers. They need a temperature of at least 60°F (15°C) to start growing. Place the pots in a bright position out of full sun; water and fertilise regularly until the flowers open in summer. *B tuberhybrida* is the species, and its variety 'Pendula' has a natural weeping habit and is used in hanging baskets. (See plate page 31).

Rhizomatous Begonias
Here we have a great variety of plants, usually propagated from cuttings of their thickened root systems which scramble everywhere over or just under the soil surface. Popular types include:

B. caroliniaefolia 'Hand Begonia'. Splendidly lobed smooth leaves, 12 in (30 cm) across.
B. X 'Cleopatra' Translucent silky maple-shaped leaves patterned in green and chocolate.
B. luxurians 'Palm-Leaf Begonia'. This is a tall-growing plant for the greenhouse. Decorative leaves divided into as many as seventeen leaflets.
B. masoniana 'Iron Cross Begonia'. Hairy puckered leaves of bright green, marked with a large Maltese Cross in red-brown.
B. rex 'Rex Begonia'. These have generally wing-shaped leaves, marked in pink, red, bronze, purple and silver. Some have an iridescent effect; others are quite translucent and one or two have almost black leaves.

All are good houseplants in the warm weather, but should be wintered under glass.

BIFRENARIA
(bai fre neə' ree ə)   ORCHIDACEAE

BIFRENARIA *harrisoniae*
Bifrenaria

Here's a pleasant surprise — an Orchid that's easy to grow without a glasshouse, can cope with temperatures down to 50°F (10°C) and is over-poweringly perfumed as well. *BIFRENARIA harrisoniae* is its botanical name, and it comes from Brazil. Plant it in a small pot of fibrous, well-drained compost with plenty of sphagnum moss. Supply bright light and water in the summer (but not sun), and keep up the humidity as best you can. The leaves are handsome, evergreen and rather like a pleated *Aspidistra*. The flowers (which may appear any time from late winter on) are rich buttery cream, with a handsome red-violet lip covered in silver hairs.

BILLBERGIA
(bil bur' jə)   BROMELIACEAE

BILLBERGIA nutans
The Queen's Tears

BILLBERGIA pyramidalis
Flaming Torch

Among the easiest to grow of Bromeliads, *BILL-BERGIAS* make ideal indoor plants. Their humidity needs are not great, they're not fussy as to soil mix, and will actually grow sitting in a pot of stones or even a jar of water. The leaf rosettes are always handsome, and striking flower displays appear at many times of the year. Just remember to keep the leaf vase filled with water. Species are:

B. nutans 'Queen's Tears'. Slim, spidery grey-green leaves. Tall arching flower stems in spring, decked with navy blue and lime flowers in pink bracts. From Brazil.
B. pyramidalis 'Flaming Torch'. Open apple-green cups of spiny-edged leaves. A strong spike of

BILLBERGIA venezuelana
Fishing Pole Billbergia

70

flowers, any time from midwinter; all scarlet, gold and purple. From Brazil.

B. venezuelana   Tall vase-shaped leaf rosettes to 3 ft (90 cm), cross-banded blue-gray. The arching flower stems appear in midsummer, growing at an amazing rate of up to 6 in (15 cm) a day. They will hang down to 5 ft (150 cm) so that the potted plant must be placed on quite a tall stand. It has large hot pink bracts, flowers of grey-blue and lime. A stunning conversation piece. From Venezuela.

BLETILLA
(ble til' ə)   ORCHIDACEAE

BLETILLA striata
Chinese Ground Orchid

The miniature 'Chinese Ground Orchid', *BLETILLA* grows easily in a shallow pot filled with leaf mould, rubble and sand. Plant the snail-shaped corms in cool weather. 12 in (30 cm) pleated leaves will appear in early spring, followed quickly by wiry stems each with up to half a dozen miniature-*Cattleya*-type blooms. These are a vivid cerise with a slight striped effect. Pots can be brought indoors as soon as the first shoots appear and should be watered regularly. *BLETILLAS* can cope with a winter temperature just above freezing.

BOUGAINVILLEA
(boo gen vil' yə)   NYCTAGINACEAE

Not often thought of as a house plant, the rampant Brazilian 'Paper Vine' is quite amenable to taming, and makes a splendid specimen for balcony or sunroom. Pot up nursery-bought plants in early

BOUGAINVILLEA X 'Scarlett O'Hara'
Paper Vine

BOUGAINVILLEAS on seaside terrace

spring in a poorish soil mixture containing at least one third brick rubble and sand. Wire to shape or train it espalier fashion on a framework, and place in full sun. Give copious quantities of water in the hot weather but allow almost to dry out in winter. *BOUGAINVILLEA* is deciduous, so the colourful bracts (which almost hide the insignificant white flowers) will appear before the leaves, on new wood. The pot can be brought indoors as these begin to enlarge, but should be kept in a warm sunny position. Prune back after flowering. Re-pot rarely, but scrape away the surface soil every two years and top dress. Plants are available in every imaginable shade of pink, red and purple, with newer named varieties in shades of yellow, orange and white. Variegated leaves on some varieties. (See also plate page 47).

BRASSAIA
(brə sae' ə)   ARALIACEAE

BRASSAIA *actinophylla*
Octopus Tree

From tropical Queensland and Polynesia, the easy-to-grow 'Octopus Tree' makes a spectacular indoor plant with outstanding architectural qualities. It can be grown from seed, or from semi-ripened cuttings in a standard house plant mix (a little on the heavy side). It endures neglect surprisingly well. Keep it moist, but do not over-water. Each leaf consists of a number of shiny leaflets on separate stems. The blood-red flowers (which will only appear on a mature specimen in good light) are in a series of panicles arranged rather like extended octopus tentacles. BRASSAIA needs winter shelter and protection from full summer sun. Even indoors, BRASSAIA is a large plant and should be used as a floor specimen. (See also plate page 26).

BRASSOCATTLEYA
(bras oh kat lae' ə)   ORCHIDACEAE

BRASSOCATTLEYAS are possibly the most beautiful of all Orchids — hybrids between *Brassavola* and *Cattleya* with great ruffled flowers up to 8 in (20 cm) across. Varieties are available in delicious shades of mauve, lime, pink, crimson and white, usually with a fringed and contrasting lip. They are grown under shelter except in the tropics, but can be raised successfully in a sunny room with mild winter heat (keep the temperature around 50°F or 10°C). Epiphytic by nature, they are best grown in heavy pots or baskets filled with broken crocks, chunks of fern bark and other rough organic matter.

Let them almost dry out during winter; give occasional deep soakings in diluted fertiliser as the weather warms up. The majority of species will produce flowers in late summer and autumn.

BRASSOCATTLEYA *mossiae*
Brassocattleya

BRODIAEA
(broh dee ae' ə)   ALLIACEAE

BRODIAEA *ida-maia*
Firecracker Flower

Delightful North American bulbs highly suited to pot culture, BRODIAEAS give spectacular spot colour in spring and summer. Pot them up in a mixture of loam, sand and bulb fibre. Soak deeply and withhold water until the bulbs shoot.

Additional bulbs can be raised from seed, which sets freely; or by the small offset bulbs which develop if the plants are allowed to ripen properly after flowering. Colourful species include:

B. *californica*   Rosy-purple flowers. 12 in (30 cm).
B. *coronaria*   'Triplet Lily'. Violet-blue. 10 in (25cm).

B. ida-maia 'Firecracker Flower'. Scarlet and green. 9 in (23 cm).
B. laxa Purple-blue. 24 in (60 cm).
B. uniflora 'Spring Starflower'. Lilac. 6 in (15 cm).

THE BROMELIADS
(bro mel' ee adz) BROMELIACEAE

BROMELIADS — mixed planting on driftwood in terracotta trough

Members of the numerous family of colourful and exotic *BROMELIADS* are often seen as companions of rare Orchids in hothouse displays. Surprisingly, they are quite easy to grow. They are mostly tree-dwelling and have the characteristic shape of a pineapple top. This is hardly remarkable, for the Pineapple is itself a member of the family. The rosette of leathery leaves may be plain, striped, spotted, blotched or variegated in a number of colours in-cluding red, purple, yellow, white, grey and brown. The flowers may be small, almost hidden inside the cup, or borne proudly in spikes of the most unlikely colour combinations; black and orange, blue and lime-green, violet and scarlet; the colours are almost endless. Colourful berries often follow the flower display.

The roots of most *BROMELIADS* merely attach the plant to some other surface, so they are often grown wired to pieces of driftwood or old tree branches. They can however be grown in small pots supported by combinations of charcoal, rubble, peat moss, leaf mould and broken pots. Watering of these peculiar plants is done by continually filling the natural vase-like centre of the leaf rosette. An occasional dilution of weak chemical fertiliser in the water stimulates healthy growth.

Propagation is generally done by means of suckers or offshoots, for once a *BROMELIAD* rosette has flowered it will never do so again. *BROMELIADS* you will find in this book include colourful species of: *Aechmea* (Vase Plant), *Ananas* (Pineapple), *Billbergia* (Flaming Torch), *Cryptanthus* (Earth Stars), *Guzmania*, *Neoregelia* (Heart of Flame), *Nidularium* (Friendship Plant), *Portea, Tillandsia* (Spanish Moss) and *Vriesia* (Lobster Claw). (See also plate page 16).

BROWALLIA
(broh wol' ee ə) SOLANACEAE

BROWALLIA speciosa
Amethyst Flower

The true *BROWALLIAS* are compact spring and summer flowering annuals and perennials. The commonly named Browallia is actually an orange-flowered shrub called *Streptosolen.*

Raise *BROWALLIAS* from seed or cuttings planted in earliest spring under glass. They prefer a well-drained sandy compost mixed with leaf mould.

Water lightly and give weekly doses of weak liquid fertiliser. A new series of plants can be raised from cuttings in early summer to provide autumn and winter colour, for they will grow happily in temperatures as low as 45°F (7°C).

B. speciosa Major is the commonly seen variety, growing to 18 in (45 cm), and producing masses of violet-blue flowers. There are varieties with white and variegated blossom as well. All from South America.

BUXUS
(buk' səs)   BUXACEAE

BUXUS microphylla Japonica
Japanese Box

The many varieties of Box or *BUXUS* are often raised in containers of lime-dressed potting mix and clipped to formal shapes — their dense evergreen foliage looks particularly well in classic urns and similar formal pots placed at entryways or around a furnished terrace. Box is fast growing, completely frost-hardy and can be raised from cuttings. Pruning to shape is done in spring, and the growing plants should be fed often to keep them in good health. *B. microphylla,* the tiny-leafed 'Japanese Box', branches and rebranches prolifically and is particularly amenable to formal shaping. It has many forms with narrow or wide leaves, gold or variegated foliage.

THE CACTI
(kak' tai)   CACTACEAE

Typical of desert *CACTI* is
OPUNTIA microdasys

The indoor cultivation of the *CACTUS* family is simply a reproduction of their natural climate. Almost all of the spiny types flourish indoors or on a terrace in a warm, bright, sunny position. They like a well-drained compost containing at least one third sand and grit, and require water only during the growing season from late spring to early winter. They will survive astonishing neglect and lack of moisture when you are away on vacation, shrinking away like the hump of a thirsty camel as they use up their inbuilt water storage. But then, they plump up quickly and recover when the supply of water and light is restored. All in all, they're an ideal choice for people who are away a lot. *CACTI* reward us at any time of the year with their strange shapes, and most of them produce a brilliant flower display as well.

The great majority are quite winter-hardy; some, native to high mountainsides of Mexico, Peru and Bolivia, will even resist frost.

CACTI which do *not* like the sandy compost are those with leaves or leaf-like, spineless stems. These include *Epiphyllum* (Orchid Cactus), *Nopalxochia* (Empress Cactus), *Rhipsalidopsis* (Thanksgiving Cactus) and *Zygocactus* (Crab Cactus). These are all epiphytic and come from humid jungle places. They appreciate a generally higher temperature, partial shade and a well-drained compost rich in leaf mould. Feed and water them lavishly at flowering time and give winter protection under glass.

All *CACTI*, however, need water almost daily in summer, and regular fertilising with a balanced food rich in phosphorus and potassium, such as Nitrophoska or NPK. Occasional treats of diluted fish fertiliser or liquid animal manure are beneficial.

In addition to the epiphytes listed above, other colourful and interesting *CACTI* shown in this book include *Aporocactus* (Rat's Tail), *Astrophytum* (Bishop's Hat), *Cephalocereus* (Old Man Cactus), *Cereus, Chamaecereus* (Peanut Cactus), *Cleistocactus, Echinocactus* (Hedgehog Cactus), *Echinocereus, Gymnocalycium* (Chin Cactus), *Hatiora* (Drunkard's Dream), *Heliocereus* (Sun Cactus), *Mamillaria* (Nipple Cactus), *Notocactus* (Ball Cactus), *Opuntia* (Indian Fig), *Parodia, Pereskia* (Lemon Vine) and *Rebutia.*

Certain of the *CACTUS* family bloom only at night, opening magnificent flowers shortly after sunset and suffusing the night with rich perfume. They make sensational houseplants and include *Hylocereus* (Princess of the Night), *Epiphyllum oxypetalum* (Belle de Nuit), *Selenicereus* (Queen of the Night). They too are illustrated farther on.

CALADIUM
(ka lae' dee əm)   ARACEAE

CALADIUM X candidum
White Caladium

CALADIUM X 'Mrs W. B. Halderman'
Fancyleaf Caladium

CALADIUM humboldtii
Miniature Caladium

Their leaf-shape clearly identifies *CALADIUMS* as members of the Arum family. Tuberous-rooted perennials, they are well within the skill of any indoor gardener. Tubers are planted in early spring in containers of a rich compost of loam, leaf mould and pulverised cow manure. The addition of sharp sand helps drainage, for the juicy tubers are inclined to rot if water should lodge around them. Keep them barely moist until the first leaves appear, then gradually increase water, and fertilise regularly with diluted liquid manure. *CALADIUMS* are spectacular indoors, or massed on the shaded terrace or lanai. The leaves unfurl into magnificent heart shapes up to a foot long (30 cm), and in colour combinations of green, white, pink, red, chocolate and silver, many with a mottled translucent effect.

Hundreds of named varieties are available, but three popular types are:

C. bicolor hybrids Basically green and red.
C. X candidum Pure white leaves with light green veins.
C. humboldtii A miniature, with silver-spotted dark green leaves.

CALATHEA
(ka lə thee' ə)   MARANTACEAE

CALATHEA insignis
Rattlesnake Plant

CALATHEA louisae
Slender Calathea

Spectacularly beautiful, mostly tropical plants, *CALATHEAS* are grown for their bizarre leaf colourings and patterns. They adapt quite well to indoor pot culture, provided the humidity is kept up. Give them bright light (but never full sun), plenty of water and perfect drainage, which is achieved by

CALATHEA makoyana
Peacock Plant

CALATHEA ornata Roseo-lineata
Pink-line Calathea

CALATHEA picturata Argentea
Silver Calathea

76

CALATHEA *zebrina*
Zebra Plant

half filling the containers with brick rubble, charcoal and sand — this still leaves plenty of room for a peaty compost, for they are shallow rooters. Propagate them by division in early spring, when re-potting must be carried out. CALATHEAS quickly exhaust the soil and do not like to be overcrowded. Readily available species include:

C. insignis 'Rattlesnake Plant'. Narrow wavy-edged glossy leaves, backed with crimson and with parallel olive markings.
C. makoyana 'Peacock Plant'. The handsome leaves of this dwarf species are patterned above in green and below in red-violet. New leaves pop up in the shape of ice-cream cones.
C. ornata 'Roseo Lineata' 18 in (45 cm) tall indoors, this species sends up glossy dark leaves on tall stems. They are marked with pairs of parallel lines in rose pink.
C. zebrina 'Zebra Plant'. Large floppy leaves on short stems, purplish on the underside, soft green above, parallel-striped in chartreuse. The leaves of this species yellow in winter and can be cut away to reveal the spring flowers, which appear in a cluster of chocolate-brown bracts rather like a globe artichoke.

CALATHEAS may die right back if the winter temperature drops below 55°F (13°C) for long periods.

CALCEOLARIA
(kal see oh leə' ree ə)   SCROPHULARIACEAE

CALCEOLARIAS are shrubby South American perennials and annuals, all with striking flowers like puffed-up breakfast cereal—or, as the popular name suggests, over-full 'Ladies Purses'. The flower colours are basically red, yellow and orange; blot-

CALCEOLARIA *herbeohybrida*
Ladies' Purses

ched and spotted with crimson, brown and black. The varieties grown for indoor use are annual hybrids classed under the name of *C. X. herbeohybrida*.

Pot them in a compost rich in garden soil, with a little sand for drainage. Water regularly and treat to a periodic weak liquid fertiliser. They need good ventilation to prevent damping off, and should be kept out of the full summer sun.

CALLISIA
(ka lis' ee ə)   COMMELINACEAE

CALLISIA *elegans*
Striped Inch Plant

The 'Striped Inch Plant', CALLISIA, is a charmer for hanging baskets or dense ground cover around mass plantings. It quite resembles the *Tradescantias* 'Spider-

77

worts' to which it is closely related. It will grow well in any standard indoor compost, but like most tropicals it needs plenty of water and part shade all through the warm weather. The dark green leaves are attractively striped with white and backed with purple. Uninteresting three-petalled white flowers appear throughout summer. It is from Mexico.

CALONYCTION
(ka loh nik' tee ən)   CONVOLVULACEAE

CALONYCTION *aculeatum*
Moonflower (Photo by Margaret Davis)

The 'Moonflower', CALONYCTION, is a sensation on a sheltered terrace or anywhere you spend summer evenings—for that is when it flowers. At sunset, the plump spiral buds begin an eerie throbbing and suddenly unfurl into 6 in (15 cm) white circular flowers, striped with lime-green and beautifully perfumed. These stay open for one night only, and fade with dawn.

The 'Moonflower' is related to the 'Morning Glories' *Convolvulus* and *Ipomoea* (which see). It is perennial, grown from large seeds which it sets profusely. The hard seed casings should be filed through before planting out. Shoots will appear within ten days, and after regular water and fertiliser the vines will grow at a great rate, reaching 12 feet (4 m) or more.

CAMELLIA
(kə mee' lee ə)   THEACEAE

CAMELLIA *japonica* 'Waratah'
Australian Waratah Camellia

CAMELLIA *sasanqua* 'Hiryu'
Sasanqua Camellia

Like *Azaleas*, the handsome *CAMELLIAS* do particularly well in containers, thriving in a compost of two parts lime-free garden soil, one part each of peat moss and sand. *CAMELLIAS* are mountain plants (one of them is the tea we drink); they love sun in winter, semi-shade in summer, and resist winter temperatures almost down to freezing. They tend to flop (as we do) when the summer temperature climbs. Mist the foliage every day in hot weather and never allow the pots to dry out. Leaf scale is the only real pest, but can be controlled with a spray of white oil. Premature bud drop is not a disease, but is generally due to a lack of water.

With careful selection, you can have *CAMELLIAS* in flower from mid-autumn to early summer. Most pot types are varieties of:

C. japonica The late winter to summer flowering types have dark glossy serrated leaves, with flowers to 5 in (13 cm) in many shades and combinations of white, pink, red and 'almost purple'. The flowers vary from fully single to fully double, some with open staminated centres, some with a formal cone of petals. (See also plate page 39).

C. sasanqua These are the autumn to winter flowering types; fast growing and altogether sturdier although of a lighter, more graceful habit. The leaves are small. The flowers, to 3 in (8 cm) across, are generally semi-double in shades of white and pink. 'Sasanqua' *CAMELLIAS* are more heat-resistant than the 'Japonicas', and their lighter branches take readily to bonsai training.

CAMPELIA
(kam peel' yə) COMMELINACEAE

CAMPELIA zanonia
Mexican Flag

Closely related to *Tradescantia* and *Zebrina* (which see) *CAMPELIA*, the 'Mexican Flag' is the big brother of the family, and worth seeking out. Summer cuttings

struck in a sharp sandy rooting medium will send fleshy-branched stems up to 4 feet (120 cm) in a warm conservatory. *CAMPELIA* enjoys a peaty compost, plenty of water in the warm weather, and protection from summer sun. The striking 12 in (30 cm) leaves are sword-shaped, striped white and green with red edges—the colours of the 'Mexican Flag' after which it is popularly named. Like other 'Spiderworts' it bears small mauve and white flowers in the leaf axils. A succulent plant, it must be given protection from winter cold.

CAPSICUM
(kap' si kəm) SOLANACEAE

CAPSICUM annuum 'Fiesta'
Ornamental Chilli

Here's a dwarf annual plant grown strictly for the ornamental value of its fiery tasting fruit. Sow seeds in spring or late winter under glass. Transfer the seedlings (several to a pot) in a loamy soil mix and they'll quickly grow to flowering size. In *CAPSICUM var. 'Fiesta'*, the fertilised flowers set into 2 in (5 cm) pointed fruits which change from green to scarlet. They persist right through winter until the tiny 'Ornamental Chili' plants look like decorated Christmas trees. In fact, they make popular Christmas gifts in the northern hemisphere. Quite hardy, these miniature *CAPSICUMS* will go in any climate, like full sun and only moderate water.

CARYOTA
(ka ree oh' tə) PALMAE

The interestingly shaped foliage of the 'Fishtail Palm' makes it quite a conversation piece in modern interiors. Native to Australia and nearby Asia, *CARYOTAS* are slow to grow from seed and are

CARYOTA rumphiana
Fishtail Palm

CATTLEYA phena Ignensis
Florist's Cattleya

usually propagated from suckers. They do best in a bright light (though not direct sun) and, like all tropical palms, soak up surprisingly large amounts of water. They rarely grow more than 4 feet (120 cm) indoors, producing shiny light green fronds with rather curious ragged edges which look as though they have been torn away. These terminate with a divided fishtail effect. *CARYOTA rumphiana* really needs a minimum temperature of 55°F (13°C) to remain in good health; and likes plenty of sand and leaf mould in the potting compost.

CATTLEYA
(kat lae' ə)   ORCHIDACEAE

CATTLEYA bowringiana
Cluster Cattleya

Gorgeous orchids from tropical South and Central America, *CATTLEYAS* are really not all that difficult to grow provided you are prepared to go along with their three main requirements: softly filtered light, (a fibreglass curtain will do), heat of around 60°F (15°C) on winter days (near a sunny window or heater), and humidity of around 50 per cent or better in summer. *CATTLEYAS* are usually grown in hanging baskets of wooden slats or tree fern, filled with a compost of fir bark chunks, broken terracotta, tree fern and other fibrous material around which they can wind their worm-like roots.

There are two principal types: the first are related to the giant-flowered *C. labiata* and have swollen pseudo-bulbs with a single leaf; the second have tall cane-like bulbs with a pair of leaves, and generally bear smaller flowers in clusters. Beyond this, they both grow from a creeping rhizome which roots at intervals. All *CATTLEYAS* are tree dwellers, and like free circulation of air and occasional top-dressing with old animal manure. Popular species are:

C. bowringiana 'Cluster Cattleya'. Many small mauve flowers to a stem.
C. citrina 'Tulip Cattleya'. Yellow flowers.
C. dowiana Rich gold with a red-purple lip.
C. labiata Giant mauve flowers with a crimson lip.

CEPHALOCEREUS
(ke fal oh see' ree əs)   CACTACEAE

The popular name 'Old Man Cactus' fully describes this extraordinarily hardy plant, covered from top to toe with a tangled mass of what appears to be snow-white hair. It grows almost anywhere in small pots of gritty compost and needs little water. Bright sunlight is a necessity however if it is not to become elongated and scraggy. The 'Old Man Cactus'

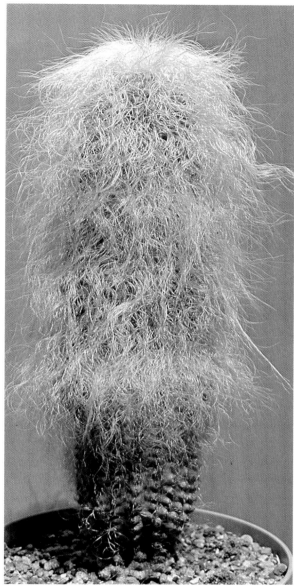

CEPHALOCEREUS senilis
Old Man Cactus

flowers at night, though rarely indoors, the blooms being usually a washed-out pink or yellow. *CEPH-ALOCEREUS* is a native of Mexico and rarely grows above 24 in (60 cm); 12 in (30 cm) is a good indoor height.

CEREUS
(see' ree 'əs)   CACTACEAE

Most of the *CEREUS* group are giant columnar Cacti, sometimes seen in courtyard gardens. A favourite with houseplant fanatics, however, is the curious variety known as 'Living Sculpture' or 'Rock Cactus'. Ribbed, twisted and crested, occasionally pierced right through, the jaw-breaking *CEREUS peruvianus Monstrosus Minor* certainly does put one in mind of some modern artist's fantasy. A curious

CEREUS peruvianus 'Monstrosus'
Living Sculpture

blueish sheen and irregular clusters of spines add to the unreal effect.

The 'Living Sculpture' is from South America, grows in a gritty compost and needs little water. Give it plenty of light, and the protection of glass in frosty weather.

CESTRUM
(ses' trəm)   SOLANACEAE

CESTRUM nocturnum
Night Jessamine

Grown solely for the unbelievable night-fragrance of its flowers, the West Indian 'Night Jessamine' is a not particularly striking plant. It grows easily from cuttings or from the readily set seeds in its white berries. It can be raised in a large container of any standard potting mix. Your *CESTRUM* will need pruning drastically from time to time, however, for it can easily reach a height of 6 feet (2 m) with regular watering. The slim stems droop under their own weight, and during the warm months are festooned with clusters of pale whitish-green tubular flowers. These partly open in the evening, releasing the heavy perfume—so heavy that some sensitive souls can't bear to be too close to it. Probably, *CESTRUM nocturnum* is best grown just outside a frequently opened door or window, but it will certainly flourish indoors if required.

CHAMAECEREUS
(ka mae see' ree əs)   CACTACEAE

CHAMAECEREUS silvestri
Peanut Cactus

Argentina's gay little 'Peanut Cactus' is seen all over the world, growing in small pots at sunny windows. The prostrate tubular stems are covered in silvery spines and grow in every direction. They should be handled carefully for they break easily, although severed pieces will root again in a few weeks. Perfectly hardy down to a temperature of 45°F (7°C), the stems of *CHAMAECEREUS* take on a reddish tone in cold weather. Grow them in shallow containers with a standard gritty cactus mix, and water lightly but regularly. The brilliant orange-scarlet flowers appear in late spring or early summer and are borne profusely.

CHAMAEDOREA
(ka mae dor' ree ə)   PALMAE

The 'Bamboo Palm', *CHAMAEDOREA erumpens*, is relatively small (6 ft or 2 m), and multiplies rapidly from suckers. It is customarily grown in a largish pot

CHAMAEDOREA erumpens
Bamboo Palm

of any standard compost and needs plenty of water to produce its handsome light green fronds and occasional sprays of small yellow fruit borne quite low down the slim trunk. Like most of the jungle palms from Central and South America, *CHAMAE-DOREA* likes diffused light and so does very well indoors. Grow it outside by all means, but be sure it has protection from full sun as it scorches easily. It will not really be happy where the minimum winter temperature drops below 50°F (10°C). The smaller plant sold as *CHAMAEDOREA elegans or Neanthe bella* will be found under *Collinia,* its correct name.

CHLOROPHYTUM
(klor oh fai' təm)   LILIACEAE

CHLOROPHYTUM comosum
Spider Plant

The 'Spider Plant', *CHLOROPHYTUM*, is grown for its rosettes of glossy foliage and curious spider-like new plantlets which form at the end of the long, arching flower stems. *CHLOROPHYTUMS* are frost-tender, but will survive outdoors provided they have overhead protection. Indoors, there's no holding them back. Pot up in a well-drained compost of loam, leaf mould and sand; leave room for the bulky, succulent root masses which form to store moisture and help the plant survive considerable neglect. *CHLOROPHYTUMS* are best placed on a tall piece of furniture or in a hanging basket, for the flower stems on mature specimens may droop to 6 ft (2 m). The new plantlets may be detached and potted up separately, but are most effective when left hanging. Popular varieties grown include:

C. comosum   Plain green leaves.
C. c. Mandaianum   Leaves edged white.
C. c. Picturatum   Leaves with central yellow stripe.
C. c. Vittatum   Leaves striped in white.

CHRYSALIDOCARPUS
(kris a lid oh kah' pəs)   PALMAE

One of the most handsome palms, *CHRYSALIDO-CARPUS*, the 'Golden Feather Palm' or 'Areca', produces a cluster of tall yellow bamboo-like stems which may reach 20 ft (6 m) in a warm greenhouse or sub-tropical courtyard, but are unlikely to pass 10 ft (3 m) indoors, which is just as well. The fronds often have a goldish tone. It needs plenty of water and diffused light and does best in a large tub of loam mixed with peat and sand. It is native to the islands of the Indian Ocean and grows readily from suckers. Like all indoor palms, *CHRYSALIDOCARPUS lutescens* benefits from regular spraying and cleaning of the leaves to remove dust and other dulling matter. (See plate page 151).

CHRYSANTHEMUM
(kris an' thə mum)   COMPOSITAE

There are several hundred species of *CHRYSANTHEMUM*, but only two of them concern us for indoor or terrace work. First is the 'Marguerite Daisy', *C. frutescens*, which grows easily from spring cuttings and should constantly be pinched back to encourage branching. The more branches the more flowers! It grows best in a large pot or tub of peaty loam and thrives with regular doses of diluted fertiliser. Just be sure you give it sun and shelter from strong winds. Flower colours are in shades of white, pink and cream.

The 'Florist's Chrysanthemum', *C. morifolium*, is grown from cuttings or divisions in much the same

CHRYSANTHEMUM frutescens
Marguerite Daisy

CHRYSANTHEMUM morifolium
Florist's Chrysanthemum

way, but is in nature an autumn flowering perennial. Nowadays, they are raised for bloom at any time of year, and treated with a dwarfing hormone to keep them at table-top size. They can be relied on to bloom over several weeks. This type of potted *CHRYSANTHEMUM* makes a delightful gift and millions of them are sold every year.

CIBOTIUM
(sib oh' tee əm)   DICKSONIACEAE

CIBOTIUMS are closely related to the *Dicksonias* of Australia and the Pacific Islands, and are grown in much the same way. They are more suited to patios and indoor gardens than actual pot use, for their great arching fronds need plenty of room and the plant demands constant humidity. This is best achieved by planting it in a moist compost of peat, sand and leaf mould. Shelter from cold draughts, and plenty of water, help *CIBOTIUM* to remain attractive the year round. Shade from hot sun is necessary, however, to prevent leaf scorch. There are several species but the 'Mexican Treefern', *C. schiedii*, is usually grown. Mature specimens will develop a trunk similar to other treeferns, but they are usually topped and the tops replanted to keep them from becoming too tall.

CISSUS
(sis´ əs)   VITACEAE

CISSUS antarctica
Kangaroo Vine

CISSUS discolor
Begonia Treebine

One of the most useful indoor trailing plants, *CISSUS antarctica* proceeds in leaps and bounds wherever you choose to put it. It is long-lived, with handsome serrated leaves, and will thrive in a pot or hanging basket of any standard indoor mix, producing cascades of fresh foliage. *CISSUS* enjoys lots of water and regular feeding and is rejuvenated every second spring by repotting. Popularly known as the 'Kangaroo Vine', it is native to Australia.

A close relative, *C. discolor*, the 'Begonia Treebine'. comes from Indonesia and Southeast Asia. It needs more winter warmth and summer humidity to do well, and is more often seen in a convervatory or heated plant window. Its leaves are beautifully marked in deep green, silver and bronze; the stems and leaf undersides are reddish. Marvellous in tropical gardens, it is worth the trouble to cultivate indoors.

CITRUS
(sit´ rəs)   RUTACEAE

CITRUS aurantifolia
Tahiti Lime

The growing of *CITRUS* fruit in containers has been practised in Europe for centuries. If they are to be more than merely decorative, they should be planted in very large pots, and you'll need a strong back to move them around. In Italy, they still make terracotta lemon pots of baroque design. These are particularly heavy, but set off the shiny leaves and colourful fruits to perfection.

Most *CITRUS* varieties are propagated by grafting onto hardy stock, usually of the fast-growing *CITRUS trifoliata*. For container use, you should choose a plant with an unobtrusive graft and a single straight trunk. This will help you train your tree to a formal standard shape, which is particularly effective. Plant in autumn in 14 to 20 inch pots (35 to 50 cm). These should be well-drained with a layer of old crocks and charcoal, and then partly filled with a

CITRUS limonia 'Meyeri'
Meyer Lemon

layer of rich, acid compost. Place your *CITRUS* plumb in the centre of the pot, vertically, and fill with soil exactly to the nursery soil mark on the trunk. This should be an inch or two (2 to 5 cm) below the rim to allow room for water and fertiliser. After tamping in the compost, water well to settle the roots and do not feed until the plant is thoroughly established.

This feeding will be with a proprietary Citrus food or old poultry manure. The general rule is a cupful for each year of the tree's growth, twice a year, in early spring and late summer. Water before scattering the fertiliser, fork in and water deeply again. From then on, the secret of success with *CITRUS* is a constant level of moisture all year, but never keep the soil too wet. The fragrant blossom appears at any time, but most heavily in spring. Where there are bees, you won't need to worry about fertilisation, but indoors you'll have to learn how to do it with a small brush. *CITRUS* trees are really quite easy to train with light regular pruning, and in a year or two you'll have a real conversation piece.

The fruit usually begins to ripen from late summer on, and the trees should be watched for aphis (which are easily banished with soapy water) and Citrus bugs, which are large enough to be lifted off individually. Be careful of them — they can squirt a nasty stinging fluid into your eyes!

Named varieties of *CITRUS* vary from country to country, but suitable species for pot culture include:

C. aurantifolia 'Lime'. Fruits all year.
C. limonia X Meyeri 'Meyer Lemon'. A Lemon-Orange hybrid of bushy habit. Delicious thin-skinned fruits.
C. paradisii 'Grapefruit'. Needs a very large container. Fruits from a potted specimen don't grow very big.
C. nobilis 'Mandarin' or 'Tangerine'. A small leafed species easy to train to formal shape.
C. sinensis 'Sweet Orange'. 'Valencia', 'Washington

Navel' and the 'Maltese Blood Orange' are varieties of this species.
C. X Tangelo 'Tangelo' or 'Ugli'. A hybrid between the 'Tangerine' and the 'Pomelo' (a species rarely grown outside the tropics). Its juice is the most delicious of all. There are many named varieties, some with golden fruit, some almost red.

All *CITRUS* are of tropical origin and need a minimum winter temperature of 45°F (7°C) — a little higher for 'Limes'. In very hot areas, partial shade is helpful in holding the fruit, as is moving the trees to a humid, well-planted corner of your patio.

The popular 'Kumquat' is not a *CITRUS*, though closely related to them; see under *Fortunella*.

CLEISTOCACTUS
(klai' stoh kak təs)   CACTACEAE

CLEISTOCACTUS straussii
Pizzle Plant

A small genus from South America, the *CLEISTOCACTUS* grows tall and straight, although rather slowly. This is something of an advantage for pot culture, and they do quite well in a container of standard gritty Cactus mix. The commonly grown species *C. straussii*, the 'Pizzle Plant', grows into a simple, lightly ribbed column, its areoles producing compact groups of spines and fine woolly hairs. The flowers (which appear only on mature plants) are tapered, phallic cylinders covered with silvery hair. The vivid cerise petals open only far enough to reveal the stamens and make fertilisation possible. Taller potted specimens will need the support of a light stake, for they quickly become top-heavy. *CLEISTOCACTUS* is propagated by severing and replanting the offset branches which form at soil level. Handling these (like all spiny Cacti) is a bit hazardous, and best accomplished by twisting a thick cloth or wad of newspapers around the spiny limb and grasping the Cactus only by means of this.

CLEMATIS
(klem' ə tis)   RANUNCULACEAE

Provided their roots can be kept cool and shaded, the many species of CLEMATIS, or 'Maiden's Bower', make delightful flowering subjects for a sunny balcony or terrace. This apparent contradiction of sun and shade is not hard to achieve, however, for they are vines, and will quickly find their way up to the sun from a shaded position. It is enough to put their container on the shaded side of a column or heavy post. Plant them in well-drained pots of rich lime-free compost and provide climbing support: with careful choice you can have a succession of flowers from spring right through to early winter. Water and fertilise regularly once growth has started, but do not use too acid a plant food; diluted natural manure is best. Good species include:

C. X jackmanii These gorgeously flowered hybrids come in a wide range of named colours, their flowers growing to 6 ins (15 cm) and more across. Prune them back almost to ground level in winter. (See plate page 42).
C. montana A rampant grower with smaller pink and white flowers. Easiest of all.
C. orientalis A less common species with bright yellow flowers. Good for cooler climates.

CLERODENDRON
(kle roh den' drən)   VERBENACEAE

CLERODENDRON *thomsonae*
Bleeding Hearts

The sub-tropical genus CLERODENDRON or CLERODENDRUM includes many different species of shrubs and climbers that are worthwhile indoor and terrace subjects. Grow them in containers of any standard potting mix and propagate from cuttings in early summer. Shrubby types can be pruned to

compact shapes; the climbers will only produce a good display when they are given some support. CLERODENDRONS need warmth, good light and plenty of water during the warm season. Widely available species are:

C. bungei 'Mexican Hydrangea'. Shrubby, with rosy flowers in late summer.
C. fragrans 'Pleniflorum' 'Cashmere Bouquet'. Felty green leaves. Scented pink and purple blossom in late summer. A shrubby type.
C. speciosissimum 'Chinese Pagoda'. A pyramidal shrub with large, lobed, felty leaves. Loose spires of scarlet flowers.
C. splendens 'Glory Bower'. A splendid climbing plant with shiny, crinkled oval leaves. Masses of scarlet and crimson flowers in warm weather.
C. thomsonae 'Bleeding Hearts'. A climber bearing hanging clusters of white heart-shaped calyxes from which scarlet petals protrude in spring.

CLIANTHUS
(klee an' thəs)   LEGUMINOSAE

CLIANTHUS *dampieri*
Sturt Desert Pea

CLIANTHUS, the 'Sturt Desert Pea' or 'Glory Pea', is one of Australia's best-known plants. In dry outback areas it germinates freely in the scorching summer sun and rapidly covers large areas with silver-hairy stems and compound leaves. The iridescent 3 in (8 cm) scarlet pea flowers (blotched with coal black or deep crimson) appear in masses any time from midwinter.

Curiously enough, it is hardly ever seen in Australian gardens, for it is averse to humidity and will damp off in the open within a hundred miles of the coast where most Australians live.

English fanciers, however, have learned to graft it onto seedlings of *Colutea arborescens*, a related genus with much stronger roots. They then grow it in a dry atmosphere in shallow pots or hanging baskets of perfectly drained sandy compost. Specimen plants are best watered by carefully dipping their containers rather than risk damping off the delicate stems by overhead spraying.

In cooler climates, *CLIANTHUS* is more likely to flower in spring.

CLITOREA
(kli tor' ree ə)   LEGUMINOSAE

CLITOREA ternatea
Butterfly Pea

An interesting member of the legume family, the 'Butterfly Pea' *CLITOREA*, is grown for its singly borne open pea flowers of vivid cobalt-blue, quite a rare colour in the botanical world. It is strictly of tropical origin, and should be grown in a humid glasshouse from spring-sown seeds. The flowers appear throughout the warm weather, their magnificent blue contrasting with white and gold throats. A rather sparse plant, *CLITOREA* can be allowed to scramble over other plants in the glasshouse or trained on a light framework. Grow it freshly from seed each year. From India.

CLIVIA
(klai' vee ə)   AMARYLLIDACEAE

Spectacular bulbous plants with yellow-throated orange flowers, the 'Kaffir Lilies,' *CLIVIA*, are more of a novelty in the northern hemisphere than in the southern, where they flower in open gardens. For indoor use, the rather massive roots are forced into a relatively small pot (say 18 in or 20 cm). A compost of loam, decayed manure and gritty sand is then forced in around them. This is done in late summer

CLIVIA miniata
Kaffir Lily

to get them established in time for late winter flowers.

For terrace use, you may prefer to plant whole clumps in a large tub, though this is quite a formidable task. Build up the water supply after the coldest days are past, and give occasional doses of liquid manure until the flowers open. *CLIVIAS* survive winter temperatures down to 45°F (7°C) and flower better out of full sun. There are hybrid varieties available with flowers tending towards a paler apricot or a redder orange, but they are not a great improvement. Native to South Africa.

COCCOLOBA
(kok ə loh' bə)   POLYGONACEAE

COCCOLOBA uvifera
Sea Grape (Ala Moana Center, Honolulu)

Found all over the tropical world, *COCCOLOBA*, the 'Sea Grape', is native to coastal areas of the Caribbean. It can be grown in a warm conservatory, but is a rather large plant and best used on an open terrace in warmer climates — it is particularly valuable in seaside areas, for the plant is quite salt-resistant. The leaves are glossy and heart-shaped, and older plants produce hanging clusters of small white flowers with a delicious fragrance. These are followed by berries, generally green but ripening to a darker grape colour if the birds leave them alone. *COCCOLOBA* is propagated from cuttings, and does best in a well-drained peaty compost with plenty of sand. It needs a minimum winter temperature of 50°F, (10°C).

CODIAEUM variegatum 'Fascination'
Croton

CODIAEUM
(koh dee ae' əm)   EUPHORBIACEAE

CODIAEUM variegatum pictum
Appleleaf Croton

Hundreds of named varieties are available in the colourful tropical genus *CODIAEUM*, native to Southeast Asia and the Pacific Islands. More commonly known as Crotons, they are grown for their dazzling leaves which may include crimson, scarlet, pink, yellow, brown and orange shades, as well as green, white and cream. Crotons are normally propagated from cuttings and raised in pots of a well-drained peaty potting mix. The leaves colour best in bright filtered light, so I bring mine indoors for the colder weather and keep them by a large sunny window. In summer I give them a break outdoors in a shaded corner of a warm courtyard. Crotons need regular attention to stay healthy; a constant level of moisture except in midwinter; and eternal vigilance against red spider, which is hard to spot on the highly coloured leaves.

Which of the many leaf shapes you choose is purely a matter of taste, but as a general rule the

CODIAEUM X 'Gloriosum Superbum'
Rainbow Croton

broader-leafed types have more striking colourings. Popular named varieties of *CODIAEUM variegatum Pictum* include 'Appleleaf', 'Fascination' and 'Gloriosum Superbum' (See also plate page 29).

COELOGYNE
(kə loj' ə nee)   ORCHIDACEAE

Beautiful 'Angel Orchids' are certainly among the easiest to grow. My prized specimen of *COELOGYNE cristata* is thoroughly crowded into a 16 in (40 cm) glazed pot, and spills its long strings of bright green pseudo-bulbs over the rim. It lives out of doors in a breezeway sheltered from the hottest

COELOGYNE *cristata*
Angel Orchid

COELOGYNE *flaccida*
Coelogyne

COLCHICUM

(kol' chik əm)   LILIACEAE

COLCHICUM *autumnale*
Naked Boys

Often called 'Autumn Crocus', COLCHICUMS in fact belong to quite a different botanical family and are incredibly easy to grow. Newly bought bulbs will bloom as readily sitting on a saucer of pebbles as they do planted up in the most exotic bulb fibre or soil mixture. Set them out in summer (with the neck of the bulbs at soil level if planted) and the flowers will often appear with the first cold snap — usually more than one to a bulb. Plant them properly after flowering is over, so that the leaves can grow and help ripen the bulb; otherwise, they won't put on a repeat performance the following year.

The species *C. autumnale*, *C. byzantinum* and *C. speciosum* are similar, with white to mauve flowers. The more exotic *C. agrippinum* has a distinct chequered appearance on its wide pink and mauve petals. COLCHICUMS are native to the mountains of North Africa and the Caucasus, and are not affected by winter temperatures so long as they are covered against frost. They can be propagated either from seed or by separating the bulblets.

COLEUS

(koh' lee əs)   LABIATAE

Easy-to-grow COLEUS can be raised from seed, or from cuttings left in a glass of water, where they root readily. This is the easiest means of keeping them over winter in cold areas where they die off at the first touch of frost. Native to several tropical areas around the Indian Ocean, they are grown for their many brilliant leaf colours. Any flower heads are pinched away to encourage further growth. They like a well-drained, rich leafy compost, must be watered regularly and given a weekly dose of

sun, and is watered only occasionally with the garden hose. I bring it indoors in winter as the flower spikes develop from last season's pseudo-bulbs. These open into perfect hanging sprays of fragrant icy-white flowers, 3 in (8 cm) across, with three to seven to a spray. The display lasts for up to six weeks. My COELOGYNE *cristata* grows in a well-drained mixture of old coke, leaf mould and treefern, and gets an occasional dose of diluted fish emulsion as a special treat. Related *C. flaccida*, with sprays of beige and yellow flowers, grows under similar conditions with perhaps a fraction more winter protection. It also flowers in winter and spring.

COELOGYNES survive winter temperatures down to 38°F (3°C), for they are native to the high mountain valleys of northern India.

COLEUS *blumei*
Painted Nettle

COLEUS *rehneltianus*
Red Trailing Queen

diluted fertiliser indoors to keep the leaves colourful and healthy.

C. blumei 'Painted Nettle'. In its many leaf varieties is the most commonly grown species for indoor decoration.

C. rehneltianus 'Red Trailing Queen'. This 'Creeping Coleus' makes a spectacular ground cover in group plantings, or spilling from hanging baskets. (See also plate page 30).

COLEUS should be grown in bright light, but not direct sun. They may need potting up several times in a season with fresh compost and milled cow manure, for they rapidly exhaust the potting medium.

COLLINIA
(kol in' ee ə)   PALMAE

COLLINIA *elegans*
Parlour Palm

Known variously as *Neanthe bella* and *Chamaedorea elegans*, the dainty 'Parlour Palm' from Mexico is currently named COLLINIA *elegans*. Hardy outdoors in a winter temperature of 55°F (13°C), or even occasionally below, it will do perfectly well in any normal domestic interior. Grow COLLINIA in containers of standard potting mix. Keep moist, but not soaking wet, all through the warm weather, and keep out of full sun. A handy size for modern interiors, COLLINIA can grow as tall as 4 ft (120 cm), but usually much less. The drooping leaves are about 18 in (45 cm) long, and consist of medium green leaflets tapered at each end.

COLUMNEA
(kol um' nee ə)   GESNERIACEAE

COLUMNEAS or 'Column Flowers' belong to the same family as African Violets, but bear little resemblance to them. They are mostly raised in hanging baskets where the beauty of their trailing stems of red, orange or yellow flowers can be seen. Grow them in a porous leafy compost containing sphagnum moss or some similar material. Regular moisture is necessary, as is regular feeding with soluble fertiliser (such as Nitrophoska) in the growing season. COLUMNEAS should be repotted every other year. They like winter sun and semi-shade in the really hot weather. Flowers appear in spring. Showy species are:

C. X banskii Variegata   This hybrid has leaves variegated in a grey-green and white. Its flowers are duller orange than most. It is also less of a trailer.

COLUMNEA *gloriosa*
Showy Column Flower

COLUMNEA X *banksii Variegata*
Variegated Column Flower

C. gloriosa 'Showy Column Flower'. Has tubular flowers of vivid orange-scarlet, 2 in (5 cm) long. (See also plate page 32).
C. microphylla 'Goldfish Vine'. Very tiny leaves. Red and yellow flowers.
C. tulae Flava Bright yellow flowers.

CONVALLARIA
(kon və leə' ree ə)   LILIACEAE

Native to all continents of the northern hemisphere, 'Lily of the Valley' is the very symbol of spring in many lands. For the French, May Day would never be the same without bunches of the fragrant *'Muguet de l'Isle'*. Try it as a short-term house plant yourself.

CONVALLARIA *majalis*
Lily of the Valley

Nurserymen sell plump 'pips' (budding roots) in late autumn or early winter. These can be forced into early bloom by being planted in bowls of damp sphagnum moss or a light peaty mix. Keep them in a dim warm place, (about 60°F or 15°C), and at a constant level of moisture until the leaves develop. When the flower spikes begin to appear, move gradually to a light but still warm place. After this treatment, the pips will be exhausted, but give them to a friend to plant out and ripen in a shady garden spot and they'll bloom another year. CONVALLARIA *majalis* is the grown species.

CORDYLINE
(kor di lain')   LILIACEAE

CORDYLINE *australis*
New Zealand Cabbage Tree (Hotel Tahara'a, Tahiti)

CORDYLINE terminalis
Ti

COSTUS speciosus
Crepe Ginger

Many species of *CORDYLINE* are grown for the beauty of their leaves, and they make excellent pot plants when young. All of them are native to Australia and New Zealand except the spectacular *C. terminalis*. *CORDYLINES* are so easily propagated that pieces of stem are sold in Hawaii to tourists as the 'Magic Hawaiian Log' which 'springs to life in a dish of water'! Rooted cuttings of *CORDYLINE* can be planted up in containers of leaf mould, damp peat and sand mixed with rich garden soil. Keep these moist and warm from early spring on and they'll grow at a great rate. Popular species include:

C. australis 'New Zealand Cabbage Tree' or 'Sago Palm'. This has narrow leathery dark leaves. A mature plant bears panicles of tiny sweet-scented cream flowers in summer.
C. stricta A dwarf species, which can be encouraged to branch with judicious pruning. Very long narrow leaves. Panicles of pale blue flowers.
C. terminalis The 'Ti' plant of Polynesia. This needs higher temperatures and humidity to make a good display. The leaves may be plain green, dark red, or variegated with many shades of scarlet, pink, white, yellow, purple and bronze. 'Ti' plants can be allowed to dry out in winter, and if too leggy can be 'topped' and the severed tops struck afresh in sharp sand.

COSTUS
(kos' təs)   ZINGIBERACEAE

COSTUS are a genus of rhizomatous perennials within the Ginger family. The majority are South American, but the more commonly seen 'Crepe Ginger', *COSTUS speciosus*, is in fact from India. *COSTUS* really needs the conditions of a warm greenhouse or conservatory to flourish, but can be

brought into the house or sheltered patio at flowering time in the warm months. 'Crepe Ginger' grows best in a moist peaty compost and needs shade from direct sun. The tissue-thin white blossoms have the finely pleated effect of crepe fabric, and are marked in orange.

COTYLEDON
(koh til ee' don)   CRASSULACEAE

COTYLEDON macrantha
Pig's Ears

Mostly South African, the succulent, fleshy-leaved *COTYLEDONS* are great for open terraces or patios — anywhere you can give them full sun and fresh air. They grow in a sandy, well-drained compost and need regular water, but never applied from above for it will spot the leaves. *COTYLEDONS* produce drooping flower stems in spring but are usually grown for the sculptural quality of the rounded leaves. Strike them from cuttings in late summer. Good species include:

C. macrantha 'Pig's Ears'. Shiny green, red-margined leaves. Red and yellow flowers.
C. orbiculata Grey-green, red-edged leaves. Red flowers.
C. paniculata Grey-green leaves in a rosette at the end of a tall stem. Red and green flowers.
C. undulata Greyish wavy-edged leaves. Orange-yellow flowers.

CRASSULA
(kras' yoo lə)   CRASSULACEAE

CRASSULA arborescens
Silver Dollar

CRASSULA argentea
Jade Tree

CRASSULA cornuta
Horn Plant

Native to South Africa, *CRASSULAS* make splendid houseplants because they can cope with dry conditions and careless owners. Just remember that too much water makes the leaves bloat, then they shrivel and become unsightly when moisture is withheld. Little and often is the watering rule. Grow them in containers of sandy, well-drained compost in full light; propagate from stem or leaf cuttings. Several species have a branching shrubby habit and assume the appearance of ornamental Chinese 'Jade Trees' — hence their popular name. These include:

C. arborescens 'Silver Dollar'. Bronzy-green leaves, red-margined. White flowers.
C. argentea 'Jade Tree'. Glossy green leaves. Pink flowers.
C. X 'Hummel Sunset' Red-edged gold and green leaves. Pink flowers.

Other useful *CRASSULAS* include:

C. cornuta Plump grey boat-shaped leaves.
C. falcata Sickle-shaped grey leaves. Scarlet flowers.
C. multicava Spoon-shaped deep green leaves. Pink and white flowers on long stems. A popular rockery plant.

CRINUM
(krai' nəm)   AMARYLLIDACEAE

Semi-tropical members of the Amaryllis family, *CRINUMS* grow easily from their gigantic bulbs, planted with at least the neck above soil level. Pot them in large containers of leafy, well-drained compost, and wait for growth to start before watering begins. Spray the foliage as it develops to increase the humidity level, and shade from hot sun at all times. *CRINUMS* are native variously to Africa, Asia, Australia and the United States; but you'd

CRINUM *asiaticum*
Poison Lily

CRYPTANTHUS are the dwarves of the Bromeliad family, low-growing and earth-hugging for the most part. They are incredibly easy to grow indoors in all but the coldest of climates. Use a container of any standard potting mix — pebbles mixed with moistened peat, or even of damp moss or fibre. So long as regular moisture and humidity are there the leaves stay fresh. New plants are easily grown from offsets which are liberally produced. Just pop them on the compost and they'll take off. CRYPTANTHUS are valuable plants for terrariums. Good species are:

C. *bivittatum* 'Green Star'. Darker-striped, drab-green leaves, flushed pink.
C. *bromelioides Tricolor* 'Rainbow Star'. A more upright plant with leaves striped in rose, white and green.
C. *fosterianus* Brown and silver-banded leaves.
C. X 'It' The brilliant wavy-leafed hybrid of the photo. It colours most brightly in shade.
C. X *zonatus* 'Zebra Plant'. Wavy brown and green leaves, greyish markings.

better check before you buy — some of them grow really enormous. Good species are:

C. *asiaticum* 'Poison Lily'. Fragrant white flowers on tall stems from an enormous pale-green leaf rosette. To 6 ft (2 m).
C. *augustum* 'Milk and Wine Lily'. Known as 'Queen Emma's Lily' in Hawaii. Darker green leaves. Crimson and white long-stemmed flowers. To 4 ft (120 cm).
C. *moorei* Pink bell-shaped flowers, rather like a 'Belladonna'. To 30 in (75 cm).

CRYPTANTHUS
(krip tan' thəs)   BROMELIACEAE

CRYPTANTHUS X 'It'
Rainbow Star

CTENANTHE
(se tə nan' thee)   MARANTACEAE

CTENANTHE *lubbersiana*
Bamburanta

Splendidly marked foliage plants for indoors, the CTENANTHES are closely related to *Calathea* and *Maranta* (which see). The leaves, however, are produced on tall, hairy stems. Grow them in a standard potting mix kept evenly moist, and ensure that the daytime winter temperature doesn't drop below 50°F (10°C). They quite enjoy crowding, so don't re-pot too often. Freshen them up with an occasional overhead sprinkling in warm weather and feed with diluted liquid fertiliser bimonthly. Three types are commonly grown indoors:

CTENANTHE oppenheimiana
Never Never Plant

C. lubbersiana 'Bamburanta'. Has yellow-marked green leaves on tall forking stems.
C. oppenheimiana 'Never Never Plant'. This has mid-green leaves, reversed in purple, with translucent bands of silver tapering from mid-rib to edge. The leaves have a curious habit of turning upside down on cold evenings.
C. oppenheimiana var. Tricolor Similar to the above, but with the leaves spectacularly blotched with pink and cream.

All species produce small, insignificant flowers, generally white.

CUSSONIA
(kus oh' nee ə)   ARALIACEAE

CUSSONIA spicata
Cabbage Tree

Small trees often grown indoors for their dramatic leaf display, the South African *CUSSONIAS* enjoy the same conditions as the closely related *Fatsia* and *Trevesia* (which see). The many-lobed, variable leaves attract caterpillars which seem to appear on them even indoors. Mealy bug can also be a problem. *CUSSONIA spicata*, the 'Cabbage Tree', may reach 10 ft (3 m), and should be protected in cold weather as the leaves yellow and drop.

CYCAS
(sai' kas)   CYCADACEAE

CYCAS revoluta
Sago Palm

CYCAS, popularly known as Cycads, are striking semi-tropical plants related to the conifers, but looking more like palms. Grown in pots of sandy compost in bright light, they appreciate a constant level of moisture all year, tapering off in winter. Cycads form a large rosette of stiff leathery fronds on top of a woody trunk, and mature plants produce a decorative cone of tough, fleshy fruits. They are cold-resistant, though not frost-hardy. They are only suitable for indoor use while young, for older plants may reach 10 ft in height and 6 ft across (3 x 2 m). The only popularly grown species is *CYCAS revoluta*, the 'Sago Palm' from China and Japan.

CYCLAMEN
(sai' klə men)   PRIMULACEAE

CYCLAMEN are ideal winter-flowering plants for indoor use, flourishing down to 40°F (5°C). The many hybrids of the principal species, *C. persicum*, grow from fleshy circular tubers pressed into a compost rich in leaf mould, charcoal and sand, for they are woodland plants and need perfect drainage. Water regularly until the leaves appear, and then give diluted liquid fertiliser at bi-weekly intervals

CYCLAMEN neapolitanum
Alpine Violet

CYCLAMEN persicum
Shooting Star

until the flower buds develop during the colder months. Mist the plants regularly in dry indoor conditions, but do not over-water. An occasional deep soaking in the sink is of far more value. Most plants are discarded after a single season, but they can be used again if you leave the pots on their sides in a dry place for the summer. When leaves begin to appear again, re-pot and start the cycle all over.

C. persicum 'Shooting Star' or 'Florist's Cyclamen'. Makes a 12 inch (30 cm) plant with leaves often marbled and marked in white and silver. The flowers are in every shade of red, pink, white and mauve, sometimes ruffled or edged with contrasting tones. (See also plates pages 15, 51).
C. neapolitanum 'Alpine Violet'. A much smaller plant with violet-sized autumn flowers, generally pink or white. The patterned leaves appear later as tightly wrapped spirals.

CYMBIDIUM
(sim bid' ee əm)   ORCHIDACEAE

CYMBIDIUM Hybrid
Cymbidium Orchid

CYMBIDIUM Miretta X pumilum
Miniature Cymbidium

CYMBIDIUMS are undoubtedly the most improved of all Orchid genera, and probably the most widely grown in temperate climates. They are hardy to a winter temperature of 40°F (5°C), and are generally planted in large pots or tubs of special cymbidium compost which simulates the natural conditions they enjoy in rotted logs.

CYMBIDIUMS need humidity and shade in summer, and all the sun they can get in winter when the flowers develop. The flower spikes may be up to 5 ft (150 cm) long, appearing at varying times from midwinter to summer. The colour range includes white, pink, gold, red, green and brown, many of the blossoms being attractively shaded, striped and spotted. There are literally thousands of hybrids.

Hybridists have also been busy producing a race of miniature CYMBIDIUMS, rarely more than 12 in (30 cm) in height. These are related to the species C. pumilum, and are still quite expensive, though worth seeking out. The best colours so far include marvelous brick-reds and bronzes.

In hard winter climates, the CYMBIDIUMS must be brought indoors to a conservatory or sunroom, and will probably not flower until later than in warmer temperate areas. (See also plate page 17).

CYPERUS
(sai pə' rəs) CYPERACEAE

CYPERUS alternifolius
Umbrella Grass

CYPERUS are decorative grassy plants from both American continents, Europe and Africa, where the 'Egyptian Papyrus Plant', CYPERUS papyrus, became a dominant element in Ancient Egypt's art and architecture. All CYPERUS need a rich compost and as much water as you can give. Indoors it is best to stand the pots in a large dish of water so they can help themselves whenever thirst strikes. CYPERUS grow from creeping rhizomes, which send up triangular hollow stalks at intervals. These are crowned with narrow grassy leaves radiating like the spokes of an umbrella, and a starburst of tiny green summer flowers on wiry stems. Several species are grown:

C. alternifolius 'Umbrella Grass'. 30 in (75 cm).
C. diffusus 'Dwarf Umbrella Plant'. Only 12 inches (30 cm) in height.
C. papyrus 'Egyptian Papyrus'. 12 ft (4 m).

CYRTOMIUM
(sur toh' mee əm) POLYPODIACEAE

CYRTOMIUM falcatum
Holly Fern

The tough 'Holly Fern', CYRTOMIUM falcatum, grows from a creeping rootstock and produces shiny, leathery dark green fronds, the tips spiky as any holly. It is almost completely hardy and needs no winter heat, merely glass protection from frost. Grow it in containers of peaty loam with a little sand or grit to improve the drainage. Repotting is done in early spring and CYRTOMIUM does best out of full sun. Water regularly in summer, taper off as the weather cools down. If unexpected frost does strike this hardy fern, don't despair. Leave the burnt fronds until after winter, then clip them away as the new ones appear. It is native to Japan.

DATURA
(da tyoo' rə)   SOLANACEAE

DATURA *suaveolens*
Angels' Trumpets

Large tropical shrubs in the open garden, *DATURAS* make splendid tub plants. They should be propagated from cuttings in the spring and potted up in any standard mix with sand for good drainage. Water them deeply and rarely rather than often and lightly. Give *DATURAS* plenty of light short of full sun, and fertilise occasionally with diluted animal manure. They flower best outdoors, but can be persuaded to do so inside, producing enormous hanging blossoms — to 8 in (20 cm) and richly perfumed. *DATURAS* are said to be hardy only down to 55°F (13°C), but I have grown them outdoors in the south of Tasmania where winter frosts and ice are quite the rule. Caterpillars of all kinds find the leaves attractive, possibly because of some narcotic content as in others of the Nightshade family *(SOLANACEAE)*, so keep a spray handy. Some species are:

D. cornigera   Cream flowers, horn-like projections on their petals.
D. mollis   Pale salmon-pink flowers.
D. sanguinea   Scarlet, smaller flowers.
D. suaveolens   'Angels Trumpets'. Enormous white flowers to 12 in (30 cm) long.

DAVALLIA
(də val' ee ə)   POLYPODIACEAE

The 'Rabbit's Foot Ferns' or *DAVALLIAS* grow from furry brown rhizomes which climb and hang all over their containers and produce delicate lacy fronds at regular intervals. Grow them in hanging baskets lined with sphagnum moss and filled with a peat-based compost. Hang *DAVALLIAS* in bright light, but out of direct sun. Keep the basket evenly moist,

DAVALLIA *fejeensis*
Fiji Fern

and mist the fronds in hot weather. They are easily propagated by pressing divisions of the rhizome into damp sand. *DAVALLIAS* are hardy only down to about 50°F (10°C). Some useful species are:

D. canariense   'Hare's Foot'. Tough, dissected 12 in (30 cm) fronds.
D. fejeensis   'Fiji Fern'. Dainty pale green 15 in (38 cm) fronds.
D. mariesii   'Ball Fern'. This can be trained to cover a globular basket, making a perfect ball of feathery 8 in (20 cm) fronds.

DENDROBIUM
(den droh' bee əm)   ORCHIDACEAE

DENDROBIUM *bigibbum*
Cooktown Orchid

DENDROBIUM kingianum
Pink Rocklily

DENDROBIUM pierardii
Hanging Dendrobium

DENDROBIUM nobile
Dendrobium

DENDROBIUM thyrsiflorum
Golden Dendrobium

Undoubtedly the most diversified of Orchid genera, *DENDROBIUMS* are native to almost all parts of Asia, and out into the Pacific. More than a thousand species have been catalogued. Most of them are tree dwellers and can be grown around the house. (See also plates pages 15, 32). There are two principal divisions -- the evergreens (including most of the Australian natives), which should never be allowed to dry out completely, and the deciduous tropical types, which need a definite rest from water corresponding to the dry tropical winter. Their individual likings, habits and compost requirements are too complicated for the scope of this book. Suffice it to say that the cane-stemmed types are usually grown in heavy pots of porous, well-drained compost. Hanging types like *D. pierardii* and *D. bigibbum* need a more tropical treatment and glass protection for they flower around winter. The small Australian epiphytic types such as *D. kingianum* do well in a shallow pan of packaged orchid compost and pebbles or small firbark pieces. Of the myriad exquisite species available, I have been able to show only five for your pleasure.

D. bigibbum 'Cooktown Orchid'. The State Flower of Queensland, this produces showy arching flower stems lined with 3 in (8 cm) butterfly flowers in deepest cerise. These have a marvellous crepe-like texture.

D. kingianum 'Pink Rock Lily'. This is a most variable species with white, red, mauve and pink varieties, plain and spotted. It is easy to grow in any temperature area, and flowers very early in spring.

D. nobile From North India. An 18 in (45 cm) cane-stemmed type, flowering candelabra-style in

early spring. Many hybrids in shades of pink, white and mauve with dark, velvety lip markings.
D. pierardii A splendid hanging species with long bare stems of delicate mauve and white flowers in spring. These may hang down as far as 8 ft (2.4 m), but only on mature specimens under glass.
D. thyrsiflorum 'Golden Dendrobium'. Another cane-stemmed species with hanging clusters of cream and egg-yellow flowers in late spring. An untidy plant most of the year, it is stunning when in full bloom . From Burma.

DICHORISANDRA
(dai ko ri san' drə)   COMMELINACEAE

DICHORISANDRA thyrsiflora
Blue Ginger

Large perennial members of the Spiderwort family, showy *DICHORISANDRAS* are much grown in conservatories for their spectacular leaves and flower spikes. As they need winter heat of at least 55°F (13°C), however, this makes them something of a problem in cold winter areas. *DICHORISANDRAS* are propagated from cuttings or divisions of the tuberous roots, and grow best in a peaty indoor compost with sand and leaf mould. Give them plenty of water in the warm weather, but withhold it almost completely in the winter when they go dormant. Popularly grown species include:

D. reginae Small leaves marked with silver and red-violet. Lavender flowers.
D. thyrsiflora Glossy dark green leaves. Sends up a tall flower spike to 4 ft (120 cm). The late summer flowers are blue-violet.
D. thyrsiflora Variegata Leaves striped lengthwise with silver or cream.

DIEFFENBACHIA
(dee fən bah' kee ə)   ARACEAE

DIEFFENBACHIA amoena
Striped Dumb Cane

DIEFFENBACHIA leoniae
Dumb Cane

Showy tropical foliage plants producing tall stems of drooping tapered leaves, *DIEFFENBACHIAS*, are interestingly marked in green, gold, white and silver. They are easy to grow and maintain indoors — any standard compost will suit them provided it is both moisture-retaining and well-drained. Give them bright light and plenty of summer water, tapering off in the cold weather when they are fairly dormant. Watch out for fungus diseases which seem to strike in the cooler months when the plants' resistance is not so high, and spray with a good fungicide. *DIEFFENBACHIAS* really need minimum winter heat of 60°F (15°C) to look happy, but I've found they survive quite well in night temperatures down to 45°F (7°C). Stem cuttings are easily struck

DIEFFENBACHIA picta 'Roehrsii'
Painted Dumb Cane

DIPLADENIA X 'Alice S. du Pont'
Mexican Love Vine

in spring, and older leggy plants can be chopped off and the tops struck again to produce a more compact, leafy plant. A myriad species and varieties are available, varying only in leaf colours. Some of the more popular are:

D. amoena Dark green, parallel vee-shaped markings in cream, white. Flourishes in poor light.
D. leoniae Dark green with irregular silver blotches that gradually feather out to the edge.
D. picta 'Exotica' Dark green with yellow markings, the veins also in green.
D. picta 'Roehrsii' Chartreuse leaves. Mid-rib and edges in darker green.

DIPLADENIA
(dip lə dee' nyə)   APOCYNACEAE

Charming South American vines, *DIPLADENIAS* respond well to indoor culture. Propagate them from cuttings and grow in any standard potting mix with the support of a wire frame or small lattice to which they can be attached. Keep the compost moist at all times except towards winter when the plant can be allowed almost to dry out for a couple of months. *DIPLADENIAS* prefer humid conditions and sun except in high summer, and produce a succession of trumpet-shaped rose-pink flowers from late spring to late summer. They can be kept to compact size in a pot by pinching back, but if grown in a conservatory or glasshouse allow them to assume their natural twining habit. The 'Mexican Love Vine', *D. splendens,* is commonly grown; its hybrid *'Alice S. du Pont'* has richer flower colouring.

DIZYGOTHECA
(di zee goth' ik ə)   ARALIACEAE

DIZYGOTHECA elegantissima
Threadleaf Aralia

The 'False' or 'Threadleaf Aralia' is rarely sold under its true botanical name, which is certainly a little hard to spell. It is a charming houseplant when young, with an airy, graceful habit. Use normal peaty indoor compost, but don't over-pot — it rather likes to be crowded. Keep the compost moist and give the plant good light at all times, without summer sun. *DIZYGOTHECA elegantissima* will grow to 6 ft (2 m) indoors, but can be cut back to force a more branching habit. Native to the New Hebrides, it is grown for its spidery, toothed compound leaves, which are dark green with a metallic purplish sheen. Re-pot only every two or three years.

DRACAENA
(dra see' nə)   LILIACEAE

DRACAENA *deremensis*
Fountain Plant

DRACAENA *fragrans*
Corn Plant (Royal Hawaiian Hotel, Honolulu)

DRACAENA *fragrans* 'Massangeana'
Golden Corn Plant

DRACAENA *godseffiana*
Gold Dust Dracaena

DRACAENAS are valued for the profuse fountain effect of their beautifully marked foliage. They need a standard tropical compost of peat, leaf mould and sand, and should be kept out of hot summer sun. They present few heating problems and are quite happy in any household temperature which would suit humans. Naturally, however, they grow taller, faster and more consistently in the humid conditions of a glasshouse or conservatory. Keep the soil evenly moist, and wipe the leaves down occasionally to keep them free of dust. Commonly grown species are:

D. *deremensis* 'Fountain Plant'. Very popular in modern interiors. The 18 in (45 cm) drooping leaves are double-striped in silver.
D. *fragrans Massangeana* 'Corn Plant'. Arching leaves of green and chartreuse. May grow to 10 ft (3 m).
D. *godseffiana* 'Gold Dust Dracaena'. A 12 in (30 cm) dwarf with branching habit. New leaves appear as tightly rolled cones, unfurling to show beautiful creamy yellow markings.
D. *marginata* 'Red Edge Dracaena'. Spiky 18 in (45cm) dark green leaves, red margins.
D. *sanderiana* 'Ribbon Plant'. A tall grower with relatively small drooping leaves, grey-green with white margins. Often planted in groups.

102

DREJERELLA
(dre jə rell'ə)   ACANTHACEAE

DREJERELLA guttata
Shrimp Plant

DREJERELLA guttata 'Yellow Queen'
Yellow Prawn Plant

The 'Shrimp' or 'Prawn Plant', *DREJERELLA guttata,* (formerly *Beloperone*) is a useful indoor subject that flowers at any time of the year. Grow it out of full sun in a standard potting mix. Use several plants in a larger container for a profuse effect. It is easily multiplied by means of stem cuttings. Quite handsome at any time, with leaves of fresh, soft green, *DREJERELLA*'s chief beauty is in the arching spikes of overlapping bracts from which peep tiny white flowers. These bracts may be a warm pinkish-brown (very much the colour of a cooked shrimp) or a clear chartreuse. From Mexico, *DREJERELLA* appreciates winter warmth and summer humidity.

ECHEVERIA
(esh ə veə' ree ə)   CRASSULACEAE

ECHEVERIA glauca
Hen and Chickens

ECHEVERIA meridian
Painted Lady

Mostly from Mexico, the *ECHEVERIAS* or 'Painted Ladies' are valued for their formally shaped leaf rosettes, which may be green or highly coloured with an almost iridescent bloom or finish. They should be grown in compost with 50 per cent grit or sand. Water regularly in summer, either by careful trickling around the plants or by soaking the container in a large vessel of water. Do not sprinkle from above as the leaves rot easily. Chemical fertilisers of the nitrogen phosphorus type are suitable in diluted quantities. Arching stems of bell-like flowers may appear any time from early spring on, after which new plants are propagated from basal shoots. *ECHEVERIAS* are winter-hardy down to about 40°F (5°C), but owing to their succulent nature can be badly damaged by frost. Splendid species for a sunny balcony or open courtyard are:

E. cotyledon Mealy-white leaves. Yellow flowers.
E. elegans Pale bluish leaves. Pink or red flowers, sometimes yellow-tipped.
E. glauca Grey-green leaves. Yellow flowers tinged red.
E. meridian 'Painted Lady'. Beautifully fluted and rippled leaves, highly coloured with red.
E.X Perle von Nurnburg Pale violet-toned leaves. Reddish flowers.

There are more than 150 known species of *ECHEVERIA* and an incredible number of hybrids, some of unknown origin.

ECHINOCACTUS
(e kin oh kak' təs)   CACTACEAE

ECHINOCACTUS grusonii
Golden Barrel

Named from the Greek word for hedgehog, *ECHINOCACTUS grusonii* is a prickly customer indeed. The popular names 'Golden Barrel' and 'Hedgehog Cactus' describe them perfectly — barrel-shaped, and vertically ribbed with strong pale gold spines, they grow to 4 ft (120 cm) in height, but before that stage is reached you'll have found them a little uncomfortable to have around the house. Smaller plants are best for indoor or balcony culture, grown in shallow pots of well-drained gritty cactus compost. Give them plenty of water through the warm weather growing season, tapering off as autumn comes to an end. Full sun and fresh air keep pests at bay.

The open yellow flowers are rarely produced when *ECHINOCACTUS* is grown in pots, but appear directly out of the top. *E. horizonthalonius,* a much smaller species, has red spines and profuse pink flowers in spring. They are both hardy down to 45°F (7°C).

ECHINOCEREUS
(e kin oh see' ree əs)   CACTACEAE

ECHINOCEREUS tubiflora
Hedgehog Cactus

Like the previous entry, *ECHINOCEREUS* are also known as 'Hedgehog Cactus', or occasionally 'Rainbow Cactus' because of the brilliance of the flowers in many species. They are ribbed cylindrical growers, sometimes several feet high, and easily grown in wide, shallow containers of a standard, well-drained cactus mix. Give them full sun, and water sparingly. Most *ECHINOCEREUS* species branch and bloom well on a terrace or at a sunny window. The flowers, generally appearing in summer, may be white through pink to red-violet and even purple in colour, with several in shades of yellow-green. Hardy down to 50°F (10°C), all species are native to Mexico and the southern United States.

ENDYMION
(en dim' ee ən)   LILIACEAE

Showy 'Spanish Bluebells' (long known as *Scilla campanulata,* but now *ENDYMION hispanicus*) grow easily in shallow pots of rich acid compost. Just make sure there's a good layer of broken crocks and charcoal to help drainage and prevent the compost souring. Plant the succulent white bulbs (at least an inch or 2.5 cm in diameter) 2 inches or 5 cm below the surface in late autumn. Water and keep them in a dim shaded place until the leaf shoots appear, then bring gradually into the light and water regularly until the flower stems are fully grown (about 15 inches or 38 cm). Taper off the water after flowering until the leaves ripen naturally, then plant them out in a friend's garden to recover. Bluebells like bright light, but not full sun. They are winter-hardy, but also grow in climates far warmer than that of Europe.

ENDYMION hispanicus
Spanish Bluebells

EPIDENDRUM
(ep i den' drəm)   ORCHIDACEAE

EPIDENDRUM radicans
Crucifix Orchid

EPIDENDRUMS form a large and widely variable genus of the Orchid family, and their name means simply 'upon a tree'. Beyond the fact that they all originate in the tropical Americas, they differ more widely among themselves than any other orchid group. The vast majority are specialist plants. The minority group with which we are concerned for pot culture are 'Crucifix Orchids'. *EPIDENDRUM radicans* send up tall leafy cane-like stems, supported by worm-shaped aerial roots. These stems may ultimately reach 7 to 8 ft (215 to 245 cm), and the plants are usually grown in a large container with the sup-

port of a wire frame. The small flowers are produced in a cluster at the end of each stem, and open progressively for many months in the warm weather. Thanks to the work of hybridists, they are available in many shades: red, pink, orange, yellow, white and mauve. Normally they seem to be upside down, with the crucifix-shaped lip uppermost, but in their native jungle the flower stems hang down of their own weight and the blossoms appear right way up. Grow them in a container of stone rubble, sphagnum and orchid fibre and keep constantly moist.

EPIPHYLLUM
(ep i fil' əm)   CACTACEAE

EPIPHYLLUM X 'London Prince'
Hybrid Orchid Cactus

EPIPHYLLUM X 'Pink Nymph'
Pink Orchid Cactus

EPIPHYLLUM oxypetalum
'Belle de Nuit'

EPISCIA cupreata
Flame Violet

No indoor plant collection should be without one of the gorgeous 'Orchid Cacti', which are incredibly easy to grow in containers of a rich, fast-draining compost. This could be leaf mould, sand, peat, brick rubble and a little animal manure. They strike easily from severed branchlets of the flattened stems (which may look like leaves, but are not). Grow them in heavy pots (so they don't overbalance) or hanging baskets. They need semi-shade, plenty of water in summer and as much humidity as you can manage. They will survive winter down to 35°F (2°C). *EPIPHYLLUMS* in nature are usually night or evening flowers, but they have been crossed with other genera such as *Heliocereus* and *Nopalxochia* (which see) to produce daytime flowers as well. These blossoms are unbelievably beautiful — up to 9 in (23 cm) across with iridescent waxy petals in a wide spectrum of orange, scarlet, pink, white, cream and purple. Some are entrancingly perfumed. The night-flowering species *E. oxypetalum*, the *'Belle de Nuit'*, is one of the easiest to grow — and what a conversation piece! The giant flowers unfurl on summer nights, spreading their fragrance for yards around as they glow in the moonlight like some strange sea-creature. A short life but a gay one — for they are dead by dawn!

EPISCIA
(e pis' kee ə)   GESNERIACEAE

Another dazzling group of Gesneriads, the *EPISCIAS* or 'Flame Violets' are jungle-dwellers that revel in humidity and are certainly not suitable for growing on an open balcony. But raise them by all means in a sunny bathroom or among other plants in a glassed-in sunporch or indoor plant corner with good light. They'll do best in hanging containers of porous peaty indoor plant mix, where they can trail

about and hang over the edge. If you can keep up the warmth (60°F or 15°C minimum) they'll keep going throughout the winter. New plants for old from cuttings or divisions. Good species include:

E. X 'Cameo' Iridescent rosy leaves. Orange flowers.
E. X 'Chocolate Soldier' Hairy brown and silver leaves. Red flowers.
E. cupreata 'Flame Violet'. Bronzy leaves felted with silver hair. Scarlet flowers.
E. dianthiflora Small pale green leaves. Feathery white-fringed flowers.
E. lilacina Viridis Green hairy leaves. Lilac flowers.

ERANTHEMUM
(e ran' the m əm)   ACANTHACEAE

Here's a charming Indian shrub that's easy to grow and bursts into masses of blue flowers in winter or early spring. It has heavily veined handsome green leaves that persist all year, and pushes ahead from spring cuttings struck in a glass of water. Plant several to a large container filled with a compost of peat, sand and rich soil, with a little milled animal manure. Keep up the water throughout the warm weather and taper down very gradually till flowering time, after which you can prune the plants right back and give them a rest till late spring. The purple-eyed blue flowers appear in long terminal spikes from among pale green bracts. They must be kept warm (at least 55°F or 13°C) in cold weather. *Eranthemum* (commonly known as 'Blue Sage') grows to 4 ft (120 cm) in a warm temperate garden, but is best kept pruned back to half that height indoors to stimulate multiple flower spikes.

ERANTHEMUM pulchellum
Blue Sage

EUCHARIS
(yoo' kə ris)　　　AMARYLLIDACEAE

EUCHARIS amazonica
Amazon Lily

The magnificent 'Amazon Lily' can only be flowered if you ensure summer humidity and a minimum winter temperature of 55°F (13°C). Grow it in large pots of well-drained peaty compost, with extra quantities of sand, leaf mould and a little milled cow manure. It needs plenty of water, and could even be stood in a dish of wet pebbles to ensure humidity around the leaves. Regular misting of the foliage helps stimulate flowering, which may occur several times in the hot season. *EUCHARIS amazonica* has large oval-pointed 12 in (30 cm) leaves on 18 in (45 cm) stems, and sends up a 3 ft (90 cm) stem with

from three to six flowers. These are sweet-smelling, and resemble snow-white daffodils with brilliant lime-green markings and a fringed white trumpet. Propagate from bulb offsets in spring, but only re-pot every three years, for they resent root disturbance.

EUPHORBIA
(yoo for' bee ə)　　　EUPHORBIACEAE

EUPHORBIA caput-medusae
Gorgon's Head

EUPHORBIA milii
Crown of Thorns

More than a thousand different *EUPHORBIAS* have been recorded — many with little resemblance to one another. They come from almost every corner of the world and often have only two features in common. These are an unpleasant milky sap usually poisonous; and small stubby uninteresting flowers.

107

EUPHORBIA obesa
Baseball Plant

EUPHORBIA pulcherrima
Poinsettia

EUPHORBIA lactea cristata
Milk Stripe Euphorbia

Doesn't sound very exciting? But wait till you see the dazzling bracts that surround the flowers on many species, and the bizarre shapes and growth habits of others. Best of all, they are easy to grow, mostly enjoying sandy soil and full sun, which makes them useful for exposed balconies and court-yards. With the exception of *E. pulcherrima*, most of them are happy with a winter temperature of 50°F (10°C) or even lower. But they are all rather suc-culent and decidedly frost tender. Some of the most interesting species are:

E. caput-medusae 'Gorgon's Head'. Produces masses of curved snake-like branches from a short trunk.
E. milii 'Crown of Thorns'. This twists along the ground, branching as it grows, the entire plant covered with vicious spines. It easily develops a hanging habit and is grown in window boxes or terrace planters. The attraction is the bright scarlet-bracted flowers which appear all year.
E. obesa 'Baseball Plant'. This botanical curiosity looks like a sewn leather ball, both in size and shape. Its small flowers appear along the rib lines.
E. pseudocactus 'Dragon Bones'. Has a remarkably cactus-like appearance, with four-angled spiny branches. Mature specimens look like some prehistoric skeleton. (See plate page 22).
E. pulcherrima 'Poinsettia'. From Mexico, this needs rather different treatment. Give it a more tropical compost and a minimum winter temperature of 55°F (13°C). Poinsettias need good light (but not full sun) and must not be placed where they receive a spillover of night light from a street or a house window. This is because their flowering is stimulated by winter shortening of the daylight hours. Bring them indoors only when the flower-heads are fully developed. Scarlet is the usual bract colour, single or fully double. But there are also named varieties with white, cream, pink, crimson or multicoloured bracts. Poinsettias give brilliant winter colour, and most plant shops can supply dwarfed specimens at any time of the year. These have been chemically dwarfed in special dark houses, and rarely remain small after repotting.

X FATSHEDERA
(fats hed' ə rə)   ARALIACEAE

X FATSHEDERA lizei
Tree Ivy

The 'Tree Ivy', *X FATSHEDERA*, is a bigeneric cross (the uncommon hybrid of two different plant *genera*): *Fatsia* (the 'Japanese Aralia') and *Hedera* (the 'European Ivy'). It has the large leaf size of one, and the scrambling habit of the other. Grown as a shrub or a vine, it makes a very decorative indoor plant indeed, and its leaves best retain their velvety gloss out of direct sunlight. *FATSHEDERA* cuttings strike easily in sharp sand, and several planted in the one pot will add bulk and help avoid a natural leggy habit. Cultivate in a rich compost based on garden loam, and let it dry out between waterings. The small pale green flowers which appear in winter are sometimes used in flower arrangements. Two varieties only are grown:

X F. lizei   Plain glossy green leaves.
X F. lizei Variegata   This has white leaf edges.

FATSIA
(fat' see ə)   ARALIACEAE

More commonly known as 'Aralia' in many countries, *FATSIA* is a hardy shrubby plant that produces magnificent leaves in almost any conditions. It is ideal for shaded patios and indoor gardens where the sun never penetrates, and grows well in any standard indoor compost. It can be raised from suckers or seed, and can be cut back hard in winter if it becomes too leggy. Give *FATSIA* regular water and liquid fertiliser, but never allow it to remain sodden. Like the preceding *Fatshedera,* of which it is a parent, *FATSIA* produces terminal clusters of greenish-white flowers in autumn. There are several varieties in leaf shape, and a variegated type which is particularly effective in shaded places.

FATSIA japonica
Japanese Aralia

FAUCARIA
(foh keə' ree ə)   AIZOACEAE

FAUCARIA tuberculosa
Pebbled Tiger Jaws

Savage-looking succulent plants from South Africa, *FAUCARIAS* are planted to best effect in shallow pans or miniature succulent gardens, and placed where they can be seen at eye level. The plump green leaves appear in pairs, their spiny jagged edges interlocked like clenched jaws. As they grow, the leaf pairs open and fold back, revealing a new pair of tightly locked leaves. As the 2 in (5 cm) yellow flowers appear in autumn, you should step up the water supply from midsummer on. *FAUCARIAS* like full sun and a well-drained gritty compost. They are hardy down to 40°F (5°C) in winter. The only common species are:

F. tigrina 'Tiger Jaws'. Has leaves finely dotted in white, with about ten hooked teeth each.
F. tuberculosa The leaves are covered with warty growths on the underside, and rarely have more than five teeth each. The flowers are a little smaller.

THE FERNS
DICKSONIACEAE, POLYPODIACEAE

FERNS — typically delicate fronds of *CIBOTIUM, POLYPODIUM* and others in a courtyard planting.

FERNS have a strange and delicate beauty all their own. They not only look different from other plants, they *are* different, for they bear no flowers and set no seeds.

Ferns reproduce from spores — tiny sexless particles contained in spore cases on certain of their leaves known as fertile fronds. When these fronds ripen, the cases split, distributing millions of the dust-like spores into the moving air. Spores that land in moist positions develop through several intermediary stages into new plants which explains why it is that Ferns seem to appear quite spontaneously.

Ferns can be grown in containers indoors or (more usually) in a sheltered patio, courtyard or shade — house. They need protection from direct sunlight, and regular spraying with water to keep every part of them moist. One blast of drying hot air and the delicate fronds will dry right out, never to revive.

They are not particular about the type of compost you use, so long as it is cool and moist, but an addition of fine leaf mould and a little sharp sand will work wonders.

Re-pot them in very early spring as soon as new fronds appear, and don't make the container too large, for Ferns enjoy a restricted root run. Just give them a good drainage layer of broken crocks and charcoal to carry away excess water, for their delicate roots can decay easily.

The ideal indoor position for Ferns is in full light of a window *without* direct sunlight. Good ventilation is essential, but without a direct draught.

Hanging Ferns are usually grown in wire baskets lined with a moisture-retaining layer of sphagnum moss, but they are really only seen at their best in the moist atmosphere and filtered light of a shade-house. When they are brought indoors, they must be syringed regularly.

Ferns are not improved by the use of chemical fertilisers, and much prefer occasional watering with diluted (though rather evil-smelling) fish emulsion to keep them in a healthy condition.

Quite possibly the most popular plants sold and grown as Ferns are not in fact Ferns at all. These are the many attractive species of *Asparagus*, which grow from a clump of tuberous roots. While the long shoots of most varieties open into delicate-appearing fern-like fronds, these are not leaves, but modified stems with all the drought resistance of Cacti. They are therefore completely suited to indoor use or to life on an open balcony.

Unlike true Ferns, the *Asparagus* varieties *do* bear flowers and follow up with a splendid winter display of scarlet berries on some types.

Ferns described and illustrated individually in this book include:

Adiantum (Maidenhair), *Asplenium* (Bird's Nest and Mother Fern), *Cibotium* (Mexican Tree Fern), *Cyrtomium* (Holly Fern), *Davallia* (Fiji Fern), *Lycopodium* (Tassel Fern), *Nephrolepis* (Boston Fern), *Phyllitis* (Hart's Tongue), *Platycerium* (Stag's Horn), *Polypodium* (Polypody), *Pteris* (Brake Fern) and several varieties of *Asparagus*.

FICUS
(fai′ kəs)   MORACEAE

FICUS benjamina
Weeping Laurel

FICUS elastica 'Decora'
India Rubber Plant

The *FICUS*, or 'Figs' are a useful evergreen genus for tropical effect and leaf interest. They grow fast in a standard peaty compost and should be shaded from direct sun in summer. The tree and shrubby types are usually air-layered; but like the climbers, can be grown from summer cuttings. Mostly of tropical origin, *FICUS* need a winter temperature of at least 55°F (13°C), but this is consistent with average indoor heating anyway. Keep them moist in summer, but taper back the watering in the colder months. If kept indoors for long periods, their leaves should be wiped down occasionally with plain water. Popular indoor types include:

F. benjamina 'Weeping Fig' or 'Weeping Laurel'.

FICUS elastica 'Schryveriana'
Variegated Rubber Plant

FICUS lyrata
Fiddle-leaf Fig

This is an ideal indoor tree with a slim straight trunk and slender weeping branches of glossy green, 4 in (10 cm) leaves.
F. elastica 'Decora, 'India Rubber Plant'. Has beautiful 12 in (30 cm) leaves of leathery texture and high gloss. New leaves are encased in a wine-red sheath. This needs occasional cutting back.

F. elastica 'Schryveriana' An elegant cultivar of the above. Pale yellow leaves, irregularly marbled and flecked with dark green and grey. A really beautiful plant.
F. lyrata 'Fiddle Leaf Fig' or 'Banjo Fig'. A handsome indoor plant when young, but older specimens appear scraggy, for the leaves are held only towards the end of branches. These are around 15 in (30 cm) long, wavy-margined and shaped very much like a violin.
F. radicans Variegata 'Rooting Fig'. Pretty as a

FICUS *radicans Variegata*
Rooting Fig

basket plant or among other larger plants grouped in large containers. It has a trailing habit, and roots from the stem at intervals. The slender leaves, greyish-green, are edged and blotched with cream.
F. retusa 'Nitida' 'Indian Laurel'. Some confusion exists in the correct identification of this plant, which is so popular in California. It appears to be an erect-growing variety of *F. microphylla*, a popular Australian tree more usually seen in its variety *'Hillii'*, with a more weeping habit. The leaves in both varieties are 2 in (5 cm) long, pointed and brilliantly glossy. (See plate page 28.)

FITTONIA
(fi toh' nee ə)   ACANTHACEAE

FITTONIA *verschaffeltii* and
FITTONIA *v. 'Argyroneura'* (top)
Painted Net Leaf and Silver Nerve Plant

Dwarf plants from the Peruvian jungle, *FITTONIAS* are often seen in terrariums where their high humidity and temperature requirements can be met. They hate draughts and enjoy shade where their leaves are most brightly coloured. Use a moist well-drained compost with leaf mould and sand, and let the mixture dry out before rewatering — *FITTONIAS* don't like wet feet. They're easily propagated from cuttings in a pot of sharp sand, and covered with a plastic bag. Two species are grown:

F. argyroneura 'Silver Nerve Plant'. Has clearly marked white veins.
F. verschaffeltii 'Painted Net Leaf' or 'Mosaic Plant'. The veins are rose-pink. Some consider this the easier to grow, but in any case 60°F (15°C) is the minimum winter temperature for these tender plants.

FORTUNELLA
(for tyoo nel' ə)   RUTACEAE

FORTUNELLA *japonica*
Marumi Kumquat

Dwarf relatives of the edible *Citrus* (which see), *FORTUNELLAS* or 'Kumquats' are more often grown in pots because of their manageable size. In 12 in (30 cm) containers they'll rarely reach above 4 ft (120 cm). Keep up regular watering (and do sprinkle the leaves), fertilise quarterly with old fowl manure or packaged Citrus food, watered well in. 'Kumquats' can be clipped to formal standard shape, or allowed to weep naturally. They are almost completely spineless, and bear miniature flowers like orange blossom. The fruits ripen any time of year with heavy crops in winter in full sun, and in summer in semi-shade. They are thin-skinned and rather tart except in the oval-shaped species *F. margarita*, which can be eaten right off the tree or as dessert. Species are:

FORTUNELLA *margarita*
Nagami Kumquat

F. japonica 'Marumi Kumquat'. Round and bitter. Light green leaves.
F. japonica Variegata As above, with white marbled leaves.
F. margarita 'Nagami Kumquat'. Oval fruit. Dark green leaves.

All species are native to Southeast Asia.

FRAGARIA
(frə geə' ree ə)   ROSACEAE

FRAGARIA *chiloensis Ananassa*
Strawberry

Strawberries as house plants? Why not? They grow beautifully in the pockets of old-fashioned strawberry pots, which are more decorative than ever now they are glazed in bright colours. In early summer, line the bottom of the pot with crocks and other drainage material, and fill with a fast-draining compost to the level of the first pocket. Place one plant, firmly covering the roots; continue filling and planting in this manner, watering as you go. Top off with three or four more plants in the large opening. Water regularly and feed with diluted organic fertiliser. Strawberries are known botanically as *FRAGARIA chiloensis var Ananassa.* They flower and fruit from late spring on, producing the delicious berries in clusters on long-hanging stems. They top off the season with a good display of autumn colour from their handsome leaves. Strawberries are native to South America, and enjoy humidity.

FREESIA
(free' zhə)   IRIDACEAE

FREESIA *refracta*
Freesia

FREESIA Hybrids
Freesia

Difficult to raise indoors, these dainty members of the Iris family are worth persisting with for their delicious spring perfume. Grow them from seed or corms planted in early autumn, the latter about 1 in (2.5 cm) deep. Don't use packaged bulb fibre, but instead mix up your own compost: half rich loam, and the other half equal parts of sand, leaf mould and old milled cow manure. Soak well after potting, then water sparingly until the leaves appear in winter. *FREESIAS* do better in larger containers on an open balcony in warm temperate areas. They are used to spring rains and a dry summer in their native South Africa.

F. refracta Cream with a gold throat, this is the most sweetly scented, and has cultivars in pink, red, purple, beige, gold and pure white.

All need a mild winter temperature of around 50°F (10°C).

FUCHSIA Hybrid
Ladies' Eardrops

FUCHSIA
(fyoo' shə)   ONAGRACEAE

FUCHSIAS, or 'Ladies Eardrops', are difficult to keep in good condition without a cool, shaded planthouse or conservatory. Grow them in large pots or hanging baskets of rich, peaty compost mixed with sand and bone meal. Water regularly, and give them plenty of fresh air. *FUCHSIAS* enjoy bright light, high humidity (which you can help with regular leaf-spraying) and are gross feeders. Pinch back new growth regularly to force branching. The flowers should begin to appear in late spring. Colours are purple, mauve, pink, red and white, with occasional green markings. *FUCHSIAS* can be brought into the house for limited periods in warm weather, but keep up the humidity or you'll set them back for months. Grow them fairly dry in winter (when they are dormant), but under shelter. They are *not* frost-hardy, and like a mild winter temperature of 50°F (10°C).

GARDENIA
(gah dee' nyə)   RUBIACEAE

GARDENIA jasminoides
Cape Jasmine

GARDENIA jasminoides 'Florida'
Gardenia

While sympathetic to gardeners faced with really cold winters, I am sick of reading about how difficult it is to grow GARDENIAS. 'A minimum winter temperature of 60°F (15°C),' they say. Nonsense! I grow them on an open terrace with morning to midday sun, but sheltered from cold winds that come from the west in Sydney. Temperatures in the 40s (5 to 9°C) are not at all unusual here. 'Buds fail to open if humidity is below 50 per cent and if night temperatures are above 70°F (21°C) or below 60°F (15°C),' they say. Nonsense again! My terrace is sometimes dry as a bone when I am away photographing; and while the night temperatures are frequently outside those limits, the GARDENIAS go on flowering twelve months of the year. I water them when I

GARDENIA radicans
Dwarf Gardenia

think of it, but the only feeding they get is fallen flowers and leaves from nearby plants which I dump around them for convenience.

So try them and see for yourselves.

Use a rich peaty compost with sand for drainage and pot up in autumn or spring. Water them regularly and otherwise forget them. The most commonly grown varieties are:

G. jasminoides 'Cape Jasmine'. 2 in (5 cm) semi-double flowers.
G. jasminoides 'Florida' 3 in (8 cm) more fully double flowers.
G. jasminoides 'Professor Pucci' 5 in (13 cm) double, irregularly petalled flowers.
G. jasminoides 'Radicans' A dwarf ground-hugging type with 1 in (2.5 cm) flowers.

GASTERIA
(gas tee' ree ə)   LILIACEAE

South African succulents, GASTERIAS are grown mostly by specialists, yet are fascinating plants for a sunny terrace or window sill. They grow in gritty cactus mix, perfectly drained. Use plenty of water in the warm months, little or none in the winter, when they need glass protection below 40°F (5°C). Interesting species include:

G. maculata Strap-shaped leaves, blotched with white. 8 in (20 cm) stems of scarlet flowers.
G. verrucosa 'Ox-Tongue Plant'. Strap-shaped leaves with concave upper surfaces, marked all over with greyish-white raised spots. Growing in stacked pairs they rather resemble a set of automobile leaf-springs. Small red flowers on a slim stalk.

GASTERIA verrucosa
Ox-tongue Plant

GEOGENANTHUS
(gee oh gen an' thəs)   COMMELINACEAE

GEOGENANTHUS undatus
Seersucker Plant

This broad-leafed member of the Spiderwort Group is low-growing and easily propagated from cuttings struck in sand, or even a container of water. Often called the 'Seersucker Plant', *GEOGENANTHUS undatus* grows easily in any peaty potting compost, but needs warmth and humidity to develop properly. Then it produces large reddish-green leaves with deep red reverses. They have rippled surfaces rather like glossy cotton seersucker fabric. *GEOGENANTHUS* is native to Peru, needs a minimum winter temperature of 45°F (7°C) and plenty of water in the summer.

THE GESNERIADS
(gez nee' ree əds)   GESNERIACEAE

African violets are the most popular member of the GESNERIAD family.

This giant family of more than five hundred species and countless hybrids is not easy to cover under a single heading. Some grow from tubers, some from rhizomes and others have fibrous roots. Some are compact plants, others upright and some are trailers. Some are evergreen, others die down altogether. Yet there is a great similarity of appearance. They are all handsome plants, mostly with soft, velvety leaves, and are grown for their beautiful flowers, mostly bell-shaped.

The great majority of *GESNERIADS* are tropical, and enjoy a rich, well-drained peaty compost with plenty of sand and leaf mould. They need humidity, yet do not like to be watered onto the plant. It is better to place the pots in a pan of warmish water and let them soak up moisture from the roots. They need summer warmth, plenty of light and prefer to dry out and rest during the winter. Most *GESNERIADS* are propagated from leaf cuttings.

Saintpaulia, or 'African Violet', is one of the family, and is possibly the world's most popular flowering houseplant. Other beautiful *GESNERIADS* in this dictionary include:

Achimenes (Hot Water Plant), *Aeschynanthus* (Lipstick Plant), *Columnea* (Column Flower), *Episcia* (Flame Violet), *Kohleria*, *Nautilocalyx*, *Ramonda* (Balkan Primrose), *Rechsteineria* (Cardinal Flower), *Sinningia* (Gloxinia), *Smithiantha* (Temple Bells) and *Streptocarpus* (Cape Primrose).

GLORIOSA
(glor ee oh' sə)   LILIACEAE

GLORIOSA superba
Glory Lily

Exotic climbing members of the Lily family, *GLORIOSAS* grow from tuberous roots and cling to nearby support with wiry tendrils that tip their leaves. They need scant attention after planting in a deep pot of peaty compost in early spring. Give them bright light and regular water, and the first leaves should appear in around two weeks. Keep up the humidity by starting them off in a greenhouse, if possible, and bring them inside when the flowers appear in summer. These have reflexed petals, and are rather like an attenuated 'Tiger Lily'. Some species are:

G. lutea Beigy-yellow flowers.
G. rothschildiana Crimson and yellow flowers.
G. superba 'Glory Lily'. Has narrower petals, which change from green through orange and finally to red when mature.
G. virescens Grandiflora Yellow flowers.

 GLORIOSAS are frost-tender, and need a minimum winter temperature of 50°F (10°C).

GRAPTOPHYLLUM
(grap' toh fil əm)   ACANTHACEAE

A shrubby tropical member of the Acanthus family, *GRAPTOPHYLLUM's* leathery leaves are marked with curious irregular scrawls that resemble rough drawings or inkblot tests. The leaves are coloured green and yellow, or pink and red, according to variety. The purple-crimson flowers appear in short-stalked clusters. *GRAPTOPHYLLUM* strikes easily from cuttings and should be renewed regularly before it becomes too straggly. The 'Caricature Plant', as it is called, thrives in the usual tropical

GRAPTOPHYLLUM pictum
Caricature Plant

peaty soil mix with leaf mould and sand, and needs constant winter warmth, not below 55°F (13°C). *G. pictum* is from New Guinea and Indonesia.

GUZMANIA
(gooz man' ee ə)   BROMELIACEAE

GUZMANIA nicaraguensis
Red Cockade

GUZMANIAS are grown for their long-lasting cockades of red, green or yellow bracts that surround a shorter-lived spike of whitish flowers. They are raised in pots of open rubble-filled compost and make agreeable house plants. The leaf-vases should be kept filled with water all through the summer months until the flowers and bracts appear. *GUZMANIAS* flower only once. They are propagated from the suckers produced around the short parent stem. Dazzling species include:

G. lingulata   Apple-green leaves. Orange-red bracts.
G. monostachya   Shaded-green leaves. White, brown and scarlet bracts.
G. nicaraguensis   Light green leaves. Glowing scarlet bracts.

GYMNOCALYCIUM
(gim noh ka lis' ee əm)   CACTACEAE

GYMNOCALYCIUM mihanowiczii 'Hibotan'
Red Chin Cactus

Dwarf cylindrical Cacti with pronounced ribs, *GYMNOCALYCIUMS* are easy to distinguish by the pronounced bump or 'chin' that appears beneath each group of spines — hence the popular name, 'Chin Cactus'. The flowers are pale green through white to pink, and the plants are grown in a standard gritty cactus mix, watered regularly through the warmer months. The genus has a very curious freak member, which is illustrated. It is:

G. mihanowiczii Friedrichiae var. 'Hibotan' This weird plant is completely without chlorophyll, and is incapable of survival unless it is grafted onto another cactus. There it resembles a spiny orange-red fruit, and produces offsets which must in turn be grafted to survive.

There are other freak *GYMNOCALYCIUMS*, in pink, yellow and white, which require the same treatment. These strange plants are not frost-hardy, and need dry winter conditions.

GYNEURA
(gai noo' rə)   COMPOSITAE

GYNEURA aurantiaca
Velvet Plant

GYNEURA sarmentosa
Java Velvet Plant

A beautiful member of the Daisy family, the 'Java Velvet Plant' is covered from top to toe with silky purple hairs. These give the plant a curiously artificial appearance. *GYNEURA* grows easily from cuttings and should be pinched back regularly to promote branching and compact growth. Completely tropical in nature, it needs minimum winter warmth of 60°F (15°C), and water and high humidity throughout the summer. Grow it in a moist peaty compost and feed at weekly intervals to promote healthy leaves. With adequate warmth, they will produce small orange-coloured flowers in winter or early spring.

G. aurantiaca   A woody, shrubby plant to 3 ft (90 cm).
G. sarmentosa   Has a twining habit and coarsely toothed leaves. It is effective in hanging baskets.

HAEMANTHUS
(hee man 'thəs)   AMARYLLIDACEAE

HAEMANTHUS *multiflorus*
Blood Lily

'Blood Lilies' are flowering bulbs from southern and tropical Africa, and are perfectly amenable to pot culture. You may not find them commonly sold at your average plant shop, but they are often listed in the pages of garden magazines and can be ordered by mail. The large bulbs of HAEMANTHUS *multiflorus* should be planted in a light, sandy compost with a little animal manure; the neck of the bulb right at soil level. Pot up in earliest spring, keep in a semi-shaded position and water regularly till roots have developed, allowing the pot to dry out between soakings. Move the container into full sun, and the plump flower stems will appear during summer while the plant is bare of leaves. Each stem bursts into an enormous 6 in (15 cm) mass of scarlet florets, resembling a bright red Dandelion puffball.

The leaves appear later, and will die back in winter as the plant enters its dormant phase, when water can be tapered right off. HAEMANTHUS should be top-dressed with soil and manure annually. Minimum winter temperature 50°F (10°C).

HAEMARIA
(hee meə' ree ə)   ORCHIDACEAE

Unusual among the vast Orchid family, the 'Jewel Orchid', HAEMARIA *discolor*, is grown almost exclusively for the beauty of its leaves, which are a rich, velvety green with fine red parallel lines and dull red reverses. The tuberous roots are planted in early spring in a rich compost with sand and charcoal for good drainage. They need constant warmth, bright light (but not sun) and high humidity. They are often mixed with other plants in dish gardens and terrariums. Regular feeding will help keep the

HAEMARIA *discolor* 'Dawsoniana'
Jewel Orchid

leaves healthy and produce the 12 in (30 cm) stems of tiny white orchid flowers. Minimum winter temperature 50°F (10°C).

HATIORA
(hat ee or' ə)   CACTACEAE

A winter-hardy shrubby Cactus from Brazil, HATIORA is named anagramatically for its discoverer, a botanist named Hariot. It has a weeping habit and is grown in tall pots or hanging containers. These are filled with a rich compost of leaf mould, peat and sand, with a little stone rubble for good drainage. HATIORA develops a brittle trunk, branches and twigs, each of which consists of one or more tiny jointed sections like reversed beer bottles. These give the plant its common name, 'Drunkard's

HATIORA salicornioides
Drunkard's Dream

Dream'. In spring, each tiny bottle-segment bursts open into a half inch (1 cm) bright yellow daisy flower. These blossoms last for weeks but open properly only on bright sunny days.

HAWORTHIA
(hae wur thee ə)   LILIACEAE

HAWORTHIA hybrid
Haworthia

HAWORTHIAS are African succulents resembling *Aloës*, though much smaller. The plump leaves form rosettes which are usually spotted with raised white markings. *HAWORTHIAS* are really specialist plants, but worth growing on a terrace or balcony because of their great heat resistance in summer and cold-hardiness in winter. Use shallow containers of a gritty compost and water lightly but regularly. Some varieties are:

HAWORTHIA tesselata
Chequered Haworthia

H. attenuata Leaves with white markings, principally on the underside, in cross-banded lines.
H. fasciata Leaves in an erect rosette, backed with white.
H. reinwardtii var Chantinii Purple-brown leaves in which the rosette keeps growing until the mature plant looks like a skein of brown wool.
H. tesselata The leaves appear in a three-pointed star, each beautifully chequered.

HEDERA
(hed' ur ə)   ARALIACEAE

HEDERA helix in hanging basket
English Ivy

Ivies, or *HEDERA,* are an indispensable part of any indoor plant collection, and have endless decorative possibilities. Grow them on a sunroom wall, in

HEDERA *helix* trained as topiary
English Ivy

HEDERA *canariensis 'Variegata'*
Variegated Algerian Ivy

than other types.

H. helix 'English Ivy'. Plain dark green or variegated leaves in many shapes. Popular varieties include *'California Gold', 'Chicago', 'Digitata', 'Glacier', 'Goldheart', 'Green Ripples, 'Needlepoint', 'Pedata', 'Sagittifolia'* and *'Shamrock'.*

HEDYCHIUM

(he dik' ee əm)   ZINGIBERACEAE

HEDYCHIUM *coronarium*
White Ginger Blossom

hanging baskets, spilling from tall furniture, or train them as topiaries or bonsai. They are struck easily from cuttings or rooted runners at any time of year, and are planted in any standard potting compost with a little extra sand for good drainage. Ivies need cool conditions (short of freezing) and should be taken out of heated rooms. They appreciate bright light in winter, but semi-shade in summer. Water them regularly but let the soil dry out between soakings. Keep an eye on the leaves in the caterpillar season, and if there are signs of damage spray with a mixture of soapy water and white oil. There are several hundred named varieties of Ivy, most of them hybrids of:

H. canariensis 'Algerian Ivy'. Large leaves, either fresh green or variegated. These may be 6 in (15 cm) across and are more rounded and less lobed

Luxuriant tropical plants for sunny indoor corners or semi-shaded terraces, 'Ginger Lilies' are deliciously perfumed. Grow them in rich peaty compost with a little sand for drainage, and keep constantly moist after early spring planting until the flowers appear in summer. *HEDYCHIUMS* grow from shooting sections of rhizome, like 'Flag Iris', and will reach 5 or 6 feet. (1.5 to 2 m). Cut the flower stalk right back to the ground after blooming, and keep barely moist over the winter months, preferably with minimum 55°F (13°C) warmth. Several species are grown, all equally spectacular:

H. coccineum 'Scarlet Ginger Lily'. Fiery-red flowers, long slender stamens. 4 ft (120 cm) only.
H. coronarium 'White Ginger Blossom'. Open, broad-petalled flowers, marked lime yellow. Sweetest scent of all.
H. flava 'Yellow Ginger'. Pale yellow flowers, orange markings.
H. gardnerianum 'Kahili Ginger'. Yellow flowers, long scarlet stamens in immense 18 in (45 cm) heads. The most common variety.

All *HEDYCHIUMS* are native to India, and really do best with high humidity.

121

HEIMERLIODENDRON
(hai mə lee' oh den drən)   NYCTAGINACEAE

HEIMERLIODENDRON *brunonianum*
Pisonia or Para Para

More popularly known as 'Pisonia', this small tree is common to areas of Norfolk Island, Lord Howe Island, Australia and New Zealand — where its Maori name is 'Para Para'. The leaves are beautifully marked in tones of dark and grey-green, ivory and white and are brilliantly glossy. It enjoys warm temperatures and grows well in any standard indoor mix, preferably in bright light.

HEIMERLIODENDRON is a slow grower, rarely passing 5 ft (150 cm) in a container. Water it regularly and sponge down the leaves with milk and water when they become dull. 'Pisonia' produces panicles of small greenish flowers, but you are unlikely to see them indoors. Only the variegated-leaf variety is commonly sold.

HELICHRYSUM
(hel ə kris' əm)   COMPOSITAE

Useful container plants for a terrace or where the humidity is low, Australia's showy 'Paper Daisies' are available in many startling colour combinations of red, pink, brown, yellow and white. Seeds can be sown directly into containers of sandy well-drained compost in earliest spring. Shade them until germination is complete, and after thinning out and feeding with diluted liquid fertiliser, move to a sunny position. Here they will flourish with regular light watering and occasional manure. The handsome 'Paper Daisy' flowers appear in summer and last for many months. At the approach of cold weather, they can be cut, dried and used for winter arrangements. *HELICHRYSUM X bracteatum* hybrids are mostly treated as annuals, so winter temperatures are of no importance.

HELICHRYSUM *bracteatum*
Paper Daisy

HELICONIA
(hel i koh' nee ə)   MUSACEAE

HELICONIA *psittacorum*
Parrot Flower

HELICONIAS are a division of the tropical Banana family, and are difficult to bring to flower away from the humid sub-tropics. To do them justice in temperate areas, you really need a warm greenhouse or conservatory, although the smaller species *HELICONIA psittacorum*, the 'Parrot Flower', can be managed as a window plant where constant warmth and humidity can be provided. Plant in earliest spring in a rich, peaty compost, water well throughout the warmer months and give a ration of well-decayed manure from time to time.

HELICONIAS are from South America and need a 55°F (13°C) winter minimum to produce their gorgeously bracted flowers. If your home is in such a climate, you'll be well advised to seek out some of the more spectacular species. These include:

H. angustifolia 3 ft (90 cm). Orange-scarlet bracts.
H. collinsia 'Fishpole Heliconia'. To 8 ft (2.5 cm). Glorious hanging bracts on arching stems. Scarlet, green and yellow.
H. 'Bihai' 6 ft (2 m). Scarlet and yellow bracts.
H. caribaea Crimson . . yellow bracts.
H. humilis 'Lobster Claw'. Leaves and flower stems to 4 ft (120 cm). Bracts glowing red, dark green.

HELIOCEREUS
(hee' lee oh see ree əs)   CACTACEAE

HELIOCEREUS mallisonii
Sun Cactus

HELIOCEREUS or 'Sun Cactus', is an epiphyte from Central America. They are much hybridised with *Epiphyllums* and others to produce red colour breaks. Because of their sturdy nature, they are also used as stocks for weeping standards of *Aporocactus, Rhipsalidopsis* and *Schlumbergera* (which see), but they are very worth while growing on their own. Planted in wide containers of a gritty but moist compost, their stems spill over the edge and bloom generally in early summer. Flowers are mostly in tones of orange-pink, vermilion and scarlet, and remain open for several days. Winter temperature, 40°F (4°C) minimum. Grow them in full sun with regular water. Good species are:

H. cinnabarinum Vermilion flowers with green outer petals. 2 inches (6 cm) wide.
H. mallisonii Pale vermilion flowers. 3 in (8 cm) across.
H. speciosus Trumpet-shaped scarlet flowers, 6 in (15 cm) long.

HEMIGRAPHIS
(hem' i graf əs)   ACANTHACEAE

HEMIGRAPHIS colorata
Metal Plant

A decorative creeping plant from the jungles of Java, the 'Metal Plant', *HEMIGRAPHIS*, demands warmth and humidity at all times, and is used mostly in terrariums or heated conservatories. But it strikes easily in a container of plain water, and cuttings can be over-wintered this way in a warm place. *HEMIGRAPHIS colorata* spreads rapidly from runners that root at intervals in a moist compost rich in peat and leaf mould. The leaves are purplish, with a distinct metallic sheen. Small white flowers are sometimes produced in warm weather, and in a hot climate it will grow busily in the shaded side of a patio. Keep it out of full sun at all times. Winter minimum, 55°F (13°C).

HIBISCUS
(hai bis' kəs)   MALVACEAE

HIBISCUS can be used in many ways as container plants. On a sunny balcony in warm temperate areas, or in a sunroom where the going is a little cooler, they can be trained as standards or pruned as bushy shrubs. In every case, though, they need relatively large pots, (at least 10 in or 25 cm, for they need a large root mass to support the big leaves and to continue to produce flowers through the warm weather. The shrubby species used for pot culture are generally hybrids between the original 'Rose of China', *H. rosa sinensis*, and a number of small species native to the Pacific Islands, particularly Hawaii. These hybrids are potted up in early summer (never winter), particularly in the case of the large-flowered group known collectively as 'Hawaiian Hybrids'. *HIBISCUS* need a rich loamy compost with sand for drainage, and regular water. Prune them to shape in late spring and feed heavily, giving them a regular

HIBISCUS X 'Surfrider'
Hawaiian Hibiscus

HIBISCUS X 'Elegance'
Hawaiian Hibiscus

HIBISCUS X 'Firefly'
Hawaiian Hibiscus

dose of diluted fertiliser throughout the warm months. The best flowers are produced in late summer and autumn, and may be up to 10 in (25 cm) across in varieties such as *'Catavki', 'Firefly'* and *'Surfrider'*.

HIPPEASTRUM
(hip ee as' trəm)   AMARYLLIDACEAE

HIPPEASTRUM amaryllis
Barbadoes Lily

The striking 'Barbadoes Lilies', or *HIPPEASTRUMS,* are native to tropical America and make gorgeous house plants. Buy the fist-sized bulbs in early spring, and plant them up in individual 6 in (15 cm) pots, always making sure there's at least an inch (2.5 cm) of space for compost all around. This will be a rich loamy mixture with slight additions of sand and charcoal, and a layer of crocks below for drainage. Leave a full third of the bulb showing above the surface. Soak the pots deeply and put them away in a cool dim place, not watering again until the flower spike is several inches high. Then acclimatise gradually to bright light, and keep up the water until both the leaves and flowers have faded. Store dry until the first signs of next year's growth, when you must re-pot with fresh soil. *HIPPEASTRUMS* can be placed anywhere about the house and their dazzling blooms (up to 9 in or 23 cm in diameter in many hybrids) will make splendid decorator accents.

Modern hybrids bloom in every shade from deep red through scarlet to pure white. They may be striped or splashed with contrasting colours and usually show a little green and yellow towards the centre.

HOSTA
(hos′ tə)   LILIACEAE

Elegant 'Plantain Lilies' produce luxuriant foliage effects in cool, shaded positions in a courtyard or garden room. They are herbaceous perennials from Japan and China, and are propagated by division of the root mass in autumn. Pot *HOSTAS* up in containers of rich peaty compost, with good drainage, and leave in a sheltered place until the new leaves appear in spring. These will develop in many shapes and sizes (up to 20 in or 50 cm according to variety) and in combinations of white and gold as well as many shades of green.

H. plantagineum Large oval leaves of blue-green, distinctively pleated.
H. fortunei Longer pointed leaves in many colour varieties.

Tall stems of nodding bell-flowers sometimes appear in warm weather, in shades of white, pink and mauve, but the magnificent leaves are the main interest. *HOSTAS* demand regular water and feeding and eternal vigilance against snails and slugs. The entire plant will die back to the roots in autumn, and must be repotted. (See plate page 42).

HOWEA
(hou′ wee ə)   PALMAE

HOWEA is the current botanical name of the popular indoor palm known as 'Kentia'. There are two species, both native to Lord Howe Island. Both are large trees in nature, but rarely pass 7 or 8 ft (2.15 to 2.45 m) indoors. They should be planted in a compost of sand and loam in relatively small pots — the size increasing over the years as they grow. Like all palms, they need deep and regular watering and do best in a good light with shade from direct sun. Indoors, you should watch out for red spider, mealy

HOWEA forsteriana
Kentia

bug and wax scale. These are kept at bay by wiping down the fronds every other month with soapy water containing a dash of methylated spirits. Treat your *HOWEA* to a rain shower occasionally, but don't leave it out in the sun. The leaves, used to indoor conditions, will scorch badly. Winter temperature, 55°F (13°C) minimum outdoors.

HOYA
(hoi′ ə)   ASCLEPIADACEAE

HOYA bella
Beautiful Honey Plant

The 'Wax Plants' or *HOYAS*, are incredibly beautiful plants from Australia and neighbouring areas. They are hardy outdoors only to 50°F (10°C), but grow easily inside, preferably in a glassed-in

HOYA carnosa
Waxplant

HYACINTHUS orientalis
Dutch Hyacinth

balcony, for they can make an incredible mess of furniture with the sticky honeydew that drips from the flowers. Plant them in small containers of standard potting compost and re-pot only when you must, for they resent disturbance. All *HOYAS* bear superbly scented summer flower-clusters that look like wax dipped in powdered sugar. They should not be pruned, nor the flowers picked. Next year's blossoms always appear in exactly the same place. Species include:

H. bella 'Beautiful Honey Plant'. This is a shrubby species with hanging branches, and should be grown in a hanging planter where the summer flowers can be seen from below.
H. carnosa 'Waxplant'. A scrambling climber that can either be grown against a small framework or allowed to travel on the underside of a balcony roof, where it will really take off in the warm shade.
H. carnosa 'Exotica' Similar, but with leaves variegated in pink, cream and blue-green.

HYACINTHUS
(hai ə sin' thəs)   LILIACEAE

Favourite spring bulbs for indoors, 'Hyacinths' (*HYACINTHUS orientalis*) are sold all over the world already potted up and in bud. For bowl culture, buy the largest bulbs you can find in autumn and plant them five or six to a wide container. Fill with standard indoor compost and a little granulated charcoal. Put the bulbs with their tops right at soil level, soak and hide the container away in a cool dark airy place. Check from time to time, and when the shoots appear bring them gradually into stronger light and start to water. The flowers will open in early spring.

'Hyacinths' can also be grown in water, with the bulbs resting in the flared necks of special Hyacinth glasses. These need topping up as the bulbs use the water and extend their roots down into it. The bulb is sometimes covered with a paper cone to force height in the stem before the flowers open. However you grow them, their leaves must be allowed to ripen naturally. Unless this happens, there are no flowers the following year. (See also plate page 22).

HYDRANGEA
(hai draen' jə)   SAXIFRAGACEAE

HYDRANGEA macrophylla
Hydrangea

The name *HYDRANGEA* comes from two Greek words meaning 'water vessel', an allusion to their great thirst in warm weather. Rather large plants, they are most commonly bought for indoor use already potted up, and are popular gift plants. The interesting thing about *HYDRANGEA macrophylla* is that except for the white varieties you can vary the colour almost at will. Use an acid peaty mix and water with aluminium sulphate — you have blue flowers ! Use plenty of lime — they are pink! It's as simple as that. Outdoors they must be given shelter from the midday sun. Indoors they do best in a brigt but shaded room and should be fed twice a month. *HYDRANGEAS* almost exhaust themselves flowering. If you want good blooms the following year, cut each cane back to the lowest pair of buds and re-pot. You can strike new plants from the cuttings. Newly potted *HYDRANGEAS* can be placed outdoors until the following season, being kept slightly moist. Native to Japan. (See also plate page 14).

HYLOCEREUS
(hai loh see' ree əs)   CACTACEAE

HYLOCEREUS undatus
Princess of the Night

The royal title 'Princess of the Night' is perfectly applicable to the gorgeous blooms of this untidy, sprawling plant. In warmer climates *HYLOCEREUS undatus* grows easily from pieces thoroughly dried off before they are dipped in rooting hormone and set in a sharp sandy mixture. Later, after roots have developed, they need an acid compost, rich in leaf mould, and will soon go climbing straight up the wall of a terrace, patio or even sunny living room, sending out clinging roots that support them for years. The main triangular stem will branch and the creamy 9 in (23 cm) flowers form on these branches, opening after dark on warm nights and fading the following morning. The perfume of *HYLOCEREUS* is magnificent.

HYPOËSTES
(hai poh es' tees)   ACANTHACEAE

HYPOËSTES cristata
Velvet Plant

HYPOËSTES sanguinolenta
Freckle Face

HYPOËSTES, or 'Freckle Face' is a shrubby perennial from Malagasy, easily grown for its curious leaf colouring or iridescent pink spots against a dull green background. The cultivar *'Splash'* has larger spots and more pronounced colour. It is easy to raise from winter cuttings under glass, and is grown in a standard house-plant mix. Water 'Freckle Face' regularly in summer, minimally in winter. Re-pot and prune only when the days warm up.

HYPOËSTES sanguinolenta should be constantly snipped back to compact shape and will bear lilac and white long-throated flowers in warm weather. Minimum outdoor winter temperature, 50°F (10°C).

127

IMPATIENS
(im pae' shəns)   BALSAMINAE

IMPATIENS *wallerana 'Sultanii'*
Busy Lizzie

The many varieties of 'Busy Lizzie' are virtually in-
destructible, their very botanic name being an allusion to the impatience with which they grow and
multiply. Pot-planted groups in mixed colours can
be pinched back continuously to keep them within
bounds, and will continue to flower all winter long
inside a sunny window. Hanging baskets can be
grown in a glassed-in room or balcony all year. The
entire spectrum of coloured types consists of hybrids
between three varieties of IMPATIENS *wallerana.*
These are: *I. wallerana Holstii* with reddish leaves and
scarlet flowers, *I. wallerana Petersiana* with bronzy
pointed leaves and red flowers, and *I. wallerana
Sultanii,* which has green foliage and flowers in many
shades of pink, orange, mauve, red and white.
Double-flowered cultivars are now available and
also some with variegated leaves, flowers, or both.
Grow them in a well-drained peaty mix with sand,
and water well all through the warm weather. Strike
cuttings in damp sand or a glass of water any time.

    IMPATIENS prefers semi-shade at all times
except winter, and is also known as 'Snapweed'.
'Touch-me-Not', 'Patient Lucy' and 'Balsam'.

IPOMOEA
(ip ə mee' ə)   CONVOLVULACEAE

The 'Morning Glories', or IPOMOEAS, are quick-
growing warm-climate vines that can mostly be
raised from seed for annual culture on a sunny
terrace, or in a glasshouse. They include the
common 'Sweet Potato' vine (*I. batatas*), and the
ubiquitous 'Purple Winder', (*I. leari*) which has
become naturalised all over the world.

    I. horsfalliae is a vine of a different colour. Known
as the 'Cardinal Creeper' or (in Hawaii) 'Prince

IPOMOEA *horsfalliae*
Cardinal Creeper

IPOMOEA *leari*
Purple Winder

Kuhio Vine', it is only suited to warm climates or
warm indoor conditions in a sunroom of conservatory. It is perennial and bears long tubular flowers of
rosy-red any time of year. Grow it in the usual
tropical compost, moist peaty loam with sand and
leaf mould, and give it support. Conditions could
hardly be too warm for this beautiful plant.

IRESINE
(ai' re seen)   AMARANTHACEAE

Quick-growing shrubby perennials for warm places,
IRESINE are not at all resistant to frost. For pot
colour, they are treated as annuals, and autumn cut-

IRESINE lindenii
Bloodleaf

ISMENE festalis
Sacred Lily of the Incas

tings can be wintered indoors either in water or pots of damp sand. *IRESINE* enjoy a standard potting mix with perhaps extra sand, and regular water in warm weather. They should be pinched back continually for denser foliage. All *IRESINE* have small spikes of greenish flowers, but are grown particularly for the vivid leaf-colourings, and may reach 30 in (75 cm).

I. herbstii 'Blood Leaf'. Is completely red on both stems and rounded leaves, with occasional purple markings.
I. herbstii 'Aureo-Reticulata' Similar, but has yellow-veined leaves on red stems.
I. lindenii Has spear-shaped glossy red leaves, shading paler toward the centre vein.

All are from South America and colour best in a bright light.

ISMENE
(iz mee' nee)   AMARYLLIDACEAE

A showy member of the Amaryllis family from South America, *ISMENE festalis* is a charming bulb with similar cultural needs to *Eucharis* (which see). The flower stems appear directly from the bare bulb in spring or summer, and the individual flowers are rather like spidery white daffodils with greenish and raggedy-edged trumpets. Certainly it deserves its reputation as 'Sacred Lily of the Incas'! Keep up water after the flowers fade so the leaves can grow to ripen naturally. If the bulbs are lifted and stored in a warm, dry place, you'll overcome the problem of cold winters. A number of closely related species may be sold either as *ISMENE* or *Hymenocallis*.

IXORA
(ik sor' ə)   RUBIACEAE

IXORA coccinea
Flame of the Woods

A showy, shrubby plant, *IXORA* may grow to 3 ft (90 cm) indoors or in a warm glasshouse, but needs plenty of sun and moisture to do at all well. Plant it in a standard potting mix with sand for drainage, and keep regularly watered throughout the warm weather. The leaves are handsome and glossy, similar to those of *Gardenia* to which it is closely related. It can be propagated from summer cuttings struck in sharp sand. The tubular flowers, which form in dense clusters, are a brilliant pillar-box red, stimulating its popular name 'Flame of the Woods'. Native to Indonesia, it needs care and warmth during the winter months to survive, but is well worth the effort.

129

JASMINUM
(jas' min əm)   OLEACEAE

JASMINUM azoricum
Azores Jasmine

JASMINUM polyanthum
Pink Jasmine

In spite of their wonderful fragrance, 'Jasmines' are rarely grown indoors because they are supposed to need a great deal of room and support to climb. At least one exception, though, is the charming *J. azoricum*, which flowers from summer right through to winter. It is normally a climber, but I've found that it will happily assume a compact, shrubby habit with regular pruning. Grow it in rich but sandy compost in quite large pots, water and fertilise regularly, and you have a splendid specimen plant for any position out of full sun. The shrubby *J. sambac* ('Arabian Jasmine') in its single or double forms is also a suitable indoor subject, though only in a warmer climate. *J. polyanthum* is a climber with deep pink buds and masses of white flowers in early spring. It can be kept reasonably compact in a large

container with a supporting wire framework, and should be brought indoors only for its brief flowering season. After this it can be cut right back to force the next year's growth.

KALANCHOË
(ka lan' koh ee)   CRASSULACEAE

KALANCHOË beharensis
Felt Plant

KALANCHOË blossfeldiana
Flaming Katy

Possibly the most popular succulent plants for pot-growing, *KALANCHOËS* need no sun protection and will survive winters down to 40°F (5°C). Cuttings may be taken in spring and dried out before planting in damp sand. When rooted, they may be potted up in containers of perfectly drained compost including 50 per cent sand and brick rubble.

KALANCHOË *orgyalis*
Copper Spoon

KALANCHOË *tomentosa*
Panda Plant

Water them freely in summer, but hold off in winter until the leaves show signs of distress. KALAN-CHOËS are grown about equally for flowers and leaf interest — it's all a matter of taste. Among the most interesting types are:

K. beharensis 'Felt Plant'. 3 ft (90 cm). A stunning architectural plant for a warm terrace. It has large triangular leaves that appear to be covered in brown felt. Pink flowers in spring.
K. blossfeldiana May bloom several times a year. Has shiny green leaves sometimes edged with red. Showy heads of vivid scarlet flowers on thin stems to 15 in (38 cm) high. There is a dwarf variety, *'Tom Thumb'*.
K. marmorata 'Penwiper Plant'. White spring flowers. The roundish grey leaves have large sooty markings and a waxy coating.

K. tomentosa 'Panda Plant'. Grows to 15 in (38 cm). Plump leaves covered with short silvery hairs, tapering to rust at the top. Rarely flowers in pots.

KOHLERIA
(koh lee' ree ə)   GESNERIACEAE

KOHLERIA *eriantha*
Isoloma

Spectacular South American perennials, KOHLER-IAS have somewhat the appearance of European 'Foxgloves', but grow from rhizomes. They like warmth, humidity and are best grown in glasshouses in cold climate areas, or in shaded moist positions in warm temperature zones. Raise them either from summer stem cuttings struck in sand, or from divisions of the rhizome potted up in early spring. Use a moist, loamy compost with sand to improve drainage. Many species grow erect but quickly lapse into a prostrate habit without support. They scorch in full sun, and the soft, velvety leaves can spot badly either from spraying or overhead watering — it is better to soak the pots from below. Colorful species are:

K. amabilis 24 in (60 cm). Dark leaves. Rose-red flowers, spotted magneta.
K. bogotensis Same height. Downy stems and leaves with red reverses. Orange and yellow flowers.
K. digitaliflorum A dwarf with magenta and white flowers.
K. eriantha 4 ft (120 cm). Reddish stems and red edging to the leaf margins. Yellow-spotted scarlet flowers.

All species bloom in summer.

LACHENALIA
(lak ə nael' ee ə)   LILIACEAE

LACHENALIA *aloides quadricolor*
Soldier Lily

LACHENALIA *aurea*
Orange Soldier Lily

LACHENALIAS are particularly suited to pot culture in hard winter areas. Pot them up in late summer using a loamy compost with decayed manure and leaf mould. The bulbs should be just under the surface — don't be afraid to crowd them. Water thoroughly, then shut the pots away in a cool shaded place while the roots develop. As winter closes in, move them to a sunnier place with night temperature of at least 40°F (5°C), and start to water regularly. LACHENALIA's green strap-like leaves are spotted with red-brown, and the stiff winter flower spikes stand like a regiment of musical comedy soldiers. When repotting in late summer, separate any small offset bulbs under flowering size.

LACHENALIA *pendula*
Red Soldier Lily

These could be given away or planted separately for another year. Good varieties are:

L. *aloides Tricolor* 'Soldier Lily'. Flowers shade from green through yellow to red.
L. *aloides Quadricolor* As above, with purple as well.
L. *aurea* Rich orange-yellow flowers.
L. *pendula* Red flowers edged green or purple.

All are from South Africa.

LAELIA
(lae' lee ə)   ORCHIDACEAE

LAELIA *flava*
Laelia

Tropical American Orchids closely related to *Cattleyas*, LAELIAS share the same cultural requirements. Species of Mexican origin safely survive a winter temperature of 50°F (10°C). They flourish in pots or baskets filled with fir chips, orchid fibre and charcoal pieces, and like a summer temperature of between 70° and 80°F (20° to 27°C), with good ventilation. Brazilian and Central American types need higher temperatures all round, and are best left to specialists with heated glasshouses.

L. anceps Is most commonly grown. Its winter flowers are mauve with a deep red lip, borne on tall stems.

L. flava Has flowers of egg-yolk yellow.

LAELIOCATTLEYA
(lae lee oh kat lae' ə)   ORCHIDACEAE

LAELIOCATTLEYA X *'Florence Patterson'*
Laeliocattleya

LAELIOCATTLEYAS are bigeneric hybrids between the two Orchid genera *Laelia* and *Cattleya*. There are well over two thousand named varieties, including the beautiful *'Florence Patterson'* of the illustration. High humidity is needed for successful flowering, and they are grown exactly as *Cattleyas* (which see).

LANTANA
(lan tah' nə)   VERBENACEAE

LANTANA camara is often in danger of losing favour because of its rampant habits in the open garden. Pot culture is the perfect answer, using a compost of sand, loam, leaf mould and decayed manure. Plant out in early spring, and water regularly until new growth appears. This can be pinched back regularly to stimulate branching as the warm weather progresses, the plant not being allowed to

LANTANA camara 'Snowflake'
White Lantana

grow above 24 in (60 cm) either in height or width. *LANTANA* may need potting up several times in the warm weather as roots fill the old container. It begins to flower about mid-summer and there are many beautiful hybrids, including:

'Chelsea Gem' — red and orange.
'Cloth of Gold' — pure yellow.
'Snowflake' — white, yellow centres.

L. montevidensis, a related species, has a more delicate weeping habit and may be grown in hanging baskets. Its flowers are a rich lavender, borne almost all the year.

LAPEYROUSIA
(lah pae roo' zee ə)   IRIDACEAE

LAPEYROUSIA grandiflora
Flame Freesia

The showy South African 'Flame Freesia', *LAPEYROUSIA*, should be grown under exactly the same conditions as its popular namesake. I've found them a little easier to flower in pots, if anything, and they set small red seeds readily, so it is easy to increase your stock. Flowers of most species are a vivid scarlet. Species you could try include:

L. cruenta 9 in (23 cm). Red flowers.
L. grandiflora 15 in (38 cm). Larger scarlet flowers with yellow eye.
L. juncea 12 in (30 cm). Fine leaves. Deep rose-pink flowers.

LAURUS
(lor' əs)   LAURACEAE

LAURUS nobilis
Sweet Bay

The 'Sweet Bay' or 'Laurel' is surely the ideal container plant for just outside the kitchen door, where its fresh green leaves can be plucked to flavour many gourmet dishes. Yes, these are the same Bay leaves you buy at your herb counter, and they're much more flavourful when fresh. *LAURUS* is normally a large tree, but quite amenable to life in a small tub, clipped and pinched to a round or obelisk shape. It will grow in any well-drained loamy soil and does not mind if the mix is slightly alkaline. Water well and regularly, and give the leaves an extra burst with the hose to keep them clean and fresh. *LAURUS* is perfectly happy indoors or out in most areas, but may require some shelter in frosty months. (See also plate page 24).

LEWISIA
(loo is' ee ə)   PORTULACACEAE

LEWISIA Hybrid
Bitter Roof

Charming perennials from the Northwest United States, *LEWISIAS* are named for the explorer Lewis who first opened up the area — one of them is the State flower of Montana. In England, they are sometimes raised in stone sinks or other wide containers where light loamy soil can be brought to perfect drainage with sand and grit. They are lime-haters, so make sure the soil is acid. *LEWISIA* species vary greatly, and there are many hybrids both in nature and cultivation. They form dense rosettes of strap-like leaves, sometimes toothed, usually dark green. The clusters of starry flowers appear on stems from 5 to 12 inches in length (13 to 30 cm), and each plant produces many stems simultaneously. The flowers may be white, cream, pink, apricot or mauve, and have a delightful waxy sheen similar to *Portulacas*, to which they are related. *LEWISIAS* are hardy down to 40°F (5°C) or less, so are suitable for growing on a open terrace. The popular name is 'Bitter Root'.

LIGULARIA
(lig yoo lea' ree ə)   COMPOSITAE

Useful Japanese plants for a sheltered terrace or window garden, *LIGULARIAS* produce stems of bright yellow daisy flowers in summer. But they are grown principally for their foliage — large 10 in (25 cm) leaves, intriguingly blotched with yellow and white, and sometimes in palest pink. These colour best out of full sun and need a rich peaty mix, kept consistently moist. *LIGULARIAS*, easily propagated by division, are repotted in early spring. Popular varieties are:

LIGULARIA *kaempferi* 'Aureo-maculata'
Leopard Plant

L. kaempferi Argentea   White-edged leaves.
L. kaempferi Aureo-maculata 'Leopard Plant'.   Yellow-spotted leaves.

LIGUSTRUM
(lig us' trəm)   OLEACEAE

LIGUSTRUM *ovalifolium* 'Aureum'
Golden Privet

I was in two minds about including the privets in this book, for they have been proclaimed garden pests in many areas. However, in containers they can be kept under control. LIGUSTRUMS grow in literally any soil, and are propagated all too easily from cuttings, layers or from seeds. Trim them to formal or standard shape and use the plants at entryways or

to add drama to your terrace. It is better to prune lightly and often, rather than too heavily. Suitable pruning times include early spring and just after flowering (if you let them flower at all — for the pollen is distressing to many people who suffer from asthma or hay fever). Privets are evergreen, frost-hardy and salt-resistant. You are likely to grow the fancy-leafed types, such as:

L. vulgare Argenteo-variegatum   'Common Privet'. With white variegated leaves.
L. ovalifolium Aureum   'Golden Privet'. Yellow leaves.
L. lucidum Tricolor   Green, white and pink leaves.

Flowers of all species are creamy-white, like miniature lilacs. The berries that follow may be blue, purple, white or yellow.

LILIUM
(lil' ee əm)
                                                 LILIACEAE

LILIUM *speciosum*
Pink Tiger Lily

The world's most beautiful Lilies or LILIUMS, are more reliable in containers than in the open garden where the delicate many-scaled bulbs often rot due to poor drainage. They are best grown in large pots with a deep layer of broken crocks and stone rubble to carry away water. Half fill the pots with a rich loamy compost mixed with leaf mould and peat, and just a scattering of sand and charcoal. Put a handful of bone meal below the surface where roots can reach it later. The bulbs are now placed in position, several inches apart. Make sure they are fresh, plump and the largest you can buy. Place a thin bamboo stake in the middle and cover the bulbs with more of the compost, half-filling the available space. Water and place the pots in a shaded position until the first shoots show. Now completely fill the pots and leave them in a brighter, sheltered position.

Tie the tall *LILIUM* stems to the stake only when they've hardened off and reached several feet in height. The pots can be moved to their final position indoors in bright light as soon as flower buds begin to form. From then on, a weak solution of fertiliser added to the regular water will help production of super-sized blooms. These may appear any time from spring to autumn according to species. Good *LILIUMS* for pot culture include:

L. auratum 'Gold Rayed Lily of Japan'. 10 in (25 cm) white and gold flowers on 5 ft (150 cm) stems. Mid-summer.
L. longiflorum 'November Lily' of the Southern Hemisphere, 'Easter Lily' of the Northern. Long white trumpets flushed with green and gold in late spring.
L. speciosum 'Tiger Lilies'. Pink and white. Late spring.
L. X parkmanii Pink hybrids between *L. auratum* and *L. speciosum.*
L. X Aurelian hybrids. Open flowers in green, gold and yellow shades. Summer.

LITHOPS
(lith' ops)   AIZOACEAE

LITHOPS touchiana
Living Stones (Photo: Hamlyn Library)

LITHOPS, the curious little plants known as 'Living Stones' (from the Greek *lithos*, a stone) are often hard to distinguish from the pebbles scattered about them in nature. You can reproduce their environment in shallow containers of sandy potting mix rich with gravel for super drainage. Top with a layer of river pebbles and place a few larger polished stones here and there. The *LITHOPS* will never grow in height above in inch or so (2.5 cm), but will slowly spread from the roots to form clumps in colour combinations of green, grey and brown. The single daisy-like

flowers (which may be twice as big as the plant) appear in autumn. Natives to many provinces of South Africa, they are not frost-hardy and like a warm, dry, sheltered position in winter. Indoors, a sunny window ledge is ideal. Water them regularly in warm weather.

LITTONIA
(lit oh' nee ə)   LILIACEAE

LITTONIA modesta
Climbing Lily

Most intriguing for pot or terrace culture, 'The Climbing Lily', *LITTONIA modesta* climbs like the related *Gloriosa* (which see) by means of leaf tendrils. Thus it will need the support either of a small, inconspicuous trellis or a larger plant around which it can twine. *LITTONIAS* enjoy moist peaty composts with plenty of leaf mould, loam and a little sand. Plant out their tubers in early spring and the first shoots should appear a month or so later. Regular water is appreciated, and (later in growth) syringeing to increase the humidity. The flowers will appear in early summer when stems have climbed to about 3 ft (90 cm). They are bright orange-yellow bells, often followed by large pods of scarlet seeds that grow very easily though they'll take several years to reach flowering size.

LONICERA
(lon is' ə rə)   CAPRIFOLIACEAE

LONICERA, or 'Honeysuckle' has a resistance to climatic vagaries that can be a great advantage on an open balcony. Plant them in large containers and train to cover trellises or fill in between balcony railings where their dense evergreen foliage will help

LONICERA japonica 'Aureo-reticulata'
Japanese Honeysuckle

LOTOS bertholetii
Coral Gem

protect more delicate plants. 'Honeysuckles' prefer a well-drained loamy compost, and can be pruned back regularly to encourage branching and prevent sprawl. All species grow easily from spring cuttings and they include:

L. etrusca 'Italian Honeysuckle'. Bluish leaves. Red and yellow flowers. Summer.
L. hildebrandiana 'Giant Burmese Honeysuckle'. For warm positions only, and needs very strong support. Masses of 6 in (15 cm) orange flowers all through the warm weather.
L. japonica Aureo-reticulata 'Japanese Honeysuckle'. A fast grower with white flowers and beautifully yellow-veined leaves. A pest in some countries, so keep an eye on it.
L. periclymenum 'Serotina' 'Late Dutch Honeysuckle'. Has deep red buds, creamy-yellow flowers.

There are many other *LONICERA* species with flowers white, red, yellow, orange, scarlet and cyclamen.

LOTOS
(loh' təs)   LEGUMINOSAE

A silver-grey waterfall of fine needle leaves. *LOTOS* is perfect for hanging baskets where it finds the good drainage it needs. Ensure a minimum winter temperature of 40°F (5°C), plant it in a sandy compost with some leaf mould, and line the baskets with bark or thick moss to prevent it all being washed away. Grow *LOTOS* (the 'Coral Gem') in full sun with regular hot-weather watering. The vivid scarlet pea-flowers appear all over the trailing branches in spring or summer, and the plant should be allowed almost to dry out in winter. *LOTOS* is from the Canary Islands, and is fairly resistant to salt air.

LYCASTE
(lai kas' tee)   ORCHIDACEAE

LYCASTE skinneri
Virgin Orchid

Unusual Orchids from Central and South America. *LYCASTES* appear to have three petals, arranged in the form of a triangle, point up. In actual fact these are sepals, and closer observation will reveal three undeveloped petals between them. *LYCASTES* are epiphytic and grow best in baskets or pots of fir chips or chunky mixtures of treefern, orchid fibre, leaf mould and rubble. They rest during winter and are not greatly worried by low temperatures provided they are sheltered from frost. But as the days warm up, begin to water regularly and deeply, occasionally soaking the entire container. Give them bright light, shelter from direct sun and good ventilation. Best species include:

L. *aromaticum* Small golden-yellow flowers.
L. *skinneri* Generally rose-pink, but may be lighter or darker.
L. *virginalis* Snow-white, flushed with pink.

LYCOPODIUM
(lai kə poh' dee əm) LYCOPODIACEAE

LYCOPODIUM *hegmaroides 'Sala'*
Tassel Fern

Usually sold as Ferns, LYCOPODIUMS are closely related to mosses and found in every continent. They are planted in hanging baskets or pots in mixtures of peat, sand and leaf mould, and must have very high humidity in warm weather to support their delicate foliage. Greenhouses and conservatories are ideal for them, but bathrooms can be quite successful if they provide the necessary winter minimum of 45°F (7°C). Tropical types rapidly cover hanging baskets with curious tassel-like growths, slightly reminiscent of 'Norfolk Island Pine' fronds. Like Ferns, LYCOPODIUMS reproduce from spores, but will also grow from spring cuttings.

L. *hegmaroides Sala* 'Tassel Fern'.

MAMILLARIA
(mam il eə' ree ə) CACTACEAE

MAMILLARIA *bocasana*
Powder Puff

MAMILLARIA *speciosa*
Nipple Cactus

MAMILLARIAS are bought by the million because they are almost completely foolproof, and flower reliably year after year. All species are native to Mexico and the American southwest, and the great majority of them remain small enough all their lives to be grown on a sunny window-sill. They can be readily identified because exaggerated tubercles (or bumps from which the spines grow) are arranged in spiral rows rather than vertical ribs — this gives them the popular name of 'Nipple Cactus'. The flowers appear in a ring or crown around the top of the plant in early spring. MAMILLARIAS form many offsets around their bases. These can be severed and potted up separately. Look for:

138

M. bocasana 'Powder Puff'.   Greyish-green with silver hairy spines surrounding a hooked reddish spine on each tubercle. The flowers are silver and cream.

M. elegans   Cylindrical rather than globular in shape, growing to 6 in (15 cm) in height. The white spines are arranged in star patterns. The flowers are pale yellow.

M. hahniana 'Old Lady Cactus'.   Grows only 4 in (10 cm) across, covered in white curly spines. Bears purple-red flowers in summer.

M. zeilmanniana   Again a dwarf, with a bright green cylindrical shape. The flowers are mauve-pink with cream throats.

Several dozen species are sold commercially, and they all like full sun and summer water.

MANDEVILLA
(man də vil ə)   APOCYNACEAE

MANDEVILLA suaveolens
Chilean Jasmine

MANDEVILLA suaveolens, the 'Chilean Jasmine', is highly successful as a balcony or courtyard plant when you can provide a large tub for its extensive root system. Prepare the container with a 4 in (10 cm) layer of broken pots or brick rubble, a layer of peat or spagnum moss to prevent washaways, and then fill with a compost of peaty loam, sand and charcoal. Plant out in early spring, spreading the roots out as wide as possible before firming in the compost and watering deeply. With regular water and occasional liquid fertiliser, your *MANDEVILLA* will really take off and twine closely around everything in sight. A small trellis attached to your balcony wall on blocks will suit it ideally. The scented white flowers appear in profusion all through the summer months, followed by bean-like seed pods. Although evergreen, *MANDEVILLA* is usually cut back hard in winter to about four buds per stem. This helps to sort out the tangles it makes.

MARANTA
(mə ran' tə)   MARANTACEAE

MARANTA leuconeura Erythrophylla
Red Herringbone Plant

MARANTA leuconeura 'Massangeana'
Massange's Arrowroot

The 'Prayer Plants', or *MARANTAS* revel in humidity, which accounts for their curious habit of folding their leaves together at night — not so much in prayer as to funnel the condensing dew down to the roots. Grow them in a moist but well-drained compost of loam, sand and peat, and keep them continually damp. *MARANTAS* need very little light, so they are frequently grown in bathrooms, in sunless windows, on lower shelves of plant tables — and even under the benches of glasshouses. Propagate them by division of the rhizome in late winter. Popular species are:

M. arundinacea 'Arrowroot'.   A tall grower, with alternately appearing grey-green leaves, sharply pointed.

M. bicolor Dark green foliage with a lighter centre and purple reverses.

M. leuconeura 'Rabbit Tracks'. Light green leaves with purple-brown patches on either side of the central vein.

M. leuconeura Erythrophylla 'Red Herringbone Plant'. Chartreuse and dark green velvety leaves, with glossy blood-red veins.

M. leuconeura Massangeana 'Massange's Arrowroot'. Broad velvety-green leaves, with silver veins, and midrib. Violet-red and white flowers in late spring.

MEDINILLA
(med i nil' ə)   MELASTOMATACEAE

MEDINILLA magnifica
Javanese Rhododendron

Dare one say the most gorgeous of all tropical plants? I've always thought so since I saw the 'Javanese Rhododendron' in Tahiti. *MEDINILLA magnifica* is a fussy grower outside the tropics, but worth every effort when the fantastic hanging flower clusters appear in late spring. These combine strawberry-pink flowers and mauve-pink bracts with purple and yellow stamens. The stems are woody and angular, the leaves large, glossy and ribbed. *MEDINILLAS* demand a warm winter (55°F or 13°C), and have to be constantly watched for red spider. Grow them in large pots of sand, peat, well-decayed manure and powdered charcoal. They need bright light and only moderate watering, but the humidity must be around 70 per cent all summer. This really calls for a small glasshouse, but they are quite often grown in European apartments. Re-pot *MEDINILLA* in earliest spring — it may be propagated at the same time from half-ripened cuttings with a heel, struck in a sharp sandy mix under glass. Good luck!

MERYTA
(meə ree' tə)   ARALIACEAE

MERYTA sinclairii
Puka

MERYTA is an uncommon member of the Aralia family, called 'Puka' in its native New Zealand. Actually a small tree, it remains a compact size in a container, sending up a single straight stem. This produces handsome, glossy 12 in (30 cm) leaves, with irregular edges. They are arranged in a spiral fashion around the stem. The leaf stalks are blotched in brown, and the pale leaf veins are most pronounced. They say it bears panicles of small yellow flowers, but I've never seen them. Some growers list a magnificent cultivar with white and gold leaf variegations. Protect *MERYTA* from full sun, for the leaves scorch badly.

MILTONIA
(mil toh' nee ə)   ORCHIDACEAE

MILTONIA Hybrid
Pansy Orchid

MILTONIA warscewiczii
Miltonia

Vibrantly coloured South American Orchids that can be flowered without heat, *MILTONIAS* bloom in unusual shades of crimson, purple, pink and brown. The single Pansy-like flowers last well, often appearing twice a year. *MILTONIAS* (or 'Pansy Orchids') can be grown in a compost of fine fir bark and charcoal, or orchid fibre and sphagnum moss. They need shade from bright sun, moist conditions all year except winter, but humidity as high as 80 per cent in the summer. Good ventilation is also important. While *MILTONIAS* will accept winter temperatures down to 40°F (5°C), they flower more reliably if it is warmer.

MONSTERA
(mon stee' rə)   ARACEAE

MONSTERA deliciosa
Swiss Cheese Plant

MONSTERA pertusa
Philodendron pertusum

A wonderful tropic climber with almost as many popular names as it has holes in its leaves, the ubiquitous *MONSTERA deliciosa*, or 'Swiss Cheese Plant', is seen all over the world in foyers, offices and greenhouses. Yet it is quite amenable to growing around the house indoors or out, and adjusts to all but the coldest winters inside. Grow it in large containers of moist tropical peaty mix with manure, and give it regular water. *MONSTERA* will in fact grow almost as well in heavy containers of water without any soil at all. When it has something to hang onto (a wall, a moss pole or even a small stake) *MONSTERA* will climb by means of aerial roots, but in indoor conditions it is likely to hold back and develop a squat shrubby habit. MONSTERA does best in bright light and likes a high degree of humidity. The leaves should be wiped down once a month. Mature plants bear sweet-smelling flowers like golden Arum Lilies, which ripen into a delicious fruit with a flavour like a mixed fruit salad. Among other names it is called 'Ceriman', 'Hurricane Plant', 'Fruit Salad Plant' and 'Mexican Breadfruit'. (See also plates pages 9, 40).

MUSA
(myoo' sə)   MUSACEAE

MUSA *nana Variegata*
Dwarf Chinese Banana

The Bananas (MUSA spp) are not trees, but giant tropical perennials that send up fruit-bearing stems from suckers. Their foliage is so spectacular they are often grown indoors or in sheltered courtyards. You may get fruit in a warm summer, but there's no guarantee. Suckers are potted up in spring in the largest possible containers, in a soil mix rich in compost and decayed manure. They need constant water throughout the warm weather and must never be allowed to dry out. They do well in either sun or semi-shade, but they must have protection from wind, which reduces the splendid 5 ft (150 cm) leaves to shreds. Remember that once a trunk has flowered, it will never do so again. Slice it off close to soil level and give the new suckers an even break. Suitable container varieties include:

M. *ensete* 'Abyssinian Banana'. Inedible fruits. Useful pot specimens only when young.
M. *nana* 'Chinese Dwarf Banana'. 6 ft (2 m).
M. *paradisiaca Vittata* Variegated leaves.
M. *zebrina* 10 ft (3 m) Red, brown and purple leaf markings.

NARCISSUS
(nah' sis əs)   AMARYLLIDACEAE

NARCISSUS X *'King Alfred'*
Daffodil

NARCISSUS *odorus Rugulosus*
Campernelle

'Daffodils', 'Jonquils', 'Narcissi' and 'Campernelles', are all part of the genus NARCISSUS as far as botanists are concerned. All grow from autumn-planted bulbs, produce long flat or hollow leaves and a single stem of flowers. Blooms of all species have six petals and a central trumpet protecting the stamens. Beyond that, they vary widely in colour, perfume and numbers of flowers per stem. Many species are grown in pots for a short-lived display of spring colour and perfume. 'Daffodils', 'Narcissi' and 'Campernelles' are potted up as soon as the bulbs are available in a peat-based compost with their tops just below surface level. This is watered, and the pots are kept in a dark airy cupboard or storeroom until at least an inch (2.5 cm) above the soil. Then

NARCISSUS tazetta
Jonquil

NAUTILOCALYX lynchii
Nautilus Flower

gradually bring them into the light, keeping the compost barely moist. Undrained containers may be filled with commercial bulb fibre and the *NARCISSUS* grown in this with similar treatment. Such growth however, will completely exhaust the bulbs.

The many varieties of 'Jonquil' can be grown beautifully in undrained containers filled with pebbles instead of compost. The bulbs are placed on these and water added up to a level barely touching the base of the bulbs. Put them away until the roots develop, which they will — twisting every way among the pebbles and anchoring the plants firmly. When shoots begin to appear, top up the water regularly and add a little liquid fertiliser. As the bulbs grow by any of the above means, they should be put in a sunny window and the containers turned regularly so they grow straight and strong. Plant many pots at fortnightly intervals and label them with the date. You should have a succession of spring colour lasting for weeks.

NAUTILOCALYX
(nor til oh kae' liks)   GESNERIACEAE

Tropical *NAUTILOCALYX* species are cultivated principally for the beauty of their foliage. There are indeed small trumpet-shaped flowers with calyxes shaped like a nautilus shell, but they are largely hidden beneath the ruffled, waxy and often purple leaves. Grow them in a compost rich with leaf mould or peat moss and keep moist at all times. *NAUTILOCALYX* are propagated in warm weather from stem or leaf cuttings, and like a heavily humid atmosphere. Keep them out of hot sun and remember their minimum winter temperature need is around 55°F (13°C).

N. lynchii is the commonly seen type, its leaves dark purplish-red, its flowers yellow with red hairs.

NEOREGELIA
(nee oh rə jee' lee ə)   BROMELIACEAE

NEOREGELIA caroliniae
Heart of Flame

In this spectacular genus of Bromeliads, the leaf-vase itself bursts into glowing summer colour. This effect is obviously designed to attract fertilising insects to the tiny flowers, which are almost invisible, barely showing above the water collected and stored in the well of the leaves.

NEOREGELIAS are grown and propagated like other Bromeliads (see *Aechmea,, Billbergia*, etc.) but should be displayed low down where the eye can see into the vivid centre of the plant. Water regularly, keeping the central leaf-hollow full at all times. In the winter, protect from temperatures below 50°F (10°C). Interesting species include:

NEOREGELIA *concentrica Marginata*
Purple Heart

N. carolinae 'Heart of Flame'. Light olivy-green leaves, copper-red in the centre. Small blue flowers.
N. carolinae Tricolor The leaves have a cream stripe and the entire plant flushes rose at flowering time, the centre turning vivid carmine.
N. concentrica 'Marginata' Cream-edged leaves, vivid red-violet in the centre.
N. spectabilis 'Fingernail Plant'. The leaves have a red spot at the tip all year. The whole centre of the plant turns rosy-red in summer when the blue flowers open.

NEPHROLEPIS
(nef roh lae' pis)   POLYPODIACEAE

NEPHROLEPIS *exaltata 'Bostoniensis'*
Boston Fern

NEPHROLEPIS *vars. 'Whitmanii'* (back)
and *'Fluffy Ruffles'* (front)
Fishbone Ferns

Most popular of indoor Ferns, *NEPHROLEPIS* has many named varieties. All have basically a wiry mid-rib covered in brown fuzz, with rough-edged leaflets (or *pinnae*) growing on both sides at regular intervals. This gives the plant its old name of 'Fishbone Fern'. Beyond that, the leaves may be rigid or drooping, the leaflets may themselves be divided (*bipinnate*); feathery; finely cut; curled or ruffled; and may vary from chartreuse to a deep rich green. Plant *NEPHROLEPIS* in hanging baskets or large pots, using a compost with equal parts of peat, loam, sharp sand and a scattering of charcoal. Pot and re-pot in early spring. Once established, they should be watered regularly with twice-monthly additions of weak liquid manure. Hanging ferns should be syringed on hot days, and they benefit from an occasional long soak in a bucket of water. The most beautiful varieties are all cultivars from *NEPHROLEPIS exaltata*, which is native to tropical areas around the world. These include the striking *N. exaltata 'Bostoniensis'* the 'Boston Fern', on which the fronds may reach 6 ft (180 cm) in length, and droop under their own weight. Other varieties of *N. exaltata* include *'Rooseveltii'*, in which the fronds have wavy leaflets, and *'Fluffy Ruffles'*, in which the short pale green fronds are lacy and much divided, resembling ostrich plumes.

N. cordifolia is also found around the tropic zone, and in many parts of Australia. The leaves are vertical and about 24 in (60 cm) long, the leaflets sharply pointed. (See also plates pages 11, 23, 28, 50).

NERINE
(nə reen')   AMARYLLIDACEAE

Hardy bulbs from South Africa, *NERINES* enjoy mild to cool conditions and flower best outdoors at the end of a wet summer. For indoor use, plant them

144

NERINE sarniensis
Guernsey Lily

in summer in shallow containers of a loamy compost enriched with well-decayed manure, and a little sand and charcoal. The bulbs should be placed with their necks just above soil level, watered to settle in and not again until the flower spikes begin to emerge. This they do from the bare bulb, the strap-like leaves not following till later. NERINES resent disturbance and should be repotted only every three or four years. They like a bright sunny position as the flower heads open. Good species include:

N. bowdenii 'Pink Agapanthus'. Mid-pink flowers with wavy petals. Prefers cooler conditions than other species.
N. filifolia 'Grass-Leafed Nerine'. Fine grassy leaves. Spidery pink flowers on slender stems.
N. sarniensis 'Guernsey Lily'. Deep cerise flowers with an iridescent effect on the petals.

NERIUM
(nee' ree əm)   APOCYNACEAE

The profuse flowers of NERIUM *oleander* (the 'Rose Bay' or 'Oleander') explain its popularity in warm moist climates — but that is only part of the story. These handsome shrubs happily turn on the same display in drought-stricken areas and make perfect tub plants where conditions are really tough. Plant them out in spring in large containers with a good drainage layer, topped up with a compost made as follows: two parts light sandy soil, one part well-decayed manure combined with peat moss. Add extra sand for good drainage, tamp in firmly and water well. Flowering takes place in summer and autumn, after which the plant is pruned and shaped. 'Oleanders' will stay healthy enough outdoors in winters down to 40°F (5°C) — any lower and they must be brought indoors till the freeze is over and

NERIUM oleander
Oleander

watering should be tapered off. NERIUM is propagated from cuttings struck in wet sand or in a bottle of plain water. There are named colour varieties in white, cream, all shades of pink and red — double and single. A pot-grown specimen may take four years to become really spectacular. They can be trained to compact shape or make a stunning standard.

NICOTIANA
(nik oh tee ah' nə)   SOLANACEAE

NICOTIANA affinis
Ornamental Tobacco

NICOTIANA, the 'Ornamental Tobacco', seems to be enjoying a big come-back all over the world. Easy to raise from seed, they are finally potted up in three

145

parts loam and one part leaf mould, with liberal addition of bone meal and sand. *NICOTIANA* plants can be kept in bloom from mid-spring to autumn with occasional snipping back and regular dosing with diluted liquid manure. Dead flowers should be removed regularly — but be careful, and do it late in the afternoon. On warm days, the sweetly scented Tobacco flowers curl up and play dead, for they are essentially evening and night-blooming plants. *NICOTIANA affinis* is the most sought-after type, its hybrids bearing long trumpeted flowers in shades of white, pink, cerise and crimson. The most startling is a pale lime-green, perfect for flower arrangements. Tobaccos are not hardy below 50°F (10°C) winter temperature, but by this time they've usually been cut back and put under cold weather shelter till the spring. A pot or two of the 'Flowering Tobacco' hybrids by a balcony door bring waves of perfume into your living room on summer evenings.

NIDULARIUM
(nid yoo lea ree əm)   BROMELIACEAE

NIDULARIUM billbergioides Citrinum
Golden Friendship Plant

NIDULARIUMS or 'Friendship Plants', are grown more for leaf colour than flower display, like the related *Neoregelias* (which see). Epiphytes by nature, they are happy in any open fibrous mix, as long as you can give them high humidity and keep the leaf rosettes filled with water. Propagated from sucker growth of older plants, they can be displayed anywhere about the house — in group plantings, large terrariums, or sunrooms. Good species are:

N. fulgens.   Yellow-green foliage, scarlet bracts. White and violet flowers.
N. billbergioides 'Citrinum'   Central leaf rosette and bracts a brilliant yellow.

N. purpureum   Leaves flushed purple. Flowers claret-red.

All *NIDULARIUMS* need a winter minimum of 55°F (13°C).

NOPALXOCHIA
(noh pəl soh' shə)   CACTACEAE

NOPALXOCHIA phyllanthoides 'Kaiserin Augusta Victoria'
Empress Cactus

A truly magnificent plant for a hanging basket or pot, the tongue-twisting *NOPALXOCHIA phyllanthoides 'Kaiserin Augusta Victoria'* is an epiphytic Cactus from high Mexican mountains. Grown in a rich well-drained compost of peat, loam and sand, and fed regularly, it will produce masses of 3 in (8 cm) spring blossoms right along the spineless flattened stems. These flowers shade from rich carmine to delicate rose. *NOPALXOCHIA* ('Empress Cactus' for short) strikes easily from large leaf cuttings severed with a very sharp knife and dried before replanting. It is winter-hardy almost down to freezing, and likes warm humid conditions in summer. The flowers colour better and last longer in shade.

NOTOCACTUS
(noh' toh kak təs)   CACTACEAE

Easy-to-grow miniatures for a window sill, *NOTOCACTUS* species reward us with flowers of yellow, scarlet and orange, often as big as the plants themselves. Grow them in pots of perfectly drained gritty compost and put in full sun. Water regularly except in the cold months, and keep watch for flower buds in early spring. The flowers are fleeting, but worth waiting for. Good species to seek out include:

NOTOCACTUS haselbergii
Golden Ball Cactus

ONCIDIUM sphacelatum
Dancing Dolls

N. apricus 'Golden Ball Cactus'.   Yellow flowers.
N. haselbergii 'Scarlet Ball Cactus'.   Orange-red.
N. scopa   Yellow flowers.

ODONTOGLOSSUM
(oh don tə glos' əm)   ORCHIDACEAE

In Europe, *ODONTOGLOSSUMS* are popular Orchids for indoor culture. They flourish in low temperatures, short of actual freezing, because they are native to mountainous parts of the Andes. Romping along in pots of fir bark, fibre or charcoal, they need year-round water except for a few weeks either side of flowering time, which varies according to species. Give them bright light in summer, and direct sun only in winter. Sprays of *ODONTOGLOSSUM* flowers open one by one, and the blooming may extend over many weeks. Most commonly grown are hybrids of :

O. crispum 'Lace Orchid'.   Snowy white, flushed rose.
O. grande 'Tiger Orchid'.   Egg-yolk yellow, banded brown. (See plate page 148).

ONCIDIUM
(on sid' ee əm)   ORCHIDACEAE

In sub-tropical areas, *ONCIDIUMS* are quite often grown outdoors in hanging containers for their arching flower sprays (as long as 4 ft or 120 cm). On a windy day, the moving flowers explain the popular names 'Dancing Ladies' and 'Dancing Dolls'.

ONCIDIUM sultanmyre
Dancing Ladies

Away from the sub-tropics, they thrive on a glassed-in balcony, in temperatures down to 45°F (7°C), but they need constant humidity. Plant them in shallow baskets or pots, placed high up where the flowers can spill forward. Grow them in any porous, perfectly drained combination of treefern fibre, Osmunda, charcoal and sand. Water only occasionally, for the pseudo-bulbs store an adequate supply and the roots

147

rot easily. Most of the many species of *ONCIDIUM* are similarly marked in brown and yellow (though there are a few pink and white species). They vary principally in the size and number of flowers. Some bear many hundreds to a stem.

OPUNTIA
(oh punt' ee ə)   CACTACEAE

OPUNTIA vulgaris
Indian Fig

Smile when you go shopping for 'Prickly Pears', for some species have been declared noxious weeds and may be illegal. But on an apartment balcony? Well, you still see them everywhere. Most are brilliantly flowered plants of dramatic appearance. Their flattened stems or pads (they are not real leaves) spring one from another, branching readily. The flowers (mostly yellow) appear in spring along the edges of new pads on mature plants. They are followed on many species by sweet and juicy red fruits, which are most refreshing, but must be peeled carefully.

OPUNTIAS survive winter temperature of 45°F (7°C). They can be used against a sunny terrace wall for dramatic accent or indoors in a well-lighted position out of the way of regular traffic. Smaller species between 24 and 48 in (60 to 120 cm) in height include:

O. brasiliensis 'Beaver Tail'.   Spineless. Yellow flowers.
O. bergeriana 'Prickly Pear'.   Few spines. Red flowers.
O. ficus-indica 'Indian Fig'.   Yellow flowers.
O. microdasys   White or red hairs. Yellow flowers. (See plate page 74).
O. santa-rita 'Bunny Ears'.   Open yellow flowers.

THE ORCHIDS
(or' kidz)   ORCHIDACEAE

ORCHIDS — a mixed display of species including (top to bottom) *CYMBIDIUM, ODONTOGLOSSUM, MILTONIA*

Any general observation about *ORCHID* culture in a few hundred words would be so diffuse as to be virtually useless, for these extraordinary plants comprise the largest of all botanical families. There are at least five hundred genera (though relatively few of them are seen outside specialist collections) and more than 27,000 recorded species — and they come from every type of climate from high, snowy mountains to low, steaming jungles. Most are tree-dwellers, but there are many attractive terrestrial forms as well, and even a few parasites. There are swamp orchids, tree orchids, rock orchids — even underground orchids that never see the light of day — and naturally the growth requirements of these different types vary wildly.

A *CATTLEYA* hybrid

SOPHRONITIS grandiflora
Fire Orchid (see page 183)

One thing, however, must be said. Many ORCHIDS are no more difficult to grow and flower than other popular indoor plants. Some of the most beautiful — *Paphiopedilums, Odontoglossums* and *Coelogynes* require no heat at all, and need only be protected against frost, which they naturally are when indoors. *Cymbidiums* flourish on an open terrace or indoors in any warm, temperate climate. Even *Cattleyas* and their many hybrids (the giant corsage ORCHIDS one sees in florists' displays) are well within the range of any indoor gardener.

Members of the great ORCHID family vary so widely in their appearance and growth habits that many amateurs must wonder just what it is they all have in common.

It is, in fact, the structure of their flowers. All ORCHIDS have three outer petals (sepals) and three inner true petals, arranged alternately. Of the three inner petals, one (usually the lowest) is called the lip and is invariably modified in some extraordinary way. It may be fringed or divided, hooded or cupped or trumpet-shaped, enlarged or highly coloured. Sometimes it is formed with amazing vegetable mimicry to look like a bee, a butterfly, a tiny human being or any one of a number of other things.

Beyond that, ORCHIDS also have a reproductive system different from other flowers. Instead of separate male and female organs, there is a single composite fleshy structure known as the *column*, which projects from the centre of the flower, often surrounded by the lip. This column contains both male and female characteristics.

The only near botanical relations of ORCHIDS are Bananas and Lilies!

The great majority of the epiphytic or tree-dwelling ORCHIDS grow from a creeping root stock, which produces a single thickened stem called a pseudo-bulb each season. This pseudo-bulb may be long and cane-like, or short and round, and in turn develop either one or two leaves according to species. Finally, the pseudo-bulb (which is a storage chamber for plant nutrients) develops a flower or flower-stem, and growth of the root-stock resumes to form a new pseudo-bulb. Each pseudo-bulb will flower once only, and can be removed when it withers and dies after several years.

Many beautiful ORCHIDS of many types are included in this book, all of them within the range of the average indoor gardener. You will find them listed and illustrated under the following names: *Bifrenaria, Bletilla* (Chinese Ground Orchid), *Brassocattleya, Cattleya, Coelogyne* (Angel Orchid), *Cymbidium, Dendrobium* (Rock Lily), *Epidendrum* (Crucifix Orchid), *Haemaria* (Jewel Orchid), *Laelia, Laeliocattleya, Lycaste, Miltonia* (Pansy Orchid), *Odontoglossum* (Tiger Orchid), *Oncidium* (Dancing Ladies, Dancing Dolls), *Paphiopedilum* (Slipper Orchid), *Phalaenopsis* (Moth Orchid), *Phragmipedilum, Pleione, Sarcochilus* (Orange Blossom Orchid), *Sobralia* (Bamboo Orchid), *Sophronitis, Stanhopea, Vanda, Zygopetalum.* (See also plates pages 15, 17, 39).

OXALIS
(oks' ə lis)   OXALIDACEAE

OXALIS species have become hated garden weeds in some countries, though they are really harmless surface rooters. One species, however, is among the most widely sold of indoor plants, the ubiquitous 'Fiji Fire Fern', which is not from Fiji and isn't a Fern either. But would it sell, do you think, under its real name *OXALIS hedysarioides Rubra* — from Brazil? Such are the wiles of nurserymen. Anyway, those who've grown it might try a few of the other delightful *OXALIS* species in pots. There are:

OXALIS adenophylla
Adenophylla

OXALIS hedysarioides Rubra
Fiji Fire Fern

O. adenophylla This has blue-green shamrock leaves and large trumpet-shaped pink flowers, blotched crimson. Grow it in a gritty well-drained compost.
O. cernua 'Bermuda Buttercup'. Has fragrant yellow flowers on tall stems. Likes a moist standard compost.
O. gigantea A 6 ft (2 m) shrub, deciduous. In early spring its branches are covered with bright yellow flowers.
O. rubra Dark red leaves and satiny-pink spring flowers. Use a rich compst.

All *OXALIS* are frost-tender (which is why they've only become pests in the sub-tropics). Protect them when winter nights drop below 50°F (10°C).

PACHYPHYTUM
(pak ee fai' təm)   CRASSULACEAE

PACHYPHYTUM oviferum
Moonstones

Smooth, succulent *PACHYPHYTUMS* are covered with a white silky bloom, which flushes with pastel colour in summer. They mark easily, and should be handled with care. Give them a well-drained gritty compost, water in summer, but almost complete dryness in winter. Deep red bell-shaped flowers appear in late spring, but their most striking feature is the same mealy bloom of stem and sepals. *PACHYPHYTUM* propagates easily from summer stem or leaf cuttings and will need the protection of glass in really cold weather. Otherwise, a good terrace plant, commonly known as 'Moonstones'.

PACHYSTACHYS
(pak ee stak' əs)   ACANTHACEAE

PACHYSTACHYS lutea
Golden Candles

150

A relatively recent houseplant introduction, the Brazilian *PACHYSTACHYS lutea* is obviously a close relative of the 'Prawn Plant' *(Drejerella,* which see). Striking in its photographs, I have found it disappointing in performance, even though I give it the warm shade and humidity it requires. My main objection is that the admittedly handsome golden bracts and white flowers last such a short time, after which the entire spike drops off completely. Nor, in spite of regular coddling, do they flower very often for me. 'Golden Candles' and 'Lollipop Plant' are its popular names.

THE PALMS
(Pahm)   PALMAE

CHRYSALIDOCARPUS lutescens
Golden Feather Palm

Though among the most popular of plants for indoor decoration, due to their elegant tropical effect, PALMS are not really suited to livingroom conditions, since they prefer a more humid atmosphere and tend to develop patchy leaves when deprived of it. Provided, however, that their leaves are sponged regularly, and they are treated to an occasional shower (either of rain or the bathroom variety) they will do well enough indoors for a few months. After this, they should be rested in a well-lit but shaded place.

Most of the Palms sold for indoor use are merely the juvenile forms of those tropical giants that may reach 30 or 40 feet in the wild (9-12 m). Even indoors their leaves soon become over-large and out of proportion.

But there are also dainty dwarf varieties, which are worth seeking out. Generally these are slow growers, and consequently hard to propagate. Their slow reproduction rate is unfortunately reflected in the very high prices dealers must charge.

Palms need as much light as they can get and plenty of fresh air whenever it is possible. Being jungle plants, they prefer a rich compost: one part garden loam, one part leaf mould and two parts fibrous peat would suit. They need plenty of fertiliser and water, for they are heavy feeders and generally need an annual re-potting in the spring. Do not fertilise for several months after re-potting.

All Palms take a winter rest, so reduce the water in cold weather. Your indoor Palms will last longer and look fresher if they can be placed outdoors for the summer in a sheltered part-sunny position, with the pots buried up to the rim.

Popular indoor Palms included in the dictionary are *Bacularia* (Walking Stick Palm), *Caryota* (Fishtail Palm), *Chamaedorea* (Bamboo Palm), *Collinia* (Neanthe or Parlour Palm), *Chrysalidocarpus* (Golden Palm), *Howea* (Kentia Palm), *Phoenix* (Pygmy Date Palm), *Rhapis* (Lady Palm), *Trachycarpus* (Japanese Fan Palm). (See also plate page 20).

PANDANUS
(pan dan' əs)   PANDANACEAE

A common sight on beaches all around the Pacific, *PANDANUS* make useful houseplants while they are fairly young. Neither pines nor palms, in spite of their popular names ('Screw Pine' and 'Walking Palm') they have two distinctive features. First they produce razor-edged leaves in a spiral arrangement around the trunk; secondly, as they mature they develop stilt-like aerial roots. For indoor use, *PAN-DANUS* demand good light and a winter temperature no less than 55°F (13°C). They grow best in a compost of loam, peat and sand, with a little charcoal and bone meal, all above a deep layer of rubble for good drainage. Water only when the compost seems dry, but then very deeply.

P. veitchii is the popular indoor species, with handsomely variegated leaves.

PANDANUS veitchii
Walking Palm

PAPHIOPEDILUM
(paf ee oh pee' də ləm)   ORCHIDACEAE

PAPHIOPEDILUM insigne Sanderae
Yellow Slipper Orchid

The popular 'Slipper Orchids', *PAPHIOPEDILUM*, are remarkably resistant both to heat and cold, except for a few definitely tropical types. They enjoy crowding in small pots. The best compost is a moisture-retaining mixture of sandy soil, ground bark and charcoal. They bloom mostly in winter or early spring, but have no resting period and can be kept moist all year. 'Paphs' (as they are often called) rarely need re-potting but should be kept in a humid shady place in the summer months, being watered often. Strip off any old yellowed leaves periodically, and check the plants for snails if you're storing them outdoors. Good species include:

PAPHIOPEDILUM lemora X April
Slipper Orchid

PAPHIOPEDILUM venustum
Slipper Orchid

P. insigne   The commoner type. Light green, blotched with brown or white and yellow in some varieties.
P. leeanum   Rich mahogany with a white-edged dorsal petal and gold-lined slipper.
P. X Maudiae   A hybrid of *P. insigne*. The white petals are striped olive, with an olive-green slipper.
P. venustum   A smaller tropical species. The blue-green foliage is distinctively marked in white. The flowers have maroon-tipped white petals striped with green and marked with blackish warts. The flower is distinctively hairy and the petals rather reflexed.

Many modern hybrids have wider, overlapping petals, and a more dramatic colouring of burgundy and white. These are greatly sought after and are quite expensive.

PARODIA
(pa roh' dee ə)   CACTACEAE

PARODIA St. Pienna
Golden Tom Thumb

Dwarf Cacti for collectors, *PARODIAS* are easily grown in a standard gritty compost. They need the usual summer water and dry winter conditions, and they'll bloom in spring, the flowers being almost as big as the plant.

Native to Argentina, these dainty but dangerous little fellows are less worried by winter cold than other Cacti. Their spines are particularly decorative, and they are best displayed in low dish plantings. Good species are:

P. aureispina   Golden flowers, white and yellow spines.
P. microsperma   Deep-gold flowers, reddish-brown spines.
P. sanguiniflora   Red flowers, white and brown spines.

PASSIFLORA
(pas i flor' ə)   PASSIFLORACEAE

Common in sub-tropical gardens, many species of 'Passionflower' make spectacular indoor plants. Try them in a sunny glassed-in balcony, or in the background of a mass planting in a window. They'll grow in 10 in (25 cm) pots of rich, loamy compost and need light support to which their climbing tendrils can become attached. Water regularly during the warm weather and fertilise when they really start to climb. 'Passionflowers' can be pruned back for shaping during the winter, and grow from cuttings. Spectacular bloomers include:

P. alato-caerulea   'Blue Passionflower'. Has pale blue petals, a violet crown and green stamens.

PASSIFLORA alato-caerulea
Blue Passionflower

PASSIFLORA coccinea
Scarlet Passionflower

P. coccinea   Scarlet petals with a white crown, green stamens. The leaves are oval and not lobed as in other species.
P. mollissima   Soft pink flowers.
P. racemosa   Deep red-pink flowers with a double crown — one purple, one red.

PEDILANTHUS
(ped ə lan' thəs)   EUPHORBIACEAE

'Ribbon Cactus', 'Devil's Backbone', 'Zig-Zag Plant', 'Red Bird', 'Jewbush' and 'Slipper Flower' — just look at the lineup of names collected by this popular West Indian plant! *PEDILANTHUS tithymaloides*

153

PEDILANTHUS tithymaloides Variegatus
Zig Zag Plant

should be seen in any warm-climate display of indoor or terrace plants. The waxy leaves are variegated and tinted with pink; the stems (often striped) are formed in a perfect zig-zag; and the flowers consist of vivid scarlet bracts like tiny red slippers. Grow it from summer cuttings, hardened thoroughly. Plant in a compost of normal loam and gritty sand over some good drainage material.

PEDILANTHUS should be given a minimum winter temperature of 55°F (13°C), and likes a rather dry atmosphere, so it is perfectly suited to wintering in heated rooms.

PELARGONIUM
(pel ə goh' nee əm)   GERANIACEAE

PELARGONIUM domesticum
Regal Pelargonium Hybrids

PELARGONIUM peltatum
Ivy-leaf Geranium

PELARGONIUM zonale
Common Geranium

Popular window plants from cottage to penthouse, *PELARGONIUMS* and 'Geraniums' are almost too well known to need any description. They prefer a soil mix that's slightly acid, but can cope with alkaline conditions as well. They like grit and quick drainage — just see them in weekend seaside gardens where they flower with minimal attention. Too much water makes them bolt to leaf; too little, and they become stunted. It's up to you to work out the happy medium. *PELARGONIUMS* mostly prefer full sun, but since house walls become hotter than the open garden, part-shade will help them colour and last better on an open terrace or balcony. Hybrids of three particular species are commonly used for pot culture. All of them grow easily from cuttings in sharp sand, taken any time of year. These three species are:

P. X domesticum 'Regal Pelargonium' or 'Martha Washington Geranium'. These are the plants universally known as *PELARGONIUMS*. They have ribbed fan-shaped leaves with toothed edges, very woody stems, and are inclined to grow leggy. The broad, open flowers (any time from spring to autumn) are richly coloured in combinations of pink, white, red, purple and mauve, mostly in the cooler tones. Each blossom is marked or centred in a contrasting tone and there are many picoteed or rayed effects. Varieties vary from country to country, but some fairly widespread ones are:

'Azalea' — rosy red, marked with crimson and pink.
'Congo' — darkest crimson, black markings.
'Deep Purple' — rich velvety purple.
'Duchess of Kent' — white, shaded purple.
'Empress of Russia' — black and rose.
'Grand Slam' — rosy red, wavy petals.
'Lavender Queen' — lavender, deep mauve markings.
'Rhapsody' — salmon-pink and maroon.
'Springtime' — soft pink, white throat and edges.
'White Cloud' — pure white.

P. X peltatum 'Ivy-Leaf Geranium'. These are especially favoured for hanging baskets and window boxes and will even climb a certain distance. They have fragrant waxy leaves like 'ivy', unmarked but occasionally variegated. They have thick and juicy trailing stems, and the flowers appear on slim stalks from stem joints. They flower virtually the entire year, and should be pruned back regularly. Popular varieties include:

'Blue Peter' — double mauve-blue.
'Claret Crousse' — cerise red flowers.
'Comtesse de Grey' — semi-double soft pink, deeper reverse.
'El Gaucho' — cerise, crimson markings; a glorious colour.
'Jeanne d'Arc' — pale lavender.
'L'Elegante' — variegated leaves, pale lilac flowers.
'Madame Crousse' — double pale pink.
'Santa Paula' — double mauve.

P. zonale 'Common' or 'Zonal Geranium'. These have thicker stems and branches than the 'Ivy-Leaf' type, are less woody than the 'Regal Pelargoniums'. The velvet-textured leaves generally have one or more horseshoe-shaped markings or zones, parallel to the edges. A number of less sturdy varieties have two, three, or four coloured leaves in many colour combinations. Like all *PELARGONIUMS* they need winter temperatures of at least 40°F (5°C), but stand up better than the others to dry indoor conditions. Destroy any leaves marked with rust spots (a fungus disease) and spray with Zineb or other fungicides. Water only occasionally in cold weather, re-pot in early spring and prune all branches back to two or three nodes to stimulate branching. New plants struck from cuttings often flower better than the old. Good varieties include:

'Apple Blossom Rosebud' — pink and white double flowers.
'Black Vesuvius' — coral-pink flowers; almost black leaves.
'Distinction' — crimson, broad zone near leaf-edge.
'Golden Harry Hieover' — red flowers, red-zoned gold leaves.
'Marechal MacMahon' — pink flowers, red-zoned gold leaves.
'Maxine Kovaleski' — orange-red flowers.
'Mrs Cox' — pink, with green, red, purple and cream leaves.
'Paul Crampel' — scarlet flowers.
'Skies of Italy' — vermilion, with green, cream, purple leaves.
'Snowflake' — pure white flowers.

PEPEROMIA
(pep ə roh' mee ə)   PIPERACEAE

PEPEROMIA *caperata*
Emerald Ripples

PEPEROMIA *maculosa*
Radiator Plant

155

PEPEROMIA obtusifolia Variegata
Peperomia

PEPEROMIA X 'Sweetheart'
Sweetheart Peperomia

PEPEROMIAS are used in terrariums, mixed planters or in shelves by a warm, sunny window. They are waxy plants with beautifully shaped and marked leaves, producing curious long-stemmed flower spikes in warm weather. Grow them in a standard houseplant mix, moist yet porous. Keep continuously damp in the warm weather, dry off in winter. They grow easily from stem cuttings and should be repotted annually. Many dozens of species are sold, but you are most likely to see:

P. caperata 'Emerald Ripples'. Pinkish stems with rippled heart-shaped leaves of dark green.
P. griseo-argentea 'Ivy Leaf Peperomia'. Similar to the above, but leaves are grey-green.
P. maculosa 'Radiator Plant'. Long oval leaves, waxy texture. Flower spikes are 12 in (30 cm) long.

P. obtusifolia 'Variegata' A shrubby type with red and green stems. Leaves cream, marked pale green.
P. sandersii 'Watermelon Peperomia'. Broad oval leaves marked exactly like a watermelon.
P. scandens 'Variegata' A trailing type. Pink stems. Grey-green and cream heart-shaped leaves.

All *PEPEROMIAS* need a minimum 50°F (10°C) in winter, and high humidity in summer. Water from below if possible, for the leaves mark easily from spraying.

PERESKIA
(pə res' kee ə)   CACTACEAE

PERESKIA aculeata
Lemon Vine

Unusual for Cacti, *PERESKIAS* produce leaves, which are unfortunately dropped should the winter temperature go below 55°F (13°C). They are grown in a compost containing equal parts of loam, sand and peat or leaf mould. Charcoal helps sweeten the soil and improve drainage. *PERESKIAS* have woody, spiny stems, are easily grown from stem cuttings and will climb, given light support. Give them plenty of water in summer, sufficient in winter only to stop the leaves wilting.

P. aculeata 'Lemon Vine' or 'Barbadoes Gooseberry'. Most often seen. It has vivid golden-yellow leaves with cerise reverses. The open Cactus flowers of pale pink or yellow are rarely seen indoors.
P. grandifolia 'Rose Pereskia'. A heartier, more upright plant with open flowers like single pink roses.

PETUNIA
(pə tyoo' nee ə)　　　　　　SOLANACEAE

PETUNIA X 'Blue Jay'
Hybrid Petunia

PETUNIAS on Paris roof garden.

Not indoor plants at all, *PETUNIAS* are still the world's most widely planted source of summer colour in a window box, hanging basket or terrace planter. Hot climate or cold, they bloom so quickly from planting out that climatic conditions can be virtually ignored. Sow the seeds as soon as you can guarantee a minimum night temperature of 50°F (10°C). Prick them out into large boxes as soon as each plant has four or more leaves. For the final planting use a compost that's half loam, half a mixture of fine leaf mould and milled manure. Sand, bone meal and a scattering of lime will really help deliver the goods. Watering should be light and the young plants must be protected from the sun till their roots are established. After that, the hotter the summer, the better they'll produce. When the long

flower shoots begin to look untidy, cut them back almost to the roots and they'll shoot and flower again.

Old-time single-bedding varieties such as *'Rosy Morn'* and *'Rose O'Day'* are still the cheapest summer colour you can buy but many splendid new hybrid types are now available, mostly Japanese or American. The *'Cascade'* types are particularly effective, with longer flowering stems to spill over the edge of boxes and baskets. My own preference for terrace use is the enormous *'White Chiffon'*, which seems to bloom for ever, and has a pronounced perfume on summer evenings.

PETUNIAS are closely related to the 'Tobaccos' (or *Nicotiana* which see) and the leaves have the same narcotic effect. In fact, the name itself comes from 'petun', a local South American name for tobacco. (See also plate page 40).

PHALAENOPSIS
(fal ae nop' səs)　　　　　　ORCHIDACEAE

PHALAENOPSIS amabilis
Moth Orchid

PHALAENOPSIS blooms hang from long arching stems, generally coloured white or delicate pink. Not so difficult to grow if you can arrange a constant winter temperature of around 60°F to 70°F (15 to 20°C), they must also be kept out of draughts. Use a coarse compost with plenty of bark or treefern chunks into which the plants can run their worm-like roots, and give plenty of water through the warm weather. They are rather sparse in growth, with only two or three large leathery leaves, and no pseudo-bulbs. Semi-shade suits them in summer, bright light in winter. *PHALAENOPSIS* may flower at any time of year except midsummer. Repotting (when absolutely necessary) may be done in early spring. The most popular species is the snow-white 'Moth Orchid', *P. amabilis*, native to Australia and nearby areas.

PHILODENDRON
(fil oh den' dr n)   ARACEAE

PHILODENDRON X 'Florida'
Florida Philodendron

PHILODENDRON hastatum
Elephant's Ear

PHILODENDRON oxycardium
Heartleaf Philodendron

PHILODENDRON X 'Redwings'
Redwing Philodendron

Popular houseplants for more than a quarter of a century, PHILODENDRONS are admired for their magnificent glossy leaves, and most (but not all) for their rampant climbing habits. In nature (Central and South America), they'll climb the tallest tree, but in your living room be content to cover a stout pole of tree fern, or a column of chicken wire stuffed with sphagnum moss. Because they originate in deep forests, PHILODENDRONS do well in quite dim interiors, and are widely used in entryways, office foyers and other places the sun never seems to reach. Grow them in pots or tubs (but not too big — crowded conditions bring out their best). These should have a deep drainage layer of brick or tile rubble; a layer of sphagnum or large leaves to prevent washaways;

and then, equal parts of sand, peat and loam with a little charcoal. Pot them up in spring, tie lightly to their support, and water lightly until the roots get a good grip. Indoors the leaves collect dust, and should be wiped down with clean water periodically.

PHILODENDRONS can be raised from cuttings and are remarkably free from pests and diseases. Over-long runners can be pruned back in warm weather and their severed ends placed in a jar of water sweetened with charcoal. There you'll find they grow just as well, and look most attractive spilling down from room dividers or kitchen shelves. The range of PHILODENDRONS is very wide, but here are a few species worth shopping for:

P. andreanum 'Velvet Vine'. Velvety heart-shaped deep olive leaves, purple on reverse.
P. bipinnatifidum 'Tree Philodendron'. A non-

PHILODENDRON *selloum*
Tree Philodendron

PHILODENDRON *warczewiczii Flava*
Golden Selloum

climbing type. Develops a trunk. Enormous 30 in (75 cm) leaves, heavily divided and lobed.
P. cannifolium   Non-climber. Leaves like an oar blade to 18 in (45 cm).
P. X 'Florida'   Shiny green leaves divided into five lobes.
P. gloriosum   Heart-shaped silky leaves, marked red and cream.
P. hastatum 'Elephant's Ear'.   Spear-shaped leaves
P. X 'Imbe'   Spear-shaped leaves, leaves red beneath. A very large grower.
P. oxycardium 'Heartleaf Philodendron'.   Dark green, heart-shaped leaves that grow bigger the taller it climbs. Long trailing stems attach themselves to walls, furniture with sticky aerial roots.
P. panduraeforme 'Fiddleleaf Philodendron'.   Leaf shape best described by its popular name.
P. X 'Redwings'   A beautiful climbing hybrid with

leaves shaped like a spearhead. All the foliage has a reddish sheen; juvenile leaves and shoots are quite red.
P. selloum   Non-climbing. Long-stalked, deeply divided leaves. Often used as architectural feature in large buildings.
P. warscewiczii Flava 'Golden Selloum'.   Very weak in chlorophyll, this beautiful plant has leaves and stems of palest lime-yellow. Difficult to propagate, hence expensive.

Though tropical in origin, most *PHILODEN-DRONS* are satisfied with average indoor temperatures. (See also plates pages 7, 10, 11, 22).

PHOENIX
(fee' niks)   PALMAE

PHOENIX *roebelinii*
Pigmy Date Palm

PHOENIX roebelinii, the 'Pigmy Date Palm', rarely grows above 4 ft (120 cm) in a pot. It has a straight, formal shape and bears delicate but tough fronds with a pendant habit. These should be stripped off as they die and discolour. *PHOENIX* needs little care, is planted in a small pot (6 in or 15 cm width is adequate). Give them as much light as you can, soak them thoroughly but let them dry out completely before rewatering. Any porous planter mix will do, and *PHOENIX* will remain happy down to 55°F (13°C) or even below.

PHRAGMIPEDILUM
(frag mə pee' dil əm)   ORCHIDACEAE

This small genus of Orchids resembles *Paphiopedilum*, (which see), but the two main petals are twisted and elongated to a length of up to 12 in (30 cm), and

PHRAGMIPEDILUM spp.
Mandarin Orchid

flowers may be borne two or three to a stem. *PHRAGMIPEDILUMS* enjoy a winter minimum temperature of 50°F (10°C) and prefer more constant humidity, but with all of that I have found them easy to grow around the house, and most eye-catching with their striped brickish-pink flowers a great contrast to the green foliage of other plants. Plant in a moist peaty mixture with plenty of charcoal and sand. Spray in warm weather. The popular name is 'Long-Tailed Slipper Orchid'.

PHYLLITIS
(fil ai' təs)   POLYPODIACEAE

PHYLLITIS scolopendrium Cristata
Hart's Tongue Fern

A curiously shaped fern from Europe and North America, *PHYLLITIS scolopendrium* is not demanding in its temperature requirements indoors. The simple fronds are curiously twisted and buckled, and grow into quite a dense plant which must ultimately be divided. Pot them in a compost that's two thirds leaf mould and one third mixed sandy loam, sand and charcoal. Native to shaded watersides, it enjoys plenty of moisture, both on roots and fronds, which will rarely exceed 12 in (30 cm) in length. Often known as the 'Hart's Tongue Fern', *PHYLLITIS* is particularly valuable indoors because it will tolerate low levels of light for weeks on end.

PHYLLOSTACHYS
(fil' oh stae kəs)   GRAMINEAE

PHYLLOSTACHYS aurea
Golden Bamboo

Handsome container plants, 'Bamboos' are easy to raise, provided you remember their continuous need for water and more water. *PHYLLOSTACHYS* may reach 15 ft (5 m) in the open garden, but rarely exceed 6 ft (2 m) in containers. These should be of at least 12 in (30 cm) diameter, and filled with a good moisture-retaining compost based on peat, leaf mould and sand, with a few chunky pieces of brick and charcoal. I get best results planting pieces of runner in early spring, just as new shoots are bursting into life — kept continuously moist, these soon root in the pot, and continue growing. A quicker effect can be gained by planting an entire clump at once, a little later in the season. But if you do this, all over-tall stems should be cut back to ground level and the entire container placed in a large tub of water so growth will not be held back. Fertilise in spring with decayed animal manure and keep up the water at all times. Spray the foliage indoors and watch out for aphis. Notable species are:

P. aurea 'Golden Bamboo'. Has golden stems on mature growth, and leaves a delicate yellow-green.
P. nigra 'Black Bamboo'. Lacy and more delicate in its appearance, 'Black Bamboo' has an arching habit and mature canes that really are a purplish-black.

PICEA
(pai see' ə)   PINACEAE

PICEA pungens 'Kosteriana'
Koster's Blue Spruce

A gem among Conifers 'Koster's Blue Spruce' comes tall and straight, a perfect Christmas tree. It is somewhat slow-growing and usually comparatively expensive, for the fine blue leaf colour can only be propagated by grafting. Grow *PICEA pungens* 'Kosteriana' in a large container of compost heavy in sand and leaf mould. Water regularly, and spray in the summer months with Malathion and White Oil as deterrent to red spider. It is entirely frost-hardy, but may suffer on an open terrace without compensating humidity. (See also plate page 43).

PILEA
(pai' lee ə)   URTICACEAE

Dwarf evergreen *PILEAS* like a moist but well-drained soil mix, semi-shaded conditions and continuous water and fertilising from spring to late summer. They are hardier than *Peperomias* (which see) and will resist winter temperatures down to 45°F (7°C), provided they are left a little on the dry side. Popular species include:

PILEA cadierei
Aluminium Plant

PILEA mollis
'Moon Valley Pilea'

P. cadierei 'Aluminium Plant'. Its distinctive bluish-green leaves are marked with parallel silver splashes. It produces delicate masses of small white summer flowers.
P. mollis 'Moon Valley' A recent success among houseplant introductions. It has deeply quilted hairy leaves of lime-green, flushed pink and veined in red. Umbels of fluffy pink flowers appear in spring and summer.
P. muscosa Forms a spreading mass of minute fern-like foliage which takes on a reddish tone in summer from its tiny red flowers. In dry conditions, these flowers visibly discharge their pollen in all directions, hence the popular name 'Artillery Plant'.
P. nummulariaefolia 'Creeping Charlie'. Forms a low

PILEA muscosa
Artillery Plant

spreading mass of tiny leaves. Makes good ground cover in terrariums.
P. *repens* 'Black Leafed Panamiga'. Has dark bronzy leaves with purplish reverses. Its summer flowers are pale green.

PINUS
(pai' nəs)   PINACEAE

PINUS thunbergii
Japanese Black Pine

Pines are scarcely indoor plants by any stretch of the imagination — but they are among the world's most popular bonsai subjects, grown in small containers of gritty sand, loam and fine leaf mould. Even when young, the dark, textured bark of many

species has an air of solid old age. The fine needle leaves are resistant to salt air, cold and heat. Pines are prone to red spider attack, and though spraying with Malathion will generally fix this minute pest, a good wash in soapy water is sometimes almost as effective. 'Pines' need regular water, but *must* have good drainage. Good bonsai species include:

P. *mugho* 'Swiss Mountain Pine'. A dwarf slow-grower with relatively small needles.
P. *densiflora* 'Japanese Red Pine'. Fine needles in dense clusters, a naturally umbrella-like shape.
P. *parvifolia* 'Japanese White Pine'. This has tiny twisted needles, borne generally in clusters of five at the end of twigs, and is very slow growing.
P. *thunbergii* 'Japanese Black Pine'. This has tough, straight needles borne in pairs, and particularly picturesque bark. (See also page 46).

PIPER
(pai' pə)   PIPERACEAE

PIPER crocatum
Saffron Pepper

PIPER (or 'Peppers') are exotic tropical vines grown for their superb leaf patternings. They also produce the small berries that become the pepper of a thousand culinary uses. This, however, rarely happens indoors, so you'll still have to visit the supermarket. Native to the tropics of Asia and South America, peppers are hot growers as well as hot producers and need a winter temperature of at least 60°F (15°C) to survive. They like bright light (not direct sun) and can be grown in any standard moist potting mix with small additions of limestone and superphosphate. Available species are:

P. *crocatum* 'Saffron Pepper'. Handsome heart-shaped leaves veined in pink and with purple reverses.

P. nigrum   Black-green leaves, more oval in shape.
P. ornatum 'Celebes Pepper'. Deep green with pale reverse, silver-pink veining.

PLATYCERIUM
(plat ə see' ree əm)   POLYPODIACEAE

PLATYCERIUM bifurcatum
Stag's Horn

PLATYCERIUM grande
Elkhorn

Often seen in cool courtyards or conservatories, *PLATYCERIUMS* can certainly be grown indoors, though they require special attention. They are completely epiphytic and must either be attached to hanging pieces of tree trunk or wired in the sides of hanging baskets. They will need to be sprayed daily in warm weather, and the entire plant soaked regularly in a tub of water. The root mass (hidden behind the shield-shaped sterile fronds) must be packed with a mixture of moist peaty compost and sphagnum. Compost, Fern and all are then bound to the hanging support with soft wire, preferably copper. After some months the Fern will grip of its own accord and the more unsightly wires can be removed. Soon, long hanging fertile fronds appear. These give the plants their popular names. Native to Australia and nearby islands as far as the Philippines, two types of *PLATYCERIUM* are commonly grown. They are:

P. bifurcatum 'Stag's Horn'. Narrow branching fronds up to 4 ft (120 cm) in length.
P. grande 'Elk Horn'.   The sterile fronds are pleated, the fertile fronds a more triangular shape, though still heavily lobed.

PLEIONE
(plə oh' nee)   ORCHIDACEAE

PLEIONE limprichtii
Indian Crocus

Dainty Asiatic Orchids, *PLEIONES* produce miniature *Cattleya*-type flowers from pseudo-bulbs the size of your fingernail. They are spring-planted in shallow containers filled with a mixture of peaty compost, sphagnum, grit and charcoal. Keep the containers constantly moist, and in semi-shade, with a minimum temperature of 50°F (10°C). Beyond that, tropical greenhouse conditions are not required, for the flowering period is over by early summer. Then the leaves will appear, two to each pseudobulb. Propagation is by offsets, detached at early spring repotting time. Species in cultivation (and which vary in few respects apart from colour) include:

P. formosana   White to mauve flowers.
P. forrestii   Rich yellow with brown markings.
P. limprichtii 'Indian Crocus'.   Reddish-pink.
P. praecox   Deep rose-pink, yellow lip.

PLEOMELE
(plee om' ə lee)   LILIACEAE

PLEOMELE *goldieana*
Fountain Plant

PLEOMELES are perennial foliage plants, grown for their dramatic leaf· colourings and drooping fountain-shaped foliage. Grow them from cuttings or suckers in any standard potting compost. Shelter from full sun and give moisture in the warmer months. Lovers of high humidity, they are best grown among other plants. Species include:

P. *augustifolia*   Cream-edged grey-green leaves.
P. *goldieana*   Silver cross-banded dull green leaves.
P. X *'Song of India'*   Leaves striped in green and creamy yellow.

PLUMERIA
(ploo mee' ree ə)   APOCYNACEAE

Fast-growing PLUMERIAS (or 'Frangipani') flourish in containers, provided they are top-dressed in early spring and given periodic fertiliser to replace nutrients washed out by regular water. Cut a firm branch (at least 18 in or 45 cm long, and preferably forked) in winter. Lay it aside in a dry place until the cut stem has callussed, then plant (with support) in a mixture of sharp, damp sand and peat moss. The PLUMERIA will burst into leaf and even flowers in a few months, but be warned — this is no guarantee of rooting success. The succulent branches contain adequate moisture reserves for such a surprising display.

Ultimately, however, the rooted and growing branches can be potted up to large permanent containers, preferably broader than they are deep. Frangipani branches from the position of last year's terminal flower clusters, sending out as many as four new shoots, so should not be pruned. Give them a

PLUMERIA *acutifolia*
Frangipani

PLUMERIA *obtusifolia*
Singapore Plumeria (State Capitol, Hawaii)

deep drainage layer (they rot easily) then fill pots with a sandy compost rich in leaf mould and a little decayed manure. Frangipanis look bare and grotesque in winter, and must be sheltered from outdoor frosts. Bring them indoors or place about your terrace as the first buds show. There are many different colour varieties.

PODOCARPUS
(poh' də kah pəs)   PODOCARPACEAE

Hardy PODOCARPUS are native to many areas of the world. They are evergreen, with tough leaves like flattened pine needles, and are greatly valued as container plants in many different climates. They are

PODOCARPUS macrophyllus
Plum Pine

most often seen pruned to formal shape, on exposed terraces or entry positions, where their natural resistance to winds and draughts makes them especially valuable. They are also used indoors, but only in proximity to windows, for they need as much light as possible and thrive in full sun. Re-pot them in an acid peaty mix only rarely, for they seem to enjoy crowded conditions. Necessary pruning should be carried out in late winter before new shoots appear. *PODOCARPUS* bear small berries and are sometimes called 'Plum Pines'.

POLYPODIUM
(pol i poh' dee əm)   POLYPODIACEAE

POLYPODIUM aureum
Hare's Foot Fern

POLYPODIUMS are showy tropical Ferns, cultivated in a moist, well-drained mixture of leaf mould, sand and sphagnum. They grow from brown creeping rhizomes, both hairy and scaly. These branch and cross each other and crawl over the sides of the container, looking like so many furry feet. That is the meaning of *POLYPODIUM* — 'many feet'. Keep them warm and sunlit in winter, shaded and cool in summer and moist at all times. The fronds, which appear at intervals along the rhizome, are simply divided, tough and leathery, and notable for the clearly visible spore casings on their undersides. Commonly seen are:

P. aureum 'Glauca' 'Hare's Foot Fern'.   Splendid fronds of a distinct blueish-green.
P. aureum Mandaianum   The fronds rippled and curled.
P. polycarpon   Yellow-green fronds.
P. subauriculatum   Fronds long and drooping.

All are popularly known as 'Polypody'.

POLYSCIAS
(pol is' kee əs)   ARALIACEAE

POLYSCIAS filicifolia
Ming Aralia

Foliage plants of the Aralia family, *POLYSCIAS* are useful indoors while young, but tend to grow straggly without the tropical heat and humidity they adore. Grow them in containers of a standard peaty mix with sand and a little charcoal, potting out in early spring. Give plenty of water in summer, little in winter and keep them out of full sun. Decorative species include:

P. balfouriana   Heart-shaped toothed leaves, light green.
P. filicifolia 'Ming Aralia'.   Leaves much divided.
P. guilfoylei var. Victoriae   The leaves lacy and finely divided, variegated white and green.

PORTEA
(por' tee ə)   BROMELIACEAE

PORTEA petropolitana Extensa
Portea

A large-growing species of Bromeliad with similar cultural requirements to *Aechmea, Billbergia,* etc. (which see), *PORTEA* grows best in a bright sunny position in a conservatory or by a large window. It should be planted in a fibrous, chunky mix and kept moist at all times to produce its spectacular rosette of leaves up to 3 ft (90 cm) across. Keep the leaf-well topped up and this splendid plant will produce heavy horizontal spikes of green and pink flowers in late summer. Minimum winter temperature of 50°F (10°C) is required and propagation is from suckers.

PORTULACARIA
(por tyoo la keə' ree ə)   PORTULACACEAE

PORTULACARIA afra
Jade Plant

Red-stemmed *PORTULACARIA* is a daintier-growing plant with far smaller, greener leaves than the other so-called 'Jade Plants' (see *Crassula*). All, however, are from South Africa, where *PORTULACARIA* is known as 'Spekboom' or 'Elephant's Food'. It is in fact relished by many animals, particularly in summer, when its succulent leaves are full of moisture. 'Spekboom' enjoys full sun, even salt air, but it rarely, if ever, produces its tiny pink flowers in a pot. Grow *PORTULACARIA* in wide containers of sandy compost enriched with leaf mould, and a deep drainage layer. Protect from freezing temperatures.

PRIMULA
(prim' yoo lə)   PRIMULACEAE

PRIMULA chinensis
Chinese Primrose

PRIMULA X Kewensis
Golden Primrose

166

PRIMULA *malacoides*
Fairy Primrose

PRIMULA *ob'conica*
Poison Primrose

PRIMULAS are woodland plants of the northern hemisphere, and many species have become indoor favourites, selling by billions every winter and spring. They are all perennial, but several, notably *P. malacoides* and *P. obconica* are treated as annuals. All enjoy a woodland compost of leaf mould, loam and sand with a little peat for moisture retention. They are potted in autumn and kept under glass, for they love cool moist conditions in their growing season. PRIMULAS are voracious feeders, revelling in a top-dressing of fine animal manure. Flower sizes are increased enormously by this special treat, and after all faded flower stems are picked off, new blossoms will appear rapidly in most species. Give them good light, but only morning or afternoon sun, and turn the pots regularly so stems grow straight and tall. Even with good care, leaves may turn yellow in the

PRIMULA X *polyantha*
Polyanthus Primrose

pot due to chemical exhaustion of the soil. This can usually be relieved by watering with half a teaspoon of ammonia to a gallon (5 litres) of water, or with diluted Epsom salts. The five best pot species for spring and winter colour are:

P. chinensis 'Chinese Primrose'. Deeply lobed hairy leaves. Flowers in pinks, reds and mauves.
P. X kewensis A charming hybrid with mealy, serrated leaves. Brilliant yellow flowers.
P. malacoides 'Fairy Primrose'. Pale green toothed leaves. Thin wiry stems of pink, white and red flowers borne in circular layers or whorls.
P. obconica 'Poison Primrose'. Very lovely, though no other plant causes more trouble to more people; the fine hairs often produce allergenic reactions on the skin and eyes. Colours white, purple and various pinks.
P. X polyantha 'Polyanthus Primrose'. This hybrid is now available in colours to suit any decor. True blues, sharp limes and warm browns have joined the older pinks, reds, yellows and whites. Most nurseries sell them potted up singly in individual colours in early spring, though this is an expensive way to buy them.

PSEUDERANTHEMUM
(syoo der ˌan' thə məm)   ACANTHACEAE

You'll find PSEUDERANTHEMUM difficult to grow without 55°F (13°C) heat in the winter. The most commonly seen species is *P. reticulatum*, the 'Golden Net Bush', from the New Hebrides. It has golden stems and bright yellow leaves with a network of green lines. The flowers are most attractive, star-shaped, snow-white, spotted with red-violet in their open throats. Raise PSEUDERANTHEMUM in warm, moist semi-shade, and bring it indoors in summer during the peak flower display.

PSEUDERANTHEMUM reticulatum
Golden Net Bush

PTERIS
(te' rəs)   POLYPODIACEAE

PTERIS ensiformis 'Evergemensis'
Silver Table Fern

Graceful small Ferns for cool places around the home or terrace, *PTERIS* need only warmth and a sandy compost-rich soil to flourish and increase naturally from spores. They are clearly identified by their wing-shaped fronds (*Pteron* = a wing), often attractively variegated. *PTERIS* are hardly only down to 55°F (13°C), and mostly need a high level of humidity to preserve their delicate fronds. Keep them away from drying heat in winter. Universally grown species include:

P. argyraea 'Silver Fern'.   Pale silvery leaves with green, lobed margins and veins.

P. cretica 'Cretan Brake'.   Deeply divided green fronds on arching stems.
P. ensiformis 'Evergemensis' 'Silver Table Fern'.   Green and silver fronds.
P. ensiformis Victoriae 'Victoria Brake'.   A delightful miniature, similar to *var. Evergemensis*, but with more white.
P. longifolia.   Simply divided fronds. This will fare better in a dry atmosphere than others.
P. tremula 'Australian Brake'.   A much larger species with rich brown stems and multiple-divided fronds up to 3 ft (90 cm) in length.

Use smaller *PTERIS* varieties in terrariums. Keep all of them out of full sun.

PUNICA
(pyoo' nik ə)   PUNICACEAE

PUNICA granatum Nana
Dwarf Pomegranate

A dainty shrub for a sunny window or terrace, the 'Dwarf Pomegranate', *PUNICA granatum 'Nana'*, rarely needs shaping to look like a perfect bonsai miniature of the fruit-bearing 'Pomegranate' tree. Best potted in a loamy soil mix with sand and leaf mould, it needs good drainage, a winter minimum of 50°F (10°C), and lots of fresh air. Water it regularly from the beginning of the growing season in early spring and fertilise with decayed animal manure to produce the orange-scarlet flowers and fruits in profusion. There are single and double varieties. Pomegranates are deciduous and generally need a little tidying up in spring.

QUAMOCLIT
(kwam' oh klit)   CONVOLVULACEAE

QUAMOCLIT lobata
Spanish Flag

QUAMOCLIT pennata
Cypress Vine

Dainty annual vines, *QUAMOCLITS* bring brilliant warm-weather colour to a sunny corner of garden rooms. Delicate in their habits, they can ramble all over large potted shrubs without damaging them in any way. Sow a few seeds in spring and they'll do their thing without any help at all from you. The popular 'Spanish Flag', *Q. lobata* (usually sold incorrectly as Mina lobata) grows easily from seed and produces long stems of tooth-shaped flowers in red and yellow, the colours of the old Spanish Empire. The dainty 'Cypress Vine', *(Q. pennata)*, has leaves of unbelievable delicacy and star-shaped cerise-scarlet flowers. These last only a day but are produced in great profusion.

RAMONDA
(rae mon' də)   GESNERIACEAE

RAMONDA myconi
Balkan Primrose

Cooler-growing than other Gesneriads, *RAMONDAS* are native to South European mountain ranges and are known as 'Balkan Primrose' or 'Pyrenean Primrose'. Grow them in shallow pots of loam, sand and leaf mould mixed with small limestone chunks to simulate their natural growing conditions. Keep them moist but never sodden, particularly in hot weather, and grow them out of full sun at all times. *RAMONDAS* quite resemble their African Violet relatives and are about the same size. The flowers are generally palest lavender, but occasionally pink or white. They appear two to six on short stems in late spring. *RAMONDA myconi* is propagated from leaf cuttings or divisions in exactly the same way as African Violet (which see). Once again, however, it does not like hot conditions.

REBUTIA
(rə byoo' tee ə)   CACTACEAE

Known as 'Crown Cactus', and from the Andes mountains, dwarf *REBUTIAS* are easy to grow in shallow dishes of gravelly compost. Their tubercles (spine-bearing bumps) are arranged in diagonal rows rather than vertical ribs, and their spring flowers appear right around the plant at ground level. Often up to 2 in (5 cm) in diameter, they are in vivid shades of scarlet, cerise and orange-yellow. *REBUTIAS* are grown in full sun with regular summer water. Species include:

R. deminuta   Orange flowers.
R. miniscula   Scarlet flowers. White spines.
R. rubriflora Orange-red flowers.   Very many spines to each areole.
R. violaciflora   Cerise flowers. Yellow-grey spines.

REBUTIA rubriflora
Orange Crown Cactus

RECHSTEINERIA
(rek stai nee′ ree ə)   GESNERIACEAE

RECHSTEINERIA cardinalis
Cardinal Flower

RECHSTEINERIAS are easier to grow than almost any other Gesneriad. Pot them up in early spring, using a standard peaty mix with sand, and leaving just the top of the circular tuber showing. Soak with water and leave to drain. When the foliage begins to appear, water and feed regularly until flowering time, when the plant can be placed near a well-lit window, providing plenty of humidity at all times. Only two species are commonly grown:

R. cardinalis 'Cardinal Flower'. Has velvety, toothed leaves. Scarlet 2 in (5 cm) tubular flowers appear in large whorls or clusters.

R. leucotricha 'Brazilian Edelweiss'. The leaves are covered in silvery white hairs. The flowers are soft coral or burnt-orange colour, and appear in whorls spaced up a tall stem.

Both species prefer a minimum temperature of 60°F (15°C), but are dormant in winter when their pots can be shut away in a warm place until spring repotting is done.

RHAPHIDOPHORA
(raf ə dof′ ə rə)   ARACEAE

RHAPHIDOPHORA aurea
Hunter's Robe

Once known as *Pothos,* then *Scindapsus,* it is now *RHAPHIDOPHORA.* With a name like that, the next change can only be for the better. So let's use the popular name everyone knows, 'Devil's Ivy'. This is one of the most versatile house-plants in the world. You can grow it up tall poles, let it hang from baskets or even pop a few stems in plain water. Off it goes, twining and vining its way around every surface in sight. 'Devil's Ivy' flourishes in any commercial peaty compost, with regular watering, and is easy to propagate from stem cuttings. The farther the plant climbs, the larger its leaves become, but indoors it will never develop the giant 3 ft (90 cm) leaves you see in tropical gardens. It loves heated home interiors in winter, provided it gets regular water. The coloured-leaf types only retain their markings in bright light, and tend to turn green as the intensity drops away from windows. Popular varieties include:

R. aurea Sometimes called 'Hunter's Robe', they have bright green leaves marbled in golden-yellow.
R. X 'Marble Queen' Leaves marbled in white. Not a strong grower.

RHAPIS
(rae' pəs)   PALMAE

RHAPIS *humilis*
Lady Palm

Why *'Lady* Palms'? Is it because they are slender,
elegant and mysterious? There are two types,
RHAPIS *humilis* and *R. excelsa* — but which is which
is, to me, the greatest mystery of all. After checking
about 30 books of botanical reference I began to
wonder if anyone knows. Both of them have trunks
from ½ to 1 in (1 to 2.5 cm) in diameter, shrouded
with mats of tough brown fibre. Each bears elegant
fan-shaped leaves consisting of from three to twen-
ty-one segments. Grow *RHAPIS* in a compost of
loam, sand and leaf mould in equal parts, with a dash
of bone meal — do not feed further for a year after
repotting, which takes place in spring each three or
four years. Give them plenty of water, a minimum
night temperature of about 50°F (10°C), and bright
light (but *never* direct sun, except in winter). Sponge
the precious leaves periodically.

RHIPSALIDOPSIS
(rip sal ə dop' səs)   CACTACEAE

Here we are playing word games again! Last time I
compiled a garden book, these jungle beauties were
called *Schlumbergera*; but the taxonomists have been
at work and now we all have to change the labels to
read *RHIPSALIDOPSIS.* Two species are commonly
grown, both with many colour varieties, and they
prefer semi-shaded conditions with plenty of
humidity. I grow mine in hanging pots on my
terrace, and use a peaty compost with plenty of leaf
mould and sand to improve the drainage. Like the
related *Epiphyllums* (which see), these leafy-looking
plants consist not of leaves at all, but flattened stems,

RHIPSALIDOPSIS *gaertneri*
Easter Cactus

RHIPSALIDOPSIS *rosea*
Pink Star Cactus

from which flowers appear at Easter in the northern
hemisphere and in spring in the southern. They need
indoor warmth in cold months, for stem segments
tend to drop when the temperature goes below
45°F (7°C). Top-dress in spring with additional leaf
mould and manure. The two principal species are:

R. gaertneri 'Easter Cactus'. Has 2 in (5 cm) scarlet
flowers, like many-pointed stars. It has several
varieties varying from a brick shade to dark red.
R. rosea 'Pink Star Cactus'. Has shorter, stubbier
stem segments, sometimes with reddish edges. The
flowers, a vivid musk-pink, have slightly reflexed
petals and often a hose-in-hose appearance. (See
plate page 33).

RHODOHYPOXIS
(roh doh hai poks' əs)   AMARYLLIDACEAE

RHODOHYPOXIS X 'Douglas'
Rose Grass

A dainty dwarf Amaryllid the RHODOHYPOXIS, or 'Rose Grass', makes a beautiful sight indoors when in bloom. Plant in shallow bulb dishes of light, sandy compost topped with fine gravel, and keep them cool but frost-free during the cold weather. The silky-haired leaves appear first, in grass-like tufts only 4 in (10 cm) high. The rose-red flowers open singly on wiry stems and are pale pink when in bud. There are several named varieties in paler shades of pink and white. RHODOHYPOXIS are not common, and must be ordered from specialist seedsmen.

RHOEO
(roh ee' oh)   COMMELINACEAE

Only one of its genus, the fascinating RHOEO spa-thacea has collected enough popular names for a whole tribe. You may know it as 'Adam and Eve', 'Boat Lily', 'Moses in the Bulrushes' or 'Moses in a Basket'. It is used mostly in sheltered indoor positions where the satiny purple leaves make a great colour contrast with lush green tropical plants. The tiny white flowers peep out of boat-shaped bracts which appear among the leaf axils. RHOEO will stay healthy in very dim light and with the most casual of watering, provided it is planted in large pots of peaty potting mix. Keep it out of dull sun, and step up the humidity in summer. Normal winter temperatures inside the home will keep it happy.

RHOEO spathacea
Moses in a Basket

ROCHEA
(roh' chee ə)   CRASSULACEAE

ROCHEA coccinea
Rochea

ROCHEA coccinea is a rather splendid South African succulent that grows well in standard gritty cactus compost. It rarely exceeds 12 in (30 cm) in height in containers, and develops many branching stems massed with four rows of triangular leaves, almost overlapping. These stems are topped with clusters of four-petalled scarlet flowers in late spring. ROCHEA loves full sun and regular water in hot weather. It is an ideal terrace or window plant.

ROSA
(roh′ zə)   ROSACEAE

ROSA minima 'Over the Rainbow'
Fairy Rose

ROSA minima spp.
Miniature Rose Garden

Perfect miniatures of garden roses, the many hybrids of ROSA chinensis 'Minima' (the 'Fairy Rose') are now available in bush, standard or climbing form, just like their big relatives. Grow them in any pot with drainage holes, using a loamy soil mixture and sand for added drainage. Keep them watered regularly and feed twice a month in spring and summer. What a delight on a breakfast table — even on your desk at work if the light's good enough. Prune lightly in winter, and feed to push the new growth in early spring. Keep them in a sunny, airy spot and watch for red spider, signalled by sudden leaf drop. This scourge of indoor plants is best controlled by a thorough spraying with Malathion, but make sure you do it out of doors — the smell is awful.

'Fairy Roses' are now available in the entire range of rose colours and even multicolours like 'Baby Masquerade' and 'Over the Rainbow'. The shrub types grow from 4 to 15 in (10 to 38 cm) according to variety, many of them being available in a choice of standard grafts with 6, 12 or 18 in (15, 30 or 45 cm) stems. The baby climbing roses normally reach around 3 ft (90 cm) and need light, decorative support. You can plant miniature rose gardens or grow them under glass, as the pictures show. (See also page 35).

RUELLIA
(roo el′ ee ə)   ACANTHACEAE

RUELLIA macrantha
Christmas Pride

Better known as winter-flowering greenhouse plants in the northern hemisphere, where they are sometimes called 'Christmas Pride', the glowing RUELLIAS are splendid indoor and terrace subjects in milder areas and in the southern hemisphere. Grow them from spring cuttings, pinched back to force bushy growth. They'll need semi-shade through the hot weather, plenty of moisture, and a periodic application of liquid fertiliser to hurry their growth along. Follow the growing instructions for Drejerella and Eranthemum (which see).

RUELLIA macrantha needs a cold-weather minimum of 50°F (10°C) and as much winter sun as it can get to force the flower production. The blooms when they open, are around 2½ in (6cm) in diameter, and are quilted in texture. They are coloured a delicious violet-pink, the throat marked in gold and vivid cyclamen. Repot them and prune back in early spring by all means, but the best display will come from newly struck cuttings.

173

SAINTPAULIA
(saent poŕ lee ə)   GESNERIACEAE

SAINTPAULIA *ionantha*
African Violet

SAINTPAULIA X *'Rochford Purple'*
African Violet

I sometimes wonder whether 'African Violets' (or *SAINTPAULIAS*) are not a great deal tougher than the experts tell us. I've read all about them being watered from below with warm water, sheltered from full sun and from draughts. But one year, a friend looked after my house while I was vacationing, and when I returned, the 'violets' were flowering as never before. He had been soaking them in a kitchen sink full of cold water, leaves and all — then standing them in a sunny window to dry out.

I also know an elderly lady who lives by the seafront. *She* grows her *SAINTPAULIAS* on an open verandah table, where they get cold wind and salt air for much of the year. She also hoses them when they dry out from the sun. They are magnificent.

So if you think I avoid giving any definite advice about these delightful plants, you're right.

I find them easy to propagate from leaf cuttings, which I cut off cleanly and stick among a layer of pebbles on top of a moist sand and peat mixture. This is so the leaves themselves don't touch the moist compost and rot.

I won't attempt to recommend any particular varieties, for these days there are several thousand, and I always seem to lose the labels. My own preference is for the original dark-leafed types with rich purple flowers (like the illustrated *'Rochford Purple')*, or for the white varieties picoteed with mauve. But there is also a wide range of pinks, reds, blues and cerises. These may be double, semi-double or single. Their velvety leaves are plain or variegated; sometimes smooth, sometimes ruffled.

The thing I dislike most is seeing each variety of *SAINTPAULIA* in its own pot — I find them happier massed about old semi-rotted pieces of wood, in simulation of their natural homes in tropical Africa. (See plates pages 35, 37, 116).

SALVIA
(sal' vee ə)   LABIATAE

SALVIA X *'Bonfire'*
Bonfire Salvia

Apart from the culinary herb 'sage' (*SALVIA officinalis*), this scarlet-flowered perennial is the only *SALVIA* to be grown in containers. Warm climate and cold, the fiery blossoms of 'Bonfire Salvia' are seen in window boxes, terrace planters and tubs of every kind. A summer bloomer in nature, it can be forced into producing winter flowers if you keep up a minimum temperature of 55°F (13°C). For winter bloom, the growing plants are plunged, pot and all, into a large box of sand over summer, and any flower buds religiously pinched off. As the weather cools down, bring them indoors and feed weekly with weak liquid fertiliser until new buds form.

For summer use, plant either seedlings or rooted cuttings in containers of well-drained sandy compost. Water and fertilise regularly and pinch out new growth to force branching and heavier flower yield. *S. splendens* is a native of Brazil and may suffer badly outdoors in cold weather — for this reason it is customary to raise fresh plants from autumn cuttings.

SANCHEZIA
(san chez' ee ə)   ACANTHACEAE

SANCHEZIA nobilis glaucophylla
Sanchezia

SANCHEZIA is grown for its splendid ornamental leaves, which are golden-green with vivid red ribs and strongly resemble the related *Aphelandra*, both in size and markings. Raise it in deep containers of standard peaty compost, from midsummer cuttings struck in sharp sand. This is an annual process because the plant is grown for foliage alone and becomes leggy after the first season. It can, however, be allowed to produce stunning heads of tubular yellow flowers and red bracts. *SANCHEZIA* is from the jungles of Ecuador, and suffers badly in temperatures below 55°F (13°C). It signals this by dropping its leaves. Humidity should be kept up at all times and regular water and liquid fertiliser given throughout the hot months.

SANSEVIERIA
(san sev ee eə' ree ə)   LILIACEAE

Like the *Aspidistra* to which it is related, the ubiquitous 'Mother-in-Law's-Tongue' will survive an astonishing degree of neglect and lack of water.

SANSEVIERIA hahnii 'Golden'
Golden Birds Nest

SANSEVIERIA trifasciata 'Laurentii'
Mother-in-Law's Tongue

Plant them in groups in broad containers filled with a rich peaty compost. This should have a deep layer of pot rubble for super drainage. The *SANSEVIERIAS* should be watered regularly, but allowed to dry out before the next soaking. Soon, they will send up fresh new leaves as suckers from various points in the root system. All leaves should be misted occasionally, for they love humidity and abhor being coated with dust.

It may come as a surprise to learn that they produce stems of delightful flowers during the warm weather. These look like pale greenish-white tuberoses, and have a faint fragrance. *SANSEVIERIAS* come in many species, with varying leaf shapes and colourings, and several types can be grouped together for a more interesting effect. Worthwhile varieties include:

SANSEVIERIA trifasciata flower
Mother-in-Law's Tongue

S. hahnii Leaves in a small rosette about 6in (15 cm) high. Dark green with gold markings.
S. hahnii X 'Golden' Rosette almost completely gold with darker markings.
S. trifasciata Stiff 24 in (60 cm) Sword-like leaves, cross-banded with yellow and green.
S. trifasciata 'Laurentii' As above, but with rich cream borders down each side of the leaves.

All species do best with a minimum winter temperature of 55°F (13°C).

SARCOCHILUS
(sah koh kai' ləs)   ORCHIDACEAE

SARCHOCHILUS falcatus
Orange Blossom Orchid

SARCOCHILUS fitzgeraldii
Pink Orange Blossom

Most beloved of Australia's native Orchids, SAR-COCHILUS of the moist coastal valleys are now widely cultivated in many temperate parts of the world. They spread by means of white worm-like aerial roots and are fairly easy to establish on old sections of tree trunk, shallow pots of treefern chunks, or fibre and charcoal. SARCOCHILUS love moisture, and should be sprayed regularly and kept damp and shaded the entire year. The evergreen SARCOCHILUS species produce clusters of shiny, sickle-shaped leaves and arching stems of strongly perfumed 1 in (2.5 cm) flowers in spring. These include:

S. falcatus 'Orange Blossom Orchid'. White flowers, gold-marked lip.
S. fitzgeraldii White flowers, spotted cerise.

SASA
(sah' zə)   GRAMINEAE

Not all 'Bamboos' produce tall cane-like growth (see *Phyllostachys*). The SASAS are a dwarf genus with fine arching stems and handsome bamboo leaves, often variegated. These are hardy plants; and although deciduous in cold weather, they can be relied on to produce fresh new growth in spring. SASA make attractive subjects for indoor planters. They are propagated from root divisions planted in very early spring in containers of moist peaty mix with a little sand, and need plenty of water right through the growing season. In time, the pot may become overcrowded and the loose wiry effect of the slender stalks may be lost. That is the time to prune, thinning out the stems at soil level, to make an interestingly spaced pattern.

SASA japonica
Dwarf Bamboo

S. fortunei   Has green and white striped leaves.
S. japonica   Has glossy green and gold striped leaves.

SAXIFRAGA
(saks' i frae gə)   SAXIFRAGACEAE

SAXIFRAGA sarmentosa
Roving Sailor

What shall we do with a 'Roving Sailor'? Pot him up in a well drained compost of sand, loam and leaf mould and let him have his head! These charmers, botanically named *SAXIFRAGA sarmentosa*, produce rosettes of long-stemmed furry leaves veined with

silver-grey and with rosy-pink reverses. They send out fine red runners from which new plants develop, much along the lines of the common Strawberry. These baby plants can be detached and potted up, or allowed to hang suspended over the side of the container. As can be imagined, they are most attractive in hanging baskets. In late spring, and if they are kept constantly moist, the *SAXIFRAGAS* produce slender 12 in (30 cm) stems of dainty white and pink raggedy flowers. 'Roving Sailor' or 'Strawberry Geranium' is native to Japan, becomes very untidy in hot summers and needs a winter minimum of about 50°F (10°C).

SCHIZANTHUS
(shi zan' thəs)   SOLANACEAE

SCHIZANTHUS pinnatus
Poor Man's Orchid

Delicate, lacy plants, *SCHIZANTHUS* are used for indoor colour in late spring and summer, but require a great deal of attention to raise to good flowering condition. They are gradually potted up to larger-sized containers, using a compost of sand, loam and leaf mould with a little bone meal. This is done in three stages, and the plants thoroughly pinched back each time, several weeks *after* they have become established in the new containers. This is to encourage a densely branched habit and maximum flower display — without it, the delicate *SCHIZAN-THUS* seedlings grow very leggy and just flop. Known as 'Poor Man's Orchid', and natives of Chile, they do not like extremes of summer heat and humidity and must be watered carefully to avoid damping off 50°F (10°C) is quite high enough as a winter temperature.

Strictly annual, they should be discarded after flowering.

SCINDAPSUS
(skin dap′ səs)   ARACEAE

SCINDAPSUS pictus Argyraeus
Satin Pothos

Once classed in the same generic group as the more spectacular *Rhaphidophora* (which see), the slower-growing 'Silver Vine' has quite a different appearance. It is known botanically as *SCINDAPSUS pictus 'Argyraeus'*, and the leaves have a matte satiny look about them, and are more definitely heart-shaped. They are a dull green, delicately blotched with soft silver-grey, and have curved, pointed tips. They use the same compost as other Aroids, and climb walls or stakes easily with short aerial roots.

SEDUM
(see′ dəm)   CRASSULACEAE

SEDUMS have more than three hundred listed species, native to the northern hemisphere. Many are remarkably resistant to winter temperatures, and also suited to pot culture on an open balcony or sunny window, where conditions are very hot in summer. Grow them in poor quality, sandy compost with perfect drainage. Give regular water but allow to dry out between soakings. *SEDUMS* are very easy to propagate, for the tiniest dropped fragment will fight for survival and send out roots. Useful and popular species include:

S. acre 'Yellow Stonecrop' or 'Gold Moss Sedum'.   Popular in the crevices of stone-paved terraces, and needs no soil beyond what it collects from wind-borne debris. It has slim fleshy leaves, and blazing heads of yellow flowers in late spring.
S. morganianum 'Burro's Tail'.   Develops dense rope-like stems of fleshy, conical leaves. It is grown in hanging containers. Large clusters of

SEDUM adolphii
Stonecrop

SEDUM morganianum
Burro's Tail

SEDUM pachyphyllum
Propeller Plant

pinkish flowers appear at the end of the tails in summer.

S. pachyphyllum   Blue-grey leaves, somewhat spade-shaped. Bears yellow flowers in spring.

S. rubrotinctum 'Jelly Beans' or 'Coral Beads'. Develops a mass of juicy jellybean leaves that turn bright red in full sun. The yellow starry flowers are borne in late spring.

S. sieboldii 'Japanese Stonecrop'.   Has greyish flat leaves arranged in threes. Heads of pinkish flowers appear in autumn. The variety *'Medio-variegata'* is a popular basket plant, its leaves splashed with gold.

SELENICEREUS
(se len ə see' ree əs)   CACTACEAE

SELENICEREUS pteracanthus
Queen of the Night

Beautiful and fragrant flowers that open in the dead of night are the principal charm of fascinating *SELENICERUS*. Grow them as you would a prize Philodendron — in a large pot with a rough-textured branch or pole for climbing support. The ideal soil mixture is well-drained, with plenty of brick rubble and leaf mould. Water lightly in the cold weather; as much as you can in spring and summer. Keep them where you'll be sure to catch the unbelievable flower display — it's for one night only, and the flowers close at dawn. *SELENICEREUS* are easily propagated from stem cuttings, dried off a day or two before planting in sandy soil. Many species are grown:

S. boeckmannii   White 8 in (120 cm) flowers, yellow-green sepals.

S. grandiflorus   7 in (18 cm) flowers, white inside, delicate salmon-pink outside.

S. pteracanthus 'Queen of the Night'.   Fragrant white flowers, 12 in (30 cm) in diameter. Reflexed reddish sepals.

S. wercklei   Twelve-ribbed stems, spineless. White fragrant flowers.

Though tough plants, *SELENICEREUS* are truly tropical and will need protection from temperatures below 55°F (13°C).

SEMPERVIVUM
(sem' per vai vəm)   CRASSULACEAE

SEMPERVIVUM arachnoideum
Cobweb Houseleek

SEMPERVIVUM X 'Wayland'
Red Houseleek

Dainty sun-loving succulents from the Mediterranean area, *SEMPERVIVUMS* are remarkably resistant to harsh conditions, and are a great success on windy terraces or in shallow dish gardens filled with stones and just enough compost to root in. They are really easy to propagate. Just pull away a small leaf

179

rosette and stick it on some soil. So long as it stays right way up it will form roots and begin to multiply, the baby new leaf rosettes appearing from underneath the leaves of the old. That's where the popular name 'Hen and Chickens' comes from. Mature rosettes of *SEMPERVIVUM* send up relatively tall stems of flowers in midsummer, after which the parent plant dies. Some of the best species are:

S. arachnoideum 'Cobweb Houseleek'. This has tiny rosettes in many shades of red and green, the leaves spanned by masses of white cobweb-like threads. Red summer flowers.
S. calcareum Blue-grey leaves, tipped brown.
S. montanum Dark small leaves, densely haired. Flowers white or purplish-blue.
S. tectorum 'Hen and Chickens'. Very variable. It may grow large rosettes up to 6 in (15 cm) in diameter. The flowers are mostly pink with some mauve tones.

Regular water but perfect drainage is the rule with *SEMPERVIVUMS*. Try planting a collection in a terracotta strawberry jar.

SENECIO
(se nes' ee oh)   COMPOSITAE

SENECIO cruentis
Cineraria

The enormous variety of daisy-flowered plants called *SENECIO* make splendid garden subjects — but very few have achieved popularity as indoor plants. Those that have are not fussy as to soil (light and sandy, with leaf mould) and, with the exception of *SENECIO cruentis*, they all enjoy full sun. With the same exception, they are propagated from midsummer cuttings struck in sharp sand. The *SENECIOS* for indoor use are:

SENECIO cineraria
Dusty Miller

SENECIO jacobsenii
Wax Daisy

S. articulatus 'Candle Plant'. This is a succulent type with bluish jointed stems — rather like a spineless cactus. It has sparse, fern-like grey leaves and pale yellow summer daisy flowers.
S. cineraria 'Dusty Miller'. This handsome perennial with deeply divided silver leaves, is often used for terrace or window box planting. It is valued principally for foliage contrast.
S. cruentis 'Cineraria'. This is a winter-flowering annual raised from seed and sold annually in pots, ready to bloom. It needs regular feeding from early autumn, and flowers best in sheltered positions with morning sun. The dazzling flower colours include blue, purple, red, pink, brick and white, often with contrasting centres.
S. jacobsenii A sprawling succulent plant suited to hanging baskets. The fleshy stems are packed with

spoon-shaped, upward-pointing leaves that colour at various times of the year.

S. mikanoides 'German Ivy'. This is a climbing plant for conservatories, sunny windows or warm terraces. It demands a winter minimum of 45°F (7°C), has leaves exactly like Ivy and pale lemon daisy flowers in spring and summer.

S. rowleyanus 'String of Beads'. This is more of a novelty than anything else, grown in hanging baskets by collectors of unusual plants. It has long wiry stems connecting a series of bead-like leaves.

SETCRAESEA
(set krae' see ə)   COMMELINACEAE

SETCRAESEA purpurea
Purple Heart

SETCRAESEA purpurea (the 'Purple Heart') is closely related to *Callisia, Tradescantia* and *Zebrina* (which see). Propagated from pieces of jointed stem that snap off easily, it grows best in a moist, peaty compost with sand for drainage, needs plenty of water in warm weather and prefers warm humid conditions. *SETCRAESEA'S* handsome leaves are a curious violet-green with royal purple undersides, and are covered with fine silky hairs. The leaves overlap in the manner of *Dracaenas,* each new one appearing from the centre of the old. *SETCRAESEA* contrasts dramatically with white pots and is successful in hanging containers. Avoid watering on top of the leaves, which mark badly.

SIDERASIS
(sid ə rae' səs)   COMMELINACEAE

SIDERASIS is of tropical origin and needs a rich peaty compost and moisture at all times. It really does best in a greenhouse of 60°F (15°C), but can be

SIDERASIS fuscata
Brown Spiderwort

used in large terrariums where the humidity is high. An almost stemless plant, it bears magnificent 8 in (20 cm) leaves. These are velvety-green with a broad silver stripe and crimson reverse; the whole top surface is covered densely with crimson hairs. Three-petalled violet-blue flowers appear on short stems in warm weather.

SINNINGIA
(sə nin' jee ə)   GESNERIACEAE

SINNINGIA speciosa Hybrid
Gloxinia

As the Cyclamen is to winter, the velvety *SINNINGIA* is to summer — the most exciting and popular of flowering indoor plants. Tubers are started in early spring in pots of peaty humus mixed with sharp sand and should be watered with a light hand until leaf growth appears. *SINNINGIAS* are usually called 'Gloxinia', and may be propagated from slices of tuber with a growing eye, or from leaf cuttings like African Violets (which see). Modern Gloxinia flowers have an open trumpet shape and are in shades of scarlet, crimson, purple, blue, pink and white, usually with contrasting throats. Some types are double, some finely marbled or mottled. After blooming, water is reduced and the tubers are stored in their pots in a cool dark place over the winter months. A window display of individually potted Gloxinias will last for many weeks with' regular water and removal of old flower stems. They often form part of the Christmas decorations in the southern hemisphere.

SMITHIANTHA
(smith ee an' thə)   GESNERIACEAE

SMITHIANTHA Hybrid
Temple Bells (Photo: Hamlyn Library)

Grown from small rhizomes like *Achimenes* (which see), *SMITHIANTHAS* are potted up in spring in a standard peaty houseplant mix and kept moist until the first leaves appear late in the season. Then step up water and fertiliser until the flowering period in late summer. *SMITHIANTHAS* (or 'Temple Bells') form pyramids of large velvety leaves with a purple sheen. The flowers are long hanging bells in shades of scarlet, orange, yellow, pink and cream, often with spotted throats. They appear in tall, branched spikes up to 24 in (60 cm) in height. *SMITHIAN-THAS* like humid warmth, with a winter minimum of 60°F (15°C). They are brought into the drier indoor conditions only when about to flower.

SOBRALIA
(so brae' lee ə)   ORCHIDACEAE

SOBRALIA macrantha
Bamboo Orchid

SOBRALIAS (the 'Bamboo Orchid') can be raised anywhere, if you guarantee them a winter temperature of 55°F (13°C). They grow rapidly from a clump of large fleshy roots potted up in a porous mixture of broken pots and brick rubble, charcoal or old grass sods, mixed with sand and sphagnum moss. Give them plenty of water through the warm weather and they'll send up tall reed-like stems to about 3 ft (90 cm). The showy Cattleya-like blooms appear at the end of these, lasting only a few days. The flowers may become a deep purplish-pink, white or yellow according to species.

SOLANUM
(so lah' nəm)   SOLANACEAE

The genus, which includes the edible Potato and Eggplant, is represented indoors by the showy 'Jerusalem Cherries'. They are woody sub-shrubs with dark green leaves of a slightly wavy appearance. Small white potato-flowers appear in summer profusion and are followed by ½ in (1 cm) berries. Yellow at first, they ripen to orange and red during the cold weather. They make popular Christmas decorations in the northern hemisphere and may be pruned back and repotted in early spring. Two species are grown:

S. capsicastrum   Smooth wavy leaves, slightly hairy stems.
S. pseudocapsicum   Velvety leaves, hairless stems, a slightly stronger growing plant.

Both are known as 'Winter', 'Christmas' or 'Jerusalem Cherry'.

SOLANUM pseudocapsicum
Jerusalem Cherry

SONERILA
(son ə ree' lə) MELASTOMATACEAE

SONERILA margaritacea
Frosted Sonerila

Small perennials from Southeast Asia, *SONERILAS* really need humid glasshouse conditions for their summer leaf display. *SONERILA margaritacea* is the most popular, a dwarf grower with reddish stems, and leaves exquisitely marked with silvery-green between the dark olive veinings of the upper surface. The reverses are palest pink shaded green, with purple-red veins. The rosy-pink blooms are borne in many-flowered clusters in summer. *SONERILAS* demand a winter minimum of 55° (13°C), and protection from summer sun. They are potted in a rich mix of peat, sphagnum or leaf mould

and sand. As the leaves colour best on young plants, it is customary to raise fresh plants of *SONERILA* from tip-cuttings each spring.

SOPHRONITIS
(sof ron ai' təs) ORCHIDACEAE

SOPHRONITIS grandiflora is a delightful small-growing epiphytic orchid from Brazil — but as it is found at high altitudes, it is more easily managed than many of the other South American beauties. It grows from a mass of dwarf 1 in (2.5 cm) pseudobulbs, each bearing one leaf. The flowers, a vivid scarlet, appear on short stems in winter or early spring, from the junctions of pseudobulbs and leaves. *SOPHRONITIS* enjoy a moist atmosphere and are frequently grown in chunky, free-draining composts of osmunda fibre, tree-fern, fir bark and charcoal. They may also be grown wired to slabs of tree fern into which they soon send roots, and do well with a winter minimum temperature of 45°F (7°C).

If containers are used, annual re-potting is to be avoided, because the plants are already flowering when they start the year's growth. Instead, remove faded foliage and bulbs as gently as possible, and top dress the whole container with orchid fibre, a little leaf mould and a sprinkling of dried animal manure.

Grow *SOPHRONITIS* in low orchid pots or shallow hanging baskets and give them maximum humidity. (See plate page 149).

SPATHIPHYLLUM
(spath' ə fil əm) ARACEAE

SPATHIPHYLLUM X 'Clevelandii'
Peace Lily

183

SPATHIPHYLLUM wallisii
White Sails

Frequently mistaken for *Anthuriums* (which see) the *SPATHIPHYLLUMS* are in fact a much less delicate genus, capable of surviving great extremes of temperature short of frost. Always green or white in colouring, the 'Arum'-style flowers appear at almost any time and last up to several months on the plant. *SPATHIPHYLLUMS* grow well in a standard peaty mix, and should be repotted each spring. Raise them in a warm sheltered position, and give plenty of water without flooding in the warm weather. They survive in the most unlikely places around the house where the level of indirect light is very low, and tend to look very tired in full sun. The shining spear-shaped leaves rise directly from the roots and stay fresh and glossy all year with an occasional fresh water sponging.

S. X Clevelandii 'Peace Lily'. Probably a hybrid, and may reach 3 ft (90 cm) in height. The leaves are very dark green.
S. wallisii 'White Sails'. A dwarf 12 in (30 cm) species.

SPREKELIA
(sprə kee' lee ə)   AMARYLLIDACEAE

Native to Mexico, the 'Aztec Lily', *SPREKELIA*, makes a really spectacular pot specimen. Pot them up in early spring, just showing above the compost of loam, leaf mould, decayed manure and bone meal. Water and set aside in a sheltered place until roots have had time to develop, then keep them continually moist until the flower spikes appear. This usually (but not invariably) takes place before the leaves. *SPREKELIAS* enjoy bright light, but not full sun — their flowering period is considerably prolonged by leaving them in a cool indoor position. They resent disturbance

SPREKELIA formosissima
Aztec Lily

and need repotting only every third year at the most frequent. The glowing crimson flowers may be as much as 5 in (13 cm) deep and are shaped something like a classic *Fleur-de-Lys*.

STANHOPEA
(stan hoh' pee ə)   ORCHIDACEAE

STANHOPEA wardii
Leopard Orchid

The 'Leopard Orchid', *STANHOPEA*, is suitable for basket culture only, for the gigantic flowers appear right through the bottom of the container! Wire basket frameworks are best lined with a thick layer of soft sphagnum moss, then filled with a compost of bark chips, treefern chunks, charcoal and fibre, among which the root mass is placed. The entire basket is then thoroughly soaked and hung securely in a warm, bright place. I've found *STANHOPEAS* are quite happy in a shadehouse with a winter night temperature of about 40°F (5°C), for the plants are then dormant. As the weather warms up they are moved to a humid position indoors with good ventilation.

STANHOPEAS flower mostly in summer, their curious blossoms reminding one of squids moving slowly under water. They are coloured creamy yellow with brown spots and markings and have a thick, waxy lip.

STAPELIA
(sta pee' lee ə)   ASCLEPIADACEAE

STAPELIA nobilis
Starfish Flower

The truly remarkable *STAPELIA* or 'Starfish Flower' smells very faintly of dead meat, and appears in summer clusters from velvety four-sided stems. Grow *STAPELIAS* in pots of porous gritty compost and remember that regular light watering must be observed — too much and they may rot, too little and they shrivel in hot weather. Because of the smell problem you're unlikely to grow them in the living area, but they are ideal plants for a terrace or balcony with just a little overhead protection from the hottest summer sun. Two species are:

S. nobilis The flowers, up to 9 in (23 cm) across, are a light tan in colour and marked across the five petals with parallel purplish lines, the whole covered with red hairs. The fleshy stems are bluish-green.
S. variegata The flowers are pale yellow marked with regular patterns of purplish spots. The stems are faintly marked in the same colour. A smaller plant.

STEPHANOTIS
(stef ə noh' təs)   ASCLEPIADACEAE

STEPHANOTIS floribunda
Madagascar Chaplet Flower

STEPHANOTIS flowers are as sweetly scented as those of *Stapelia* are evil-smelling — and yet they are closely related. Grow the splendid 'Madagascar Chaplet Flower' in a sunroom or conservatory in large containers of standard peaty potting mix with a solid layer of drainage material, and water well all year except in the depths of winter. It is a twining plant, twisting around its supports and producing dark green waxy leaves at regular intervals. The flower clusters appear from the leaf axils — snowy-white tubular bells with flaring petals. Long-lasting and deliciously perfumed, they appear over a long period in summer. *STEPHANOTIS* are propagated from spring cuttings struck with bottom heat and the plants are best renewed in this way every three years. Malagasy is their home, and 50°F (10°C) their minimum winter temperature.

STERNBERGIA
(stern berg' ee ə)   AMARYLLIDACEAE

The dainty 'Autumn Crocus', *STERNBERGIA*, is related to the giant *Hippeastrum* and shines with a golden light in the autumn. Bulbs are potted up in spring over a deep layer of drainage material. Pots are then filled with a compost of light sandy loam mixed with leaf mould and a handful of crushed lime-stone. Plant the bulbs about 1 in (2.5 cm) below soil level, water well and keep in a dim place until roots are established. Like many autumn-flowering bulbs. *STERNBERGIAS* like to be baked in summer with just occasional water. As the temperature drops, step up the water and both leaves and crocus-like flowers will appear simultaneously.

STERNBERGIA *lutea*
Autumn Crocus

STRELITZIA
(stre lit' zee ə)   MUSACEAE

STRELITZIA *parvifolia*
Bird of Paradise

STRELITZIAS flower just as well in containers as in the open garden, though they are essentially sun-loving plants. Grow them on your balcony or terrace in large pots (they have enormous root systems) using a rich, loamy compost and a little bone meal. Plant them out in spring and water regularly throughout the warm months. They will begin to flower in summer, sending up reddish stems from 18 in to 5ft (45 to 150 cm) in length, according to species. These finally develop into an erect series of orange and blue petals, like the crest of an exotic bird. STRELITZIAS are warm-climate plants and must have winter minimum of 55°F (13°C). There

are several species with identical flowers but quite different leaf shapes, they are all known as 'Bird of Paradise'.

S. juncifolia The leaf stems are elongated like a bull-rush, with merely the slightest suggestion of leaf at the end.
S. parvifolia Long leaf stems with paddle-shaped leaves at the end.
S. reginae The large leaves are completely paddle-shaped.

STREPTOCARPUS
(strep tə kah' pəs)   GESNERIACEAE

STREPTOCARPUS Hybrid
Cape Primrose

'Cape Primroses' are unjustly neglected for indoor use, for they flourish any place you grow Gloxinias, to which they are closely related. Young plants are potted up in early in containers of standard peaty mix or special African Violet mix. Keep them in bright light, water and feed regularly with diluted fertiliser as the leaves begin to grow. Modern STREPTOCARPUS are hybrids of original species from Africa and Asia and bloom in summer. The flowers are very similar to Gloxinias but borne several to a long stem. They come in many shades of mauve, magenta and rose and make a marvellous warm-weather display in a sunny window.

STROBILANTHES
(stroh bil an' thəs)   ACANTHACEAE

STROBILANTHES remain attractive only with a minimum winter temperature of about 55°F (13°C). The leaves will discolour and drop if it gets too cold

STROBILANTHES gossipiinus
Persian Shield

STROMANTHE sanguinea
Red Rain

—so if you can't keep them warm, don't grow them. *STROBILANTHES* are propagated from heeled cuttings struck in sharp sand, in the warmer months. Many indoor gardeners raise new plants each year, for that way the leaf colour is better. Grow them in a standard peaty indoor compost, with sand for drainage, water regularly and feed twice a month with a leaf-fertiliser like Aquasol.

S. dyerianus   Has 6 in (15 cm) toothed spear-shaped leaves that appear to have been brushed with iridescent red-violet.
S. gossipiinus   Mixes the violet leaf colour with lime and olive.
S. isophyllus   A hardier relative, more usually known as 'Goldfussia'. It has smaller red-purple leaves and pale lavender flowers in warm-weather profusion.

STROMANTHE
(stroh man' thee)   MARANTACEAE

STROMANTHES need humid warmth and semi-shade, with a mimimum winter temperature of around 50°F (10°C). The Brazilian species called *STROMANTHE sanguinea* is the most commonly seen. It grows to about 4 feet (120 cm) away from the tropics, producing stiff, branching stems of handsome spear-shaped leaves. These are glossy olive-green with lighter ribs above, a rich red-purple beneath. In late spring the taller branches develop many-stemmed flower heads. The tiny white flowers are quite overwhelmed by the mass of vivid scarlet bracts. Individual flowers are short-lived, but the head blooms over many weeks.

STRONGYLODON
(stron gil' ə don)   LEGUMINOSAE

STRONGYLODON macrobotrys
Jade Vine

Native to the Philippines, the magnificent 'Jade Vine' is a challenge to plant lovers outside tropical climates, for it really must have a winter minimum temperature of 60°F (15°C). I have seen it growing in large tubs on terraces in Hawaii and the Far East, and what a sight it is! It has thick woody stems and leaves like *STEPHANOTIS* (which see), but long hanging heads of superb sickle-shaped flowers of a colour unique in the entire plant world — soft jade green

187

lined with vivid turquoise. *STRONGYLODON macrobotrys* needs strong support for its twining stems and a rich peaty compost with plenty of water. It is propagated both from cuttings and seeds, but the latter are viable only for about two weeks after the pod has ripened.

SYNADENIUM
(sin ə den' ee əm)   EUPHORBIACEAE

SYNADENIUM grantii
African Milkbush

A curious shrub from Tanzania, *Synadenium grantii* is very suited to growing on sunny terraces of warm areas, although it needs winter protection below 50°F (10°C). It has more than a passing resemblance to *Plumeria*, with thick-branched stems and similarly shaped waxy leaves. The leaves however, are apple-green with darker veins and minutely toothed red margins. *SYNADENIUM* bears flattish heads of small dark red flowers in summer. The popular name, 'African Milkbush', refers to the thick milky sap, which is irritating to many people. Grow it in large pots of well-drained sandy loam, with a good layer of drainage material.

SYNGONIUM
(sin goh' nee əm)   ARACEAE

Formerly known as *Nephthytis*, these attractive tropical climbers have much in common with *Philodendrons*. They are happy indoors with filtered light, humidity and warm winter conditions, and should be grown in a compost of loam, peat and

SYNGONIUM podophyllum
Arrowhead

SYNGONIUM wendlandii
Nephthytis

sand. Though climbers in nature, *SYNGONIUMS* sometimes develop a self-heading habit or decide to run along the ground rooting at intervals. Their juvenile leaves are usually of a simple arrow shape, and quite different from the leaves of mature plants, which have five or seven lobes.

S. auritum 'Five Fingers'. Has golden-green leaves divided into five leaflets of quite a curious shape. It bears tiny green-spathed flowers like Arum Lilies.
S. podophyllum 'Arrowhead'. Has many cultivars with varying leaf patterns and colours. Indoors, the leaves are generally long-stalked and arrow-shaped.
S. wendlandii   Dull green leaves with silver-pink markings.

TAGETES

(tə gae' təs) COMPOSITAE

TAGETES erecta, the 'Aztec Marigolds', are the ideal annual for terrace planters and tubs — even windowboxes if you use dwarf growing types. Anywhere, they'll help light up the long, golden days of summer and autumn. There are no worries about winter cold — buy the seedlings in late spring and you'll have finished with them by the time the first frosts come. Make sure the drainage in your containers is perfect, with a deep layer of pot rubble, then coarse humus to prevent the soil being washed away. Fill with poor quality sandy soil or else they may bolt to leaf in the warmer weather. Place 'Marigolds' right out in the open (they need all the sun they can get) and do not over-water. Let the containers almost dry out between soakings. Hold off on the liquid fertiliser until the plants are well established and then dilute it more than usual. *TAGETES* have brittle stems and may need some support on exposed terraces. Better to use the dwarf-growing 'Chrysanthemum' flowering types. (See plate page 42).

TILLANDSIA

(til and' see ə) BROMELIACEAE

TILLANDSIA cyanea
Pink Quill

TILLANDSIAS are great heat-lovers, and in Europe are placed high up in windows in hanging pots, where all the rising heat of the steam radiators can reach them. This is scarcely necessary in warm temperate areas where indoor winter temperatures are unlikely to drop below their 50°F (10°C) need.

T. cyanea 'Pink Quill'. Forms a dense mass of grass-like recurved leaves. These are often reddish-

TILLANDSIA usneoides
Spanish Moss

brown in new foliage. The spectacular flower heads rise from among the leaf-rosettes on tall stems. They are shaped like a paddle and consist of overlapping pink bracts, from among which pop vivid violet-blue flowers. This type of *TILLANDSIA* should be grown in a chunky compost of treefern fibre, peat and sand and needs maximum humidity.

T. usneoides 'Spanish Moss'. This is the delicate species so often seen trailing eerily from trees in Hollywood sagas of the Deep South. It lives on air and moisture and can be merely hung from branches of larger plants. It looks like a tangled mass of grey threads, but turns green instantly when sprayed. There are tiny three-petalled yellow-green flowers in warm weather.

TOLMEIA

(tol' mee ə) SAXIFRAGACEAE

TOLMEIA menziesii is one of the sturdiest indoor plants, thriving in poor light provided the drainage is good. It is not fussy about temperature if you keep up the humidity and place it out of strong sunshine in the warmer months. *TOLMEIA* is almost unique in its method of reproduction. Buds appear at the junction of leaf and stalk and develop into new plantlets. Pin them down to develop new roots in a pot of moist sand, and you have plenty of spare plants for your admiring friends. A mature *TOLMEIA* decked with tiny plantlets clearly illustrates the popular name 'Piggy-Back Plant'. *TOLMEIA* is native to the West Coast of the United States.

TOLMEIA menziesii
Piggy-back Plant

TRACHYCARPUS
(trak' ee kah pəs)   PALMAE

TRACHYCARPUS fortunei
Japanese Fan Palm

TRACHYCARPUS fortunei is native to Japan and parts of China. It is therefore by no means tropical and requires rather different treatment to other Palms. Grow the 'Japanese Fan Palm' in containers of fibrous gritty soil with a handful or two of leaf mould and old poultry manure. Water regularly, but not too heavily, especially in winter. The leaves are an erect fan shape, bluish-green on the underside and borne on spiny stalks. It grows from a suckering trunk heavily shrouded in brown fibres, and is most decorative when young. For indoor use, the palms

are generally discarded when they begin to branch too heavily, for they are difficult to handle. *TRACHYCARPUS* is quite hardy to all but the heaviest frosts and has no special heating requirements. It can be raised either from suckers, or the decorative bluish seeds.

TRADESCANTIA
(trad əs kant' ee ə)   COMMELINACEAE

TRADESCANTIA blossfeldiana Variegata
Spiderwort

TRADESCANTIA fluminensis
Wandering Jew

If popular names are any indication of *real* popularity, *TRADESCANTIAS* must be near the top of the list. Take your pick: 'Spiderwort', 'Inch Plant', 'Wandering Jew', 'Speedy Jenny', 'Creeping Jesus',

'Chain Plant'. They are charming, easy-to-grow plants for home, conservatory or greenhouse. Try them as ground cover, in hanging baskets or even in a jar of water. Just keep them out of strong sunlight and arrange plenty of humidity. New plants are started by snapping off pieces of stem at a joint and planting them or even leaving them in water. In just a few days, roots appear and they're off! The many species vary mostly in the colour of their flowers and leaves, which may be pink, red, mauve, cream, gold or any shade of green. Popular species include:

T. albiflora A common garden plant all over the world. Plain, dark green shiny leaves. White flowers.
T. blossfeldiana 'Variegata' Green and cream striped leaves with purple reverses. Pinkish-mauve flowers.
T. fluminensis 'Variegata' Leaves striped in pale green, white and cream.

All species are grown in a standard compost of loam, peat and sand, and need plenty of water.

TREVESIA
(tre vee' see ə)   ARALIACEAE

TREVESIA palmata
Snowflake Tree

In nature a small tree from India, the striking *TREVESIA* remains manageably sized indoors. It likes the same temperatures and conditions as *Fatsia* (which see) and is grown for its remarkable leaves, which are quite irregular in shape. Those on my own specimen, have from six to nine umbrella-like ribs connected in the centre by leaf-tissue like the webbing on a duck's feet. The ribs project beyond this and develop into deeply lobed, variable leaflets.

TREVESIA enjoys humidity, shade from direct sun and produces flattened clusters of greenish-white flowers in summer. Though the leaves have a naturally half-eaten appearance, caterpillars are always trying to improve on nature, and they should be sprayed with a stomach poison if grown in the open.

TULIPA
(tyoo' lip ə)   LILIACEAE

TULIPA (Darwin Hybrid)
Darwin Tulip

Tulips make stunning temporary visitors indoors and can provide a succession of colour from mid-winter to late spring. To do this, you must buy the bulbs very early, and pay for the largest available. Pot them up at two-weekly intervals from early autumn, using a well-drained mixture of light top-soil, sand and leaf mould—and be sure to label each pot with the planting date! The bulbs should be positioned with their pointed ends just visible, and can be quite close together. The pots should then be watered deeply and stored away in a dark place for about three months to encourage deep root growth. Bring them very gradually into stronger light when the leaf shoots are almost 1 in (2.5 cm) high. Wait until these turn green before feeding with diluted liquid manure, then give them all the light you can, close to a sunny window. The warmer the position, the quicker the blooms will appear and open. Be sure never to let the pots dry out. If you have planted and stored batches of bulbs in regular succession, you will have a regular succession of blooms as you bring them out into the warmth and light. Single and double 'Early' Tulip varieties are the best for indoor culture.

191

VALLOTA
(və loh' tə)   AMARYLLIDACEAE

VALLOTA speciosa
Scarborough Lily

VALLOTAS or 'Scarborough Lilies' turn on a start-ling display when several bulbs are crowded into a small pot of sandy loam in early spring. The crowd-ing seems to force bloom, and the bulbs should be planted with their tips just showing. Water regularly, and feed with diluted fertiliser just as the buds begin to grow. Flower stems may grow from 18 to 30 in (45 to 75 cm) in length and produce about six funnel-shaped blooms of vivid orange-scarlet, normally in late summer. *VALLOTAS* enjoy the light in a sunny window, or semi-shade on a terrace. Keep the pots indoors over winter if there is any danger of freezing.

VANDA
(van' də)   ORCHIDACEAE

VANDA Orchids have become almost an Hawaiian trademark. They are in nature epiphytic (tree-dwel-ling) and monopodial — which means they keep growing from a single stem that gets longer every year. They produce overlapping rows of strap-shaped leaves, and the flowers appear from the leaf axils. They are magnificent flat open blooms up to 6 in (15 cm) across, and generally including some shade of blue in their colouring. *VANDAS* are grown in heavy pots of rubble such as stones, pot shards, coke, treefern chunks and bulb fibre. This gives perfect drainage and support to their fleshy aerial roots. They need full sun, plenty of water and as much humidity as you can arrange. Mine flower quite satisfactorily in an open courtyard close to a sun-facing wall. Temperatures sometimes drop to

VANDA arachnoides
Vanda Orchid

VANDA X 'Miss Joaquim'
Lei Orchid

the low 40s at night (5 to 7°C) and may reach 100°F (38°C) in summer, but they flower intermittently at any time of year. When *VANDAS* grow too leggy, the top can be lopped off and replanted. Popular species include:

V. caerulea 'Blue Orchid'. Pale blue flowers, marbled deeper purple. Needs all the heat, but less sun than the others.
V. X 'Miss Joaquim'. The hybrid orchid of Hawaiian trade, much used for table decoration as well as leis. The flowers are mauve-pink with a red-spotted golden throat.
V. X Rothschildiana. A hybrid between *V. caerulea* and *V. sanderiana*. The flowers are a pale amethyst with deeper veining.
V. roxburghii Pale open flowers marked with brown, the lip in a deep purple.

VANDA X sanderiana
Vanda Orchid

V. sanderiana Wonderfully coloured open flowers. The upper petals are pink, the lower a rich gold and all are marked with brown veinings.

VELTHEIMIA
(fel tai' mee ə)   LILIACEAE

VELTHEIMIA viridifolia
Veldt Lily

An attractive bulbous plant from South Africa, *VELTHEIMIA viridifolia* produces towering spikes of green-tipped rosy bells year after year. Bulbs of the 'Veldt Lily' are potted up in early autumn in a well-drained compost, their necks just above soil level. Care in filling the pot one-third with drainage rubble will be amply rewarded in minimising bulb loss from

rot. Water well and put the pot away in a shaded place with a minimum temperature of 45°F (7°C). Delay regular water until the leaves appear. *VELTHEIMIAS* need repotting only about every fourth year, but a spring top dressing of aged leaf mould is beneficial. Growing plants are happy in or by a sunny window, and will produce their long-lasting flowers in early spring.

VRIESIA
(vree' see ə)   BROMELIACEAE

VRIESIA platynema Variegata
Vriesia

VRIESIA psittacina
Painted Feather

VRIESIA X Belgium Hybrid
Flaming Sword

VRIESIAS require the same culture as other Bromeliads, but are perhaps a little hardier. Plant them in pots of compost mixed with sand. Water regularly and keep the leaf rosettes well filled. The flowers appear at all times of the year, according to species.

V. hieroglyphica Sometimes known as 'King of the Bromeliads', this plant has a rosette of golden-green leaves, superbly marked with irregular scribblings of dark green and brown.
V. psittacina 'Painted Feather'. A dwarf plant rarely exceeding 8 in (20 cm) in diameter. The red-stemmed spike of red and yellow bracts appears in winter. It is sometimes known as V. carinata.
V. splendens 'Flaming Sword'. Has handsome dark green foliage and an 18 in (45 cm) stem of brilliant overlapping red bracts. These appear in summer and may be tinted orange or yellow in various hybrid varieties.

Unlike the majority of Bromeliads, VRIESIAS are not epiphytic but live among the roots of trees in soil rich in leaf mould.

WISTARIA

(wis teə' ree ə)   LEGUMINOSAE

Familiar spring-flowering climbers, WISTARIAS also make charming pot plants. First make sure that the specimen you propose to use has bloomed before, or is a division of a mature plant. Newly grafted or seedling WISTARIAS may not bloom for years in pots, if at all. Lift the plant from its nursery container, in late winter, untangle the roots and prune at least one third of them away. Pot in a mixture of almost pure decayed manure, sand and a

WISTARIA floribunda 'Noda Fuji'
Japanese Wistaria

WISTARIA sinensis (as bonsai)
Wistaria

little leaf mould, then place in a sunny position. Water heavily, and when the flower buds begin to appear in early spring, stand the whole container in a dish of water, for WISTARIA's thirst is unbelievable. Leaves and climbing tendrils will develop after the flowers in mauve 'Chinese Wistaria' (W. sinensis), often before them in the Japanese species (W. floribunda). These tendrils should be shortened back to two leaf joints to encourage further branching. WISTARIA must be watered regularly all through the hot weather, and must be repotted every year.

XANTHOSOMA
(san the soh' me)   ARACEAE

XANTHOSOMA lindenii
Xanthosoma

Yet another tropical Aroid, *XANTHOSOMA* is difficult to grow well outside a greenhouse, for it needs a winter temperature of at least 60°F (15°C). If you can provide the warmth, give them bright light also (but not sun), a moist peaty soil mix and humidity up to the limit. *XANTHOSOMA* are propagated by early summer division of their fleshy rootstocks. Two varieties are commonly grown:

X. lindenii   Handsome 24 in (60 cm) leaves, veined in white.

X. violacea   Large pointed green leaves with purple stems and veins.

YUCCA
(yuk'ə)   LILIACEAE

North America's *YUCCAS* adapt well to courtyard plantings in modern homes and buildings, even in cold areas. They develop stiff rosettes of sharply pointed leaves, and produce spikes of creamy bell-flowers in summer. *YUCCAS* can be grown in large tubs or pockets left in the courtyard paving. They soon become over-large and are best replaced from time to time by some of their lavishly produced offsets which root in sharp sand. The many species are similar in general appearance, and are known as 'Spanish Dagger', 'Spanish Bayonet' or 'Adam's Needle'.

YUCCA aloifolia
Spanish Bayonet

ZEBRINA
(zeb ree' nə)   COMMELINACEAE

ZEBRINA pendula
Wandering Jew

Yet another genus of the 'Spiderwort' family, *ZEBRINAS* are treated exactly like *Tradescantias* (which see). They are spectacular as hanging basket subjects in lightly shaded positions. Keep them well watered and replant when they become too bare and leggy. This is done merely by breaking off joints in warm weather, and potting them in fresh compost.

Z. pendula   The commonly grown type; like several of the *Tradescantias* it is also known as 'Wandering Jew'. Its leaves are green with two silvery stripes and purple reverses.

    ZEBRINA is native to Mexico and likes a minimum winter temperature of 50°F (10°C).

ZEPHYRANTHES
(zef ə ran' thəs)　　　　AMARYLLIDACEAE

Charming dwarf bulbs, ZEPHYRANTHES or 'Storm Lilies' enjoy the crowded conditions of small pots. Use any peaty compost, plant the bulbs merely buried and almost touching each other. This can be done at any time, even when the flowers are beginning to open. Give them plenty of water from late summer on and the flowers will appear continuously, often many from each bulb. Place them in a sunny window or grow on an open terrace. There are other species blooming in pink and yellow, but white-flowered *Z. candida* is far and away the easiest.

ZEPHYRANTHES candida
Storm Lily

ZEPHYRANTHES rosea
Pink Storm Lily

ZINNIA
(zin' ee ə)　　　　COMPOSITAE

ZINNIA elegans
Mexican Aster

Dazzling ZINNIAS are ideal hot-weather plants for an open terrace. Plant them in early summer in large tubs or planters of sandy compost enriched with leaf mould and decayed manure. Water regularly. Pinch off the first growing points to encourage branching and heavy flower crops. Keep in full sun at all times, dead-head faded flowers regularly, and you'll have a display that lasts till autumn. Dwarf growing varieties of Cactus-flowered ZINNIA *elegans* the 'Mexican Aster', give the best display; *'Thumbelina'* hybrids are better for smaller containers. ZINNIAS are generally sold in mixed colours, but specialist nurseries can provide seeds of a single shade. (See also plate page 19).

ZYGOCACTUS
(zai goh kak' təs)　　　　CACTACEAE

ZYGOCACTUS *truncatus* is known in some countries as *Schlumbergera,* but whichever name you know, they are the world's most popular epiphytic Cacti. Grow them in hanging pots of peaty well-drained compost so the vivid flowers can be appreciated from below. They appear in autumn in cold winter areas (it is called 'Thanksgiving Cactus' in the United States), and during winter in milder areas where it is 'Crab Cactus'. ZYGOCACTUS should be kept in an area unused at night, for they must have twelve hours of darkness to trigger flower production. Many colour varieties are grown, ranging from cerise and pale pink, to orange, purple, crimson and white, often

ZYGOCACTUS X 'Llewellyn'
Humming Bird Flower

ZYGOCACTUS truncatus
Crab Cactus

ZYGOCACTUS X Purple Hybrid

with contrasting edges. Unlike the related *Rhipsalidopsis,* which bears open daisy-shaped flowers, *ZYGOCACTUS* blossoms are curiously flattened, and curve up at an angle from the hanging stems. They are sometimes known as 'Hummingbird Flowers' for reasons obvious in the close-up photograph. Should winter night temperatures drop below 50°F (10°C), the developing flower buds will drop along with many of the stem joints. Water regularly except in autumn.

ZYGOPETALUM
(zai goh pet' ə ləm)   ORCHIDACEAE

ZYGOPETALUM mackayi
Zygopetalum

Inevitably the last plant in any flower book, *ZYGOPETALUM mackayi* is always worth waiting for — a magnificently perfumed orchid that's easy to grow. *ZYGOPETALUM* has crested green and brown blotched petals, and an enlarged lip of white and mauve. It should be grown in pots of coarse compost incorporating brick rubble, sphagnum, and fir chips, and watered regularly throughout the year. *ZYGOPETALUM* likes moist shade for most of the year, but more light and sun as the days cool down. There's no need for heating unless your winter nights are below 50°F (10°C).

GLOSSARY

Botanists have adopted many specialised words and terms to describe accurately the many parts of a plant; its appearance, colour, shape and texture.

It is difficult to compile any garden book without using at least a few of these words. But as they are not much used in everyday English, we are also including a glossary or dictionary of them for the grower of indoor plants who is not botanically minded.

Most unfamiliar words used in this book (or for that matter, in other garden books) will be found here, together with their meanings.

Acid Soil deficient in lime.
Acute Sharply pointed, but not elongated.
Adventitious Occurring away from the usual place, e.g. aerial roots.
Aerial roots Roots appearing above soil level, to extract moisture from the air.
Air layering A method of propagation which stimulates root growth from a plant *above* ground.
Alkaline Soil rich in lime.
Allergenic Said of a plant which produces rashes, etc. on contact.
Alternate Leaves arranged along a stem on opposite sides and at different levels
Annual A plant which completes its entire life-cycle within a single year.
Anther The pollen-bearing part of a stamen.
Areole A swelling on a Cactus out of which appear the spines, branches and flowers.
Axil The point where a leaf joins a stem — upper side.
Banded A leaf striped crosswise.
Biennial A plant which completes its life-cycle in a two year period.
Bifurcate Forked.
Bipinnate A compound leaf with branches of leaflets on either side of its main axis.
Bisexual A plant with flowers having both male and female reproductive parts.
Bract A modified leaf at the base of a flower, often the most colourful part.
Budding Grafting by inserting a stem-bud of one plant into the cambium layer of another.
Bulb A fleshy growth bud consisting of overlapping layers, found underground.
Bulbil A small bulb appearing at leaf-joints, as in some Lilies.

Cactus A spine-bearing succulent plant found only in the Americas.
Calcifuge A lime-hating plant.
Calyx The outer covering of a flower, consisting of sepals. Often decorative.
Catkin A hanging spike of unisexual flowers.
Chlorosis Yellowing of the leaves.
Column Stamens and style combined into one organ, as in Orchids.
Composite Like a Daisy.
Compost A mixture of growth elements for a plant; a potting mix.
Conifer A tree or shrub in which the seeds are protected within the scales of a cone, as in a pine tree.
Conservatory A heated, humidified room for plants.
Cordate Heart-shaped.
Corm A bulb-like enlargement of the joint of a root and stem. Planted like a bulb.
Corolla The circle of outer petals of a flower.
Corymb A flat-topped flower cluster. Commences blooming from the outside.
Creeper A trailing plant that roots at intervals.
Crenate With scalloped edges.
Cyme A flat-topped flower cluster in which the centre flowers open first.
Damping off Death of young seedlings, due to overwatering or fungus infection.
Darkhouse A special plant shelter in which daylight can be excluded to stimulate unseasonal flowering of short-day plants such as Cyclamen and Poinsettias.
Deciduous Leaf-losing.
Dentate Toothed.
Dioecious Unisexual, a plant species which bears male and female flowers on separate plants.
Disbudding A process in which a number of flower buds are removed from a growing plant, generally to increase flower size in those remaining.
Division Propagation of perennial plants by splitting the root mass.
Elliptical Roughly oval, but with the widest point at the centre.
Entire A leaf margin without divisions or teeth.
Epiphyte A plant which supports itself without soil, extracting nutriment directly from the air or nearby decaying matter.
Espalier A plant trained flat against a wall or support, roughly in two dimensions.

198

Evergreen A plant which does not drop all its leaves at a particular season; rather a few at a time.

Exotic A plant which is foreign to the country in which it grows; as opposed to native.

Fern An ancient race of plants which do not bear flowers.

Fertile Bearing viable seeds or spores.

Fibrous-rooted Without any major or tap roots.

Filament The thread-like stalk of a stamen.

Floret A minute flower, hundreds of which make up the centre of a Daisy or the spadix of an Aroid.

Foliage plant An indoor plant grown specifically for leaf interest, though it may flower as well.

Frond The mature leaf stem of a fern.

Frost-tender A fleshy plant which may be destroyed when the sap freezes.

Fungicide A chemical preparation for the destruction of fungus diseases.

Fungus A parasitic vegetable organism without chlorophyll or leaves.

Garden room A simple form of conservatory; generally a living area where plants are grown.

Glabrous Completely smooth.

Glaucous Possessing a whitish coating that marks or rubs off, without damaging the surface underneath.

Glochid A hook-tipped hair or spine, often painful to remove from your finger.

Grafting When a bud or shoot of one plant is severed and joined to the rooted section of another.

Habit The most usual growth form of a plant, often modified by training.

Half-hardy A plant which will resist cold, in a sheltered position.

Hardy Frost resistant.

Head A short, compact flower spike.

Heeled cutting A cutting of new wood, still attached to portion of hardened previous year's growth.

Herb (a) any non-woody plant.
(b) a plant used for flavouring purposes.

Herbaceous A non-woody plant which dies back annually.

Hothouse A glasshouse with artificial heating.

Humus Rich debris of rotted-down vegetable and other organic matter.

Hybrid The result of crossing two different plants.

Inflorescence A generalised word describing any grouping of flowers on a plant.

Insecticide A substance, chemical or organic, which is fatal to some types of insects.

Insectivorous Plants which trap insects and absorb nutriment from them directly.

Juvenile The second leaves to appear from seed, often quite different to a plant's mature leaves.

Labellum The lip of an Orchid, differing strongly from the other petals.

Labiate Formed like a lip.

Laciniate A leaf slashed into irregular lobes.

Lanceolate Lance-shaped, a long gradually tapering leaf.

Lateral Any shoot from a main stem short of the tip.

Layering Pinning a branch down to produce new roots.

Leaf-cutting A method of propagating many tropical plants from portions of their leaves.

Leaflet A leaf-shaped segment of a compound leaf.

Leaf mould Humus consisting exclusively of rotted-down fallen leaves.

Legume A plant which produces pea-type seeds in a pod.

Linear A narrow, flat leaf with parallel margins.

Loam Friable soil containing a mixture of sand, clay and rotted down turf.

Lobe Any projection from a leaf margin.

Margin The edge of a leaf.

Membranous Thin and translucent.

Microclimate A purely local combination of climatic factors, generally different to that of nearby areas.

Monocarpic A plant that flowers once only, then dies.

Monoecious Male and female organs in separate flowers, but on the same plant.

Monopodial Unbranching plants in which a single stem grows continually longer each year. Generally of a semi-climbing habit. See *VANDA*.

Mulch A soil covering to conserve moisture, and prevent root damage by heat or cold.

Mutant A form of plant derived by sudden natural change from its parent. But not a hybrid.

Needle A specialised elongated leaf, as in conifers.

Node A joint in a stalk where leaves and sometimes flowers appear.

Oblong Longer than broad.

Obtuse Blunt at the end.

Offset A small outside division from a parent plant.

Organic Composed of live or formerly living tissue.

Ovary That part of the plant containing unfertilised seed.

Ovate Roughly egg-shaped, broadest at the base.

Palmate Leaflets arranged like a palm or hand.

Panicle A branching cluster of flowers.

Parasite An organism existing by means of another organism's food-collecting system.

Peatmoss An organic material used particularly in potting composts. Very acid and water retaining.

Perennial A plant lasting more or less permanently.

Perianth The combined calyx and corolla of a flower.

Petal One decorative segment of a flower's corolla.

Petiole A leaf stem.

pH balance The degree of acidity or alkalinity in soil.

Phyllode A stem developed into a leaf-like shape.

Pinched back To prune soft leading shoots with the finger nails to encourage branching.

Pinnae Leaflets.

Pinnate Like a feather. Specifically, a leaf with leaflets arranged on both sides of the stalk.

Pistil The prominent female organ of a flower.

Pollen The fertilizing powder contained in a flower's anther.

Pollination The placing of pollen on the stigma of a flower. Performed in nature by honey-seeking insects.

Procumbent A plant which trails without rooting at intervals.

Propagate To reproduce a plant by means of cuttings, layers or divisions, so that it comes true to type, which seedlings might not.

Prostrate Lying flat on the ground.

Pruning Selective cutting back of a plant to encourage new growth, or to adapt its shape.

Pseudobulb The thickened bulbous stem formed by some orchids for the storage of nutriment.

Raceme A long flower stem with stalked flowers.

Recurved Bent backward.

Reverse The underside of a petal or leaf.

Rhizome A root-like underground stem which produces buds of new growth at intervals.

Root-cutting A section of root used to propagate new plants of some species.

Rootbound A plant starving to death because its container is full of roots with nothing to feed on.

Rosette A cluster of leaves radiating in a circle.

Runner A trailing stem which roots at intervals.

Scale A segment of lily bulb which may be detached for propagation.

Scape A leafless flower stalk arising from the roots.

Scion The bud or shoot which is grafted onto the stock of another plant.

Segment One section of a divided plant part.

Sepal The individual segment of a calyx; an outer petal.

Serrated Toothed like a saw.

Shoot An immature combination of leaf and stem.

Shrub A woody plant, generally without the single trunk of a tree.

Simple A single-bladed leaf, the opposite of compound.

Spadix The fleshy spike of minute flowers characteristic of the Arum family.

Spathe The sheath or bract which encloses a spadix.

Sphagnum moss The dried parts of a moisture-loving moss, used in pot culture. Very water retaining.

Spike A series of flowers on a single stem, with each flower stemless.

Sporangium The spore-case of ferns.

Spore The reproductive cell of Ferns and Moss, differing from a flower's seed.

Sport A plant variety resulting from natural mutation.

Stamen The pollen-bearing or male organ of a flower.

Standard (a) The upright petals of certain flowers.
(b) A plant trained to a tall, tree-like shape.

Sterile A plant incapable of reproduction by seed.

Stock The parent plant on which the scion of another is grafted.

Stigma The female part of a flower which receives the pollen, connected to the ovaries.

Stolon A shoot which bends to the ground, forms roots, and finally separates from the parent plant.

Stomata The leaf-pores through which a plant breathes.

Sub-tropical A plant native to areas outside the true tropics, but not able to survive cold winters.

Succulent A plant with fleshy leaves and stems acting as moisture reservoirs against drought.

Sucker An adventitious shoot which appears from an underground section of a grafted plant.

Synonym An out-of-date name rejected in favour of a new one.

Tanbark The shredded bark of certain trees used for its acid content by tanners of leather. Also useful for growing acid-loving plants.

Taproot The principal feeding root of many plants, corresponding underground to the plant's trunk.

Temperate A mild, often coastal climate.

Tendril The curling, threadlike end of a leaf or stem which enables many plants to climb.

Terete Cylindrical and circular in cross section.

Terminal A shoot at the end of a stem.

Terrestrial Plants which grow on the earth's surface in contrast to epiphytic or tree-dwelling types.

Tip-cutting A cutting of new growth used for the propagation of certain perennial plants.

Topiary Ornamental pruning of densely foliaged plants such as box into sculptured shapes.

Trifoliate Leaves divided into three parts, such as Oxalis or Shamrock.

Tropical A plant native to the areas between the tropics of Cancer and Capricorn, hence needing a wet summer and dry winter.

Trunk The main stem or body of a tree-like plant.

Tuber A thickened underground stem for the storage of nutriment.

Tubercle A wart-like projection on a leaf or stem.

Twiner A plant that climbs by winding around itself or other plants.

Umbel A group of flowers growing from a common point.

Undulate Wavy-margined.

Variegation A condition in many plants where the natural green is broken by other colours, often white. Usually the result of a virus infection.

Vermiculite A sterile mineral compound, with remarkable qualities of water retention. Used in composts.

Viable Capable of germination or life.

Vine A plant of climbing habit.

Whorl A circle of leaves around a stem.

Xerophyte A plant adapted for growing in dry regions.

Zone A band or belt of a second colour, slightly in from the edge of a roughly circular leaf. See-*PELARGONIUM.*

INDEX

BOTANICAL AND POPULAR NAMES
Due to limitation of space, it has not been possible to illustrate every plant mentioned in this book — nor does every plant illustrated in the opening chapters have a corresponding description in the Dictionary section.

This alphabetical index refers you by page number to:
(a) Every *genus* of plant included in the Dictionary section (but not every *variety* mentioned therein, as these will be found within the appropriate generic entry).
(b) Any additional *genus* of plant mentioned in the opening chapters of the book, when it has not qualified for a Dictionary entry.

The name of any plant illustrated either in the opening chapters or the Dictionary section is followed by an additional page number in heavy type — that's where the colour plate appears.

Every popular name used anywhere in the book is also indexed. Each of these is cross-referenced to the appropriate botanical name entry.

Botanical generic names are listed in Italic type as elsewhere in the book. Popular names are in normal Roman type in lower case with an initial capital.

Unillustrated entries are prefixed with an asterisk.

ACKNOWLEDGEMENTS

I am indebted to the many gardening friends, both amateur and professional, who helped locate plants not readily available, or permitted me to photograph their own botanical treasures. They include:

in Australia
Brian Donges, Olwyn Ferris, Eddy Graham, Olga Henning, Rick Matthews, Alan Swavley, Kevin Wellings
Glenda's Plants, Northbridge, N.S.W.,
Gone Potty, Mosman, N.S.W.
Green Fingers Nursery, Warriewood, N.S.W.
Green Leaves, Upper Mt. Gravatt, QLD.
J. L. Krempin, Tingira Heights, N.S.W.
Pickwick's Indoor Plants, Neutral Bay, N.S.W.
Rawards' Nursery, Cumbabah, QLD.

in California
Max Eckert, Lloyd Killam, John Marion, David Wittry

in France
Roderick Cameron, St Jean Cap Ferrat
Louise Coleman, Paris

in Hawaii
John G. Allerton, Margaret Davis, Ruth Farrior, Loy Marks, Dr. William S. Stewart

in Tahiti
Jacques Rentier

Other plants were photographed at:
Chateau de Malmaison, Paris
Chelsea Flower Show, London
Huntington Gardens, San Marino, Calif.
Hyatt Regency Hotel, San Francisco, Calif.
Jardin Botanique de Tahiti
Kahala Hilton Hotel, Hawaii
Los Angeles State Arboretum, Arcadia, Calif.
Olu Pua Botanical Garden, Kauai
Pacific Tropical Botanic Gardens, Kauai
Pago Pago Americana Hotel, Tutuila,
Palais de Bagatelle, Paris
Pua Laki (Moir's Plantation Gardens) Kauai
R.H.S. Gardens, Wisley, England
Royal Hawaiian Hotel, Honolulu
Strybing Arboretum, San Francisco, Calif.
Tahara'a Inter. Continental Hotel, Tahiti
UCLA Garden, Bel Air, Calif.

Air New Zealand; Hawaiian Airlines and UTA French Airlines who helped take me where the botanical action was, and brought me home safely to my own plants.

BOTANICAL RELATIVES

Many popular Indoor Plants have a number of close relatives that do equally well in the same conditions. I thought readers might be interested to know about these relationships, so I am including the following listing of the botanical families represented in this book, together with the individual plants which belong in each of them. The botanical families are in alphabetical order and so are the plants included within them.

ACANTHACEAE (The Acanthus)
APHELANDRA, BARLERIA, DREJERELLA, ERANTHEMUM, FITTONIA, GRAPTOPHYLLUM, HEMIGRAPHIS, HYPOESTES, PACHYSTACHYS, PSEUDERANTHEMUM, RUELLIA, SANCHEZIA, STROBILANTHES.
ACERACEAE (The Maples)
ACER.
AIZOACEAE (The Fig-Marigolds)
FAUCARIA, LITHOPS.
ALLIACEAE (The Onions)
BRODIAEA.
AMARANTHACEAE (The Amaranths)
IRESINE.
AMARYLLIDACEAE (The Amaryllids)
AGAVE, CLIVIA, CRINUM, EUCHARIS, HAE-MANTHUS, HIPPEASTRUM, NARCISSUS, NERINE, RHODOHYPOXIS, SPREKELIA, STERNBERGIA, VALLOTA, ZEPHYRANTHES.
APOCYNACEAE (The Dogbanes)
ADENIUM, ALLAMANDA, DIPLADENIA, MANDEVILLA, NERIUM, PLUMERIA.
ARACEAE (The Aroids)
AGLAONEMA, ALOCASIA, ANTHURIUM, CALADIUM, DIEFFENBACHIA, MONSTERA, PHILODENDRON, RHAPHIDOPHORA, SCINDAPSUS, SPATHIPHYLLUM, SYNGONIUM, XANTHOSOMA.
ARALIACEAE (The Aralias)
BRASSAIA, CUSSONIA, DIZYGOTHECA, X FATSHEDERA, FATSIA, HEDERA, MERYTA, POLYSCIAS, TREVESIA.
ARAUCARIACEAE (The Araucarias)
ARAUCARIA.
ASCLEPIADACEAE (The Milkweeds)
HOYA, STAPELIA, STEPHANOTIS.
BALSAMINAE (The Balsams)
IMPATIENS.
BEGONIACEAE (The Begonias)
BEGONIA.
BROMELIACEAE (The Air-Pines)
AECHMEA, ANANAS, BILLBERGIA, CRYPTANTHUS, GUZMANIA, NEOREGELIA, NIDULARIUM, PORTEA, TILLANDSIA, VRIESIA.
BUXACEAE (The Boxes)
BUXUS.
CACTACEAE (The Cacti)
APOROCACTUS, ASTROPHYTUM,

CEPHALOCEREUS, CEREUS, CHAMAECEREUS, CLEISTOCACTUS, ECHINOCACTUS, ECHINOCEREUS, EPIPHYLLUM, GYMNOCALYCIUM, HATIORA, HELIOCEREUS, HYLOCEREUS, MAMILLARIA, NOPALXOCHIA, NOTOCACTUS, OPUNTIA, PARODIA, PERESKIA, REBUTIA, RHIPSALIDOPSIS, SELENICEREUS, ZYGOCACTUS.
CAPRIFOLIACEAE (The Honeysuckles)
LONICERA.
COMMELINACEAE (The Wandering Jews)
CALLISIA, CAMPELIA, DICHORISANDRA, GEOGENANTHUS, RHOEO, SETCRAESEA, SIDERASIS, TRADESCANTIA, ZEBRINA.
COMPOSITAE (The Daisies)
CHRYSANTHEMUM, GYNEURA, HELICHRYSUM, LIGULARIA, SENECIO, TAGETES, ZINNIA.
CONVOLVULACEAE (The Morning Glories)
CALONYCTION, IPOMOEA, QUAMOCLIT.
CRASSULACEAE (The Stonecrops)
AEONIUM, COTYLEDON, CRASSULA, ECHEVERIA, KALANCHOE, PACHYPHYTUM, ROCHEA, SEDUM, SEMPERVIVUM.
CYCADACEAE (The Cycads)
CYCAS.
CYPERACEAE (The Sedges)
CYPERUS.
DICKSONIACEAE (The Treeferns)
CIBOTIUM.
ERICACEAE (The Heaths)
AZALEA.
EUPHORBIACEAE (The Spurges)
ACALYPHA, CODIAEUM, EUPHORBIA, PEDILANTHUS, SYNADENIUM.
GERANIACEAE (The Geraniums)
PELARGONIUM.
GESNERIACEAE (The Gesneriads)
ACHIMENES, AESCHYNANTHUS, COLUMNEA, EPISCIA, KOHLERIA, NAUTILOCALYX, RAMONDA, RECHSTEINERIA, SAINTPAULIA, SINNINGIA, SMITHIANTHA, STREPTOCARPUS.
GRAMINEAE (The Grasses)
PHYLLOSTACHYS, SASA.
IRIDACEAE (The Irises)
FREESIA, LAPEYROUSIA.
LABIATAE (The Mints)
COLEUS, SALVIA.
LAURACEAE (The Laurels)
LAURUS.
LEGUMINOSAE (The Peas)
CLIANTHUS, CLITOREA, LOTOS, STRONGYLODON, WISTARIA.
LILIACEAE (The Lilies)
ALOE, ASPARAGUS, ASPIDISTRA, BEAUCARNEA, CHLOROPHYTUM, COLCHICUM, CONVALLARIA, CORDYLINE, DRACAENA, ENDYMION, GASTERIA, GLORIOSA, HAWORTHIA, HOSTA,

HYACINTHUS, LACHENALIA, LILIUM, LITTONIA, PLEOMELE, SANSEVIERIA, TULIPA, VELTHEIMIA, YUCCA.
LYCOPODIACEAE (The Tassel Ferns)
LYCOPODIUM.
MALVACEAE (The Mallows)
ABUTILON, HIBISCUS.
MARANTACEAE (The Arrowroots)
CALATHEA, CTENANTHE, MARANTA, STROMANTHE.
MELASTOMATACEAE (The Lasiandras)
MEDINILLA, SONERILA.
MORACEAE (The Mulberries)
FICUS.
MUSACEAE (The Bananas)
HELICONIA, MUSA, STRELITZIA.
MYRSINACEAE (The Coral Berries)
ARDISIA.
NYCTAGINACEAE (The Four O'clocks)
BOUGAINVILLEA, HEIMERLIODENDRON.
OLEACEAE (The Olives)
JASMINUM, LIGUSTRUM.
ONAGRACEAE (The Evening Primroses)
FUCHSIA.
ORCHIDACEAE (The Orchids)
BIFRENARIA, BLETILLA, BRASSOCATTLEYA, CATTLEYA, COELOGYNE, CYMBIDIUM, DENDROBIUM, EPIDENDRUM, HAEMARIA, LAELIA, LAELIOCATTLEYA, LYCASTE, MILTONIA, ODONTOGLOSSUM, ONCIDIUM, PAPHIOPEDILUM, PHALAENOPSIS, PHRAGMIPEDILUM, PLEIONE, SARCOCHILUS, SOBRALIA, SOPHRONITIS, STANHOPEA, VANDA, ZYGOPETALUM.
OXALIDACEAE (The Wood-Sorrels)
OXALIS.
PALMAE (The Palms)
BACULARIA, CARYOTA, CHAMAEDOREA, CHRYSALIDOCARPUS, COLLINIA, HOWEA, PHOENIX, RHAPIS, TRACHYCARPUS.
PANDANACEAE (The Screw-Pines)
PANDANUS.
PASSIFLORACEAE (The Passion Flowers)
PASSIFLORA.

PINACEAE (The Pines)
PICEA, PINUS.
PIPERACEAE (The Peppers)
PEPEROMIA, PIPER.
PODOCARPACEAE (The Plum Pines)
PODOCARPUS.
POLYGONACEAE (The Knotweeds)
COCCOLOBA.
POLYPODIACEAE (The Common Ferns)
ADIANTUM, ASPLENIUM, CYRTOMIUM, DAVALLIA, NEPHROLEPIS, PHYLLITIS, PLATYCERIUM, POLYPODIUM, PTERIS.
PORTULACACEAE (The Portulacas)
LEWISIA, PORTULACARIA.
PRIMULACEAE (The Primroses)
CYCLAMEN, PRIMULA.
PUNICACEAE (The Pomegranates)
PUNICA.
RANUNCULACEAE (The Buttercups)
CLEMATIS.
ROSACEAE (The Roses)
FRAGARIA, ROSA.
RUBIACEAE (The Madders)
GARDENIA, IXORA.
RUTACEAE (The Rues)
CITRUS, FORTUNELLA.
SAXIFRAGACEAE (The Saxifrages)
HYDRANGEA, SAXIFRAGA, TOLMEIA.
SCROPHULARIACEAE (The Figworts)
CALCEOLARIA.
SOLANACEAE (The Night-Shades)
BROWALLIA, CAPSICUM, CESTRUM, DATURA, NICOTIANA, PETUNIA, SCHIZANTHUS, SOLANUM.
THEACEAE (The Teas)
CAMELLIA.
URTICACEAE (The Nettles)
PILEA.
VERBENACEAE (The Verbenas)
CLERODENDRON, LANTANA.
VITACEAE (The Grapes)
CISSUS, VITIS.
ZINGIBERACEAE (The Gingers)
COSTUS, HEDYCHIUM.